The Politics of Healthcare Reform in Turkey

Volkan Yılmaz

The Politics of Healthcare Reform in Turkey

palgrave
macmillan

Volkan Yılmaz
Graduate Program in Social Policy,
Institute for Graduate Studies in Social Sciences
Bogazici University
Istanbul, Turkey

ISBN 978-3-319-85211-9 ISBN 978-3-319-53667-5 (eBook)
DOI 10.1007/978-3-319-53667-5

Softcover reprint of the hardcover 1st edition 2017

Cover illustration: Medicshots / Alamy Stock Photo

Printed on acid-free paper

This Palgrave Macmillan imprint is published by Springer Nature
The registered company is Springer International Publishing AG
The registered company address is: Gewerbestrasse 11, 6330 Cham, Switzerland

Dedicated to the memory of my mother Seyhan Yanık.

Acknowledgements

It is a pleasant duty to express my sincere gratitude to the following people for supporting this project at its different stages: Ayşe Buğra, Belgin Tekçe, Charles Dannreuther, Çağlar Keyder, Nurhan Yentürk, Gordon Crawford, Jelke Boesten, Ray Bush and Zülküf Aydın. I am grateful to the University of Leeds and the British Institute in Ankara for granting me research scholarships, without these valuable opportunities, I would not be able to complete this project. I wish to thank my dearest friends who made it all possible: Burcu Oy, Nilay Şentürk, Mehmet Baki Deniz, Pınar Gümüş, Sezen Yalçın, Sinan Eden and Zeynep Akça. My biggest gratitude lies with İslam Gezer who gave me the time and support I needed to write. Finally, I would like to thank Peggy Alptekin for her outstanding work in proofreading the manuscript.

Contents

List of Abbreviations

AK Party and AKP[1]	Justice and Development Party, Adalet ve Kalkınma Partisi
AMA	American Medical Association
ANAP	Motherland Party, Anavatan Partisi
AP	Justice Party, Adalet Partisi
BAĞ-KUR	The Pension Fund for the Self-Employed, Esnaf, Sanatkarlar ve Diğer Bağımsız Çalışanlar Sigorta Kurumu
BMA	British Medical Association
CHP	Republican People's Party, Cumhuriyet Halk Partisi
DEV-SAĞLIK-İŞ	Revolutionary Health Workers' Union, Devrimci Sağlık İşçileri Sendikası
DİSK	The Confederation of Progressive Trade Unions' of Turkey, Devrimci İşçi Sendikaları Konfederasyonu
DPT	The State Planning Organisation, Devlet Planlama Teşkilatı
DSP	Democratic Left Party, Demokratik Sol Parti
DYP	True Path Party, Doğru Yol Partisi
EMU	European Monetary Union
EU	European Union
FP	Virtue Party, Fazilet Partisi
GBP	Great Britain Pound
GDP	Gross domestic product
HDP	People's Democratic Party, Halkların Demokratik Partisi
HTP	Health Transformation Programme
IBRD	International Bank for Reconstruction and Development
ICSID	International Centre for Settlement of Investment Disputes
IDA	International Development Association
IFC	International Finance Corporation

IMF	International Monetary Fund
İTC	The Committee of Union and Progress, İttihat ve Terakki Cemiyeti
KESK	The Confederation of Public Labourers' Union, Kamu Emekçileri Sendikaları Konfederasyonu
MIGA	Multilateral Investment Guarantee Agency
MoH	Ministry of Health
NHS	National Health Service
NPM	New Public Management
OECD	Organization for Economic Cooperation and Development
OHSAD	Private Hospitals and Health Institutions Association, Özel Hastaneler ve Sağlık Kuruluşları Derneği
PFI	Private Finance Initiatives
PKK	Kurdistan Workers' Party
PPP	Public Private Partnership
RP	Welfare Party, Refah Partisi
SES	Health and Social Services Labourers Union, Sağlık ve Sosyal Hizmet Emekçileri Sendikası
SGK	Social Security Institution, Sosyal Güvenlik Kurumu
SHP	Social Democratic Populist Party, Sosyal Demokrat Halkçı Parti
SME(s)	Small and medium enterprise(s)
SPGK	The General Directorate of Health Project, Sağlık Projesi Genel Koordinatörlüğü
SSK	Social Insurances Institution, Sosyal Sigortalar Kurumu
TİP	Labour Party of Turkey, Türkiye İşçi Partisi
TİSK	The Turkish Confederation of Employer Associations, Türk İşverenleri Sendikaları Konfederasyonu
TKHK	The Public Hospitals Institution of Turkey, Türkiye Kamu Hastaneleri Kurumu
TL	Turkish Lira
TMMOB	The Union of Chambers of Turkish Engineers and Architects, Türk Mühendis ve Mimar Odaları Birliği
TOBB	Turkish Union of Chambers and Commodity Exchanges, Türkiye Odalar ve Borsalar Birliği
TSB	Insurance Association of Turkey, Türkiye Sigorta Birliği
TSK	Turkish Military Forces, Türk Silahlı Kuvvetleri
TTB	Turkish Medical Association, Türk Tabipleri Birliği
TÜİK	Turkish Statistical Institution, Türkiye İstatistik Kurumu
TÜRK-İŞ	The Confederation of Turkish Trade Unions, Türkiye İşçi Sendikaları Konfederasyonu

TÜSİAD	Turkish Industry and Business Association, Türk Sanayicileri ve İşadamları Derneği
WB	World Bank
WBG	World Bank Group
WHO	World Health Organization
WWII	Second World War

Note

1. Official abbreviation of the Justice and Development Party is the AK Party. However, abbreviations of political parties in Turkey are generally the combination of the first letters of their official name. As the word "ak" means "white" implying cleanliness and transparency, the Justice and Development Party decided to use the AK Party, rather than the AKP. However, the opponents of the AK Party still use the AKP to refer to the Justice and Development Party.

List of Tables

CHAPTER 1

The New Politics of Healthcare in Turkey

1.1 Introduction

The healthcare system in Turkey has been through a significant transformation since the launch of the Health Transformation Programme (HTP) in 2003. Given the intensity of the reform's impact on the financing, delivery and regulation of healthcare services, the reform was categorised as a 'large-scale' one (Ağartan 2015a; Sparkes et al. 2015; Akıncı et al. 2012).

While the impact of the reform on the various components of Turkey's healthcare system has been extensively researched (Ökem and Çakar 2015; Hazama 2013; Adıyok 2012; Ağartan 2012a, 2012b; Baris et al. 2011; Yaşar and Uğurluoğlu 2011; Elveren 2008; Keyder 2007a; Üstündağ and Yoltar 2007; Adaman 2003), the politics of healthcare that paved the way for the launch of the HTP and the political contestations and negotiations between different actors during the implementation of this reform process are underresearched (Ağartan 2016, 2015a; Dorlach 2015; Sparkes et al. 2015; Akıncı et al. 2012; Rosetti 2004). Most research on healthcare politics in Turkey fails to take into consideration power relations among diverse set of actors and the actors' interpretations of the reform. To address this gap in the literature, this book examines the politics of healthcare in Turkey during the launch and implementation of the HTP in the last decade.

Turkey has not been an outlier in transforming its healthcare system. The restructuring of healthcare systems worldwide has been on the agenda

V. Yılmaz, *The Politics of Healthcare Reform in Turkey*,
DOI 10.1007/978-3-319-53667-5_1

of the majority of governments for the last four decades. Contextual factors such as an ageing population and increasing health expenditures have been presented as the main drivers of healthcare reforms (e.g. Oxley and Macfarlan 1995). While these factors might create the need for healthcare reform in a given country, the mere presence of these factors cannot guarantee the introduction and implementation of reforms.

An examination of the American example reveals support for this claim. The 2000 World Health Report of the World Health Organisation (WHO) ranked the American healthcare system 37th out of 186 countries. According to the report, the country that spent the most on healthcare was the United States, yet the US healthcare system ranked 72nd in terms of health outcomes and 54–55th in fairness in financial contribution (WHO 2000). As the report clearly demonstrates, the US healthcare system needed a reform.

Skocpol points out that the low performance of the American healthcare system did not automatically lead to a healthcare reform. President Clinton's attempt at a comprehensive healthcare reform failed (Skocpol 1997), and it took more than a decade for the United States to ratify the Patient Protection and Affordable Care Act, better known as Obamacare (Jacobs and Skocpol 2010). Even the ratification of this reform did not guarantee its implementation. In the case of the National Federation of Independent Business vs. Sebelius, the United States Supreme Court upheld the power of Congress to enact key provisions of the Act, including the compulsory health insurance requirement. It is now thought that the newly elected President Trump is likely to repeal Obamacare. As the American experience suggests, the mere existence of factors that indicate the need for a healthcare reform is not sufficient to initiate and implement a healthcare reform. Even if these factors do result in a reform, the content of the reform does not necessarily remedy the shortcomings of the previous healthcare system.

In cases where reform does happen, the literature indicates that these reforms differ from one another in terms of the solutions they bring forward. For instance, Latin American and Southern European countries had similar healthcare systems with similar problems, such as a lack of universal coverage, but they followed dissimilar paths in reforming their healthcare systems. While Spain and Greece carried out healthcare reforms aimed at transforming their social insurance-based healthcare systems into tax-financed healthcare systems (Petmesidou and Guillén 2008), Argentina and Chile introduced reforms that altered the main parameters of their formerly social insurance-based healthcare systems into more private insurance-based systems (Barrientos and Lloyd-Sherlock 2000). After a significant welfare retrenchment in the 1980s and 1990s, some Latin American countries – Chile, for example – renewed their efforts to institutionalise universal healthcare (Ewig and Kay 2011). In the meantime, southern European countries fell into a financial crisis that undermined their previous ambitions to achieve universal coverage and eventually led to increases in user charges. As the above-mentioned studies on healthcare reform suggest, shared problems do not imply that a reform will indeed be introduced, nor do they predict what kind of healthcare reform will follow.

What factor, then, is the key to an understanding of the dynamics of healthcare reforms? The main factor is politics. Whether it is defined as 'the authoritative allocation of values (valued things) for a society' (Easton 1985, p. 134) or 'the study of the influence and the influential' (Lasswell 1936, p. 295), politics plays a significant role in either making healthcare reforms possible or preventing them from happening. In cases where reform is possible, politics influences the chances of a reform being implemented and helps shape its content.

Despite the fact that the literature on healthcare policy and the welfare state[1] seem to be relatively detached from one another, Moran rightly reminds us that healthcare has been the largest component of a welfare state since the end of the Second World War (2000, pp. 138–9). Moran argues that what happens to healthcare is the key to grasping what happens to the welfare state. Healthcare politics is a significant component of welfare politics in general. The literature on the politics of healthcare (e.g. Jacobs and Skocpol 2010; Klein 2010; Harrison and McDonald 2008; Giaimo 2005; Freeman 1999; Marmor 1999; Skocpol 1997; Navarro 1994; Immergut 1992; Alford 1975) is detached from the literature on welfare politics (e.g. Korpi and Palme 2003; Rothstein and Steinmo 2002; Baldwin 1999; Pierson 1996; Skocpol 1992; Korpi 1989, 1980), but both literatures approach policy reforms as critical arenas within which various actors renegotiate political bargains that back welfare systems in general and healthcare systems in particular.

A healthcare system, however, is more than just a subset of a broader welfare system. A direct link between healthcare and the healthcare industry itself makes healthcare a policy domain that cannot be reduced to a welfare state (Moran 2000, p. 139). Without ignoring the strong linkages between the broader welfare state and healthcare policy, it should be noted that, like all welfare policies, healthcare policy has its own historical trajectory and its own set of policy actors (Kasza 2002, p. 282). Therefore, changes in healthcare policies imply alteration of the welfare state as well, yet these changes might have dynamics that are relatively independent from other changes in welfare policies.

In line with worldwide trends, healthcare reform in Turkey entered the political agenda in the early 1980s. While limited yet significant changes were made in Turkey's healthcare system from the early 1980s to the 2000s, it was not until 2003 that a fundamental healthcare reform was introduced. Before that time, Turkey's healthcare system relied on a combination of social insurance-based healthcare whose governance, financing and provision were state-led. The previous model was stratified according to major occupational groups. Both the service delivery and the financing structure had been fragmented and failed to provide universal coverage (Yılmaz 2013).

The Justice and Development Party (*Adalet ve Kalkınma Partisi, AK Party*), a conservative neoliberal political party, introduced the HTP after the Party came to power as a single-party government in the 2002 general election. The three main objectives of the HTP were to ensure effectiveness, efficiency and equity (The Ministry of Health 2003). In the light of objectives that are almost universal blueprints of contemporary healthcare reforms, a series of legal changes significantly altered the main pillars of the existing healthcare system in Turkey, including the financing, provision and regulation of healthcare services.

Turkey has traditionally been a low spender on healthcare. Once the reform was launched, public healthcare expenditures increased, but Turkey still spends less on healthcare services than all other members of the Organisation for Economic Cooperation and Development (OECD) in proportion to its gross domestic product (GDP) (OECD 2012).

Drawing on this healthcare reform experience, this research is inspired by the agenda that Hall and Thelen put forward, that is, to spot alliances that can push forward reforms and to explore what factors can garner support for the reform (Hall and Thelen 2009, p. 20). I agree with their idea that distributional concerns lie at the heart of the dynamics that drive institutional change (Hall and Thelen 2009, p. 21). From this point of view, I believe in the benefits of a proper matching of politics and policy change to understand the dynamics of policy reforms.

In the light of the research agenda described above, this book asks the following questions: What political dynamics enabled the introduction of healthcare reform in Turkey? What kind of politics did healthcare reform in Turkey generate? What kind of political conflicts arose among different actors? How and to whose benefit have these conflicts been resolved?

1.2 The Contribution and Significance of the Book

The literature on the politics of healthcare is skewed towards the economically developed countries of Western Europe and North America (e.g. Klein 2010; Jacobs and Skocpol 2010; Ham 2009; Çalıkoğlu 2008; Hassenteufel and Palier 2007; Rothgang et al. 2005; Lister 2005; Giaimo 2005; Batley 2004; Freeman 1999; Marmor 1999; Moran 1999; Giaimo and Manow 1999; Wessen 1999; Freeman 1998; Immergut 1992; Moran 1992; Alford 1975). The literature on healthcare reform in emerging market economies concentrates on the impact the reforms have on access and coverage, while leaving underresearched the politics of healthcare that leads to the reform and that continues during the reform process itself (e.g. Dannreuther and Gideon 2008; Petmesidou and Guillén 2008; Lloyd-Sherlock 2006; Muntaner et al. 2006; Lloyd-Sherlock 2005; Homedes and Ugalde 2005; Guillén and Palier 2004; Laurell 2001; Barrientos and Lloyd-Sherlock 2000; Berman and Bossert 2000; Schieber and Maeda 1999; Sen and Koivusalo 1998; Reich 1995). The literature on healthcare reforms in emerging market economies tends to underestimate the role of domestic political actors (including the government) and the interplay between global and domestic actors, and to overestimate the impact of global players on the reforms.

The originality of this work derives from the empirical knowledge it produces on the politics of healthcare during a healthcare reform in an emerging market economy. In doing so, the book offers insights into the factors that motivated the actors who initiated the reform, their interpretations of the reform and the role of other actors during the reform process. In this regard, the book contributes to the healthcare politics literature in two ways. First, it sheds light on healthcare politics in an emerging market economy and thus serves to expand the literature, which has been skewed towards Western European and North American countries. Secondly, the book uncovers the complexity of a healthcare politics scene where actors' understanding of the reform is not only diverse but also rooted in the political and economic histories of specific countries.

Turkey's most recent experience of healthcare reform has attracted immense scholarly attention. The research has generally focused on the impacts of the reform on access, coverage and the working conditions of medical doctors and other health personnel (i.e. Ağartan 2015b; Ökem and Çakar 2015; Atun et al. 2013; Hazama 2013; Horton and Lo 2013; Adıyok 2012; Ağartan 2012b; Akıncı et al. 2012; Belek 2012; Çarkoğlu and Kalaycıoğlu 2012; Demirci 2012; Baris et al. 2011; Sönmez 2011; Yaşar 2011; Yaşar and Uğurluoğlu 2011; Erus and Aktakke 2010; Ucku and Elçi 2010; Teksöz et al. 2009; OECD and World Bank 2008; Kılıç 2008; Pala 2007; Soyer 2007, 2004).

The literature on healthcare politics in Turkey, however, is rather limited (Ağartan 2016, 2015a; Dorlach 2015; Sparkes et al. 2015; Ağartan 2008, 2007; Rosetti 2004). Most of the existing literature takes a stakeholder analysis approach aimed at helping the government to successfully legislate and implement the reform (Sparkes et al. 2015; Rosetti 2004). It presents the HTP as the only rational healthcare policy reform option that had to be introduced at some point, and its legislation and implementation was even delayed owing to weak coalition governments during the 1990s. From that perspective, therefore, there was no need to make a political analysis of the reform content. Because there was no legitimate or viable policy alternative to the HTP in these studies, and given the success of the HTP in delivering its promised results, the perspective researchers adopted reduced the healthcare politics analysis to a single question: How the government successfully managed to bypass all checks and balances in the Turkish political system during the reform process that were presented as obstacles to the reform?

Ağartan's work has been an exception. She examines the politics of the current healthcare reform in Turkey using an ideational approach (Ağartan 2016, 2015a, 2008, 2007). Using a policy learning approach deriving from ideational institutionalism, Ağartan underlines the significant role of the government's reform team in the preparation of Turkey's healthcare reform. While Ağartan's contribution to the literature has been significant especially in demonstrating the key role of the reform team in shaping the HTP, her work falls short of taking a comprehensive approach to healthcare politics and analysing the dynamics of power relations among different actors and their diverse understandings of the reform.

With the objective of addressing this gap in the literature, this book offers a detailed description as well as an analysis of the healthcare politics throughout the HTP. It considers the HTP as one of the reform alternatives that was available in Turkey at the time and suggests that the reason for its selection requires a political analysis. Rather than treating the HTP as a perfectly coherent policy package and a policy that reflected the most up-to-date scientific evidence on healthcare systems, the research presented in this book looks into the tensions and conflicting components within the HTP as well as the changes it has undergone over time. In this regard, it is by unveiling different actors' subjective interpretations of the reform and others' approaches to the reform that this book brings to light a vivid picture of alliances and contestations between different sets of political actors over the reform.

1.3 Methodology

This study is a historically grounded, qualitative single-country case study. As mentioned in Section 1.2, scholarly approaches to the politics of healthcare and welfare have so far been informed primarily by Western European and North American experiences. Therefore, the main methodological problem in this research and other studies on healthcare policy change and politics in emerging market economies (Walt et al. 2008) is to apply these approaches – which were originally designed to explain Western European and North American cases – to another geography with a different historical legacy.

In order to compensate for possible dissonance between the case and approaches, the methodology of this research draws on the insights from historical institutionalism. In his work on social policy regimes in the developing world, Gough argues that historical institutionalism offers a golden mean between a modernisation approach and a post-modern approach (2004, p. 240). Despite their dissimilarities, both of these approaches, in fact, limit the political possibilities in emerging market economies, either by expecting a more immature welfare system than that of Western European or North American countries, or by searching for a value in disorganised and non-universal welfare mixes. Instead of these perspectives, I believe in the universality of political ideals such as the realisation of the right to health and healthcare and the applicability of these ideals in emerging market economies, provided that the political actors are interested in applying them and have the power to do so.

This brings me to the question of how to use a historical-institutionalist perspective to integrate the historical legacy of a given country into the analysis of policy changes. In its most extreme form, historical institutionalism – when accounting for the main political factors that shape reform – generally attributes the primary agency to the political economic legacy of the country and its institutions (e.g. the argument about 'veto points' in Immergut 1992). While the focus of historical institutionalism is on the influence of history and institutions on policy-making processes, this focus has not led scholars using this approach to disregard the agency of actors to initiate political change. Scholars of historical institutionalism examine how power struggles have been mediated and framed by a particular historical and institutional context, and how these struggles change that context at the same time i.e. Rothstein and Steinmo 2002; Hall and Taylor 1996). Therefore, excluding the pure institutionalist forms, scholars of historical institutionalism study primarily the interaction between human-made institutional structures and human agency, without disregarding how and to what extent the options of the latter have been restricted by the former.

This study employs insights from historical institutionalism with the objective of integrating the political and economic legacy of Turkey into an actor-based analysis of the politics of contemporary healthcare reform. It takes a more critical stance with respect to purely institutionalist arguments and retains historical institutionalism as a way of bringing history and institutions into the final analysis without discrediting the impact of actual political struggles between political actors. Following in the footsteps of scholars of historically informed qualitative political science, the analysis made in this book is based on, in line with Vromen's suggestion, establishing linkages between the empirical data and the broader socio-cultural, economic and political frameworks (2010, p. 264).

1.4 Methods

This study relies on qualitative research methods. Qualitative research methods were selected on the basis of their ability to capture the multi-layered and complex nature of healthcare reform processes (Caronna 2010, p. 71) and the politics of healthcare, which together include alterations in the power structure, subjective interpretations of the process by major actors and changes to the formal and informal rules that operate in the healthcare service domain.

Qualitative methods (Vromen 2010) and case study research are established approaches in studies of political processes (Yanow et al. 2010) as well as in healthcare policy analysis (Walt et al. 2008). The benefit of using both qualitative methods and a case study method in this research is that it allows the integration of both historical insight and personal reflections of the actors involved in the institutions, events and processes under investigation (Vromen 2010, p. 249). The practical benefit of using a case study lies in the possibility of combining different qualitative methods such as in-depth interviews and documentary analysis to understand the intensity of lived human experience (Yanow et al. 2010, p. 109).

Scholars who generate and use large-scale quantitative data and scholars using a quantitative comparative approach generally contest the validity and reliability of case study results. Flyvbjerg summarises well-known critiques of the case study method under five headings: the limited use of context independent knowledge, the lack of generalisability in case study research, the suitability of case research for generating a hypothesis rather than testing it, the tendency of a case study to verify the hypothesis of the researcher and the inappropriateness of case study to develop general propositions or theoretical conclusions (2006, p. 221).

All of these critiques originate from a positivist take on approaching social and political issues. The majority of scholars who produce case studies using qualitative methods, however, do not share these positivist assumptions. I am convinced that the strength of social sciences lies in its ability to produce context-dependent explanations and rich knowledge (Vromen 2010, p. 257) rather than exploring the so-called objective laws of the society and politics or making predictions about the future (Flyvbjerg 2006, p. 223).

The criteria for selecting informants in case study research do not follow the logic of random selection of quantitative methods. In case study research, cases are selected with respect to the researcher's expectation about what kind of knowledge a particular interview can probably generate (Vromen 2010, p. 259; Flyvbjerg 2006, p. 230). In this regard, the subjectivity of the researcher in the case study method is more explicit. The subjective element in case study research, however, has not been dissimilar to the hidden subjectivity in quantitative research, where scholars construct categories and variables with which they conduct research and make their analysis (Flyvbjerg 2006, p. 235).

This study relies on in-depth interviews and desk research. Desk research comprised an extensive review of the literature on healthcare policies and politics in Turkey within a comparative framework. I reviewed all major legislative documents, reports and position papers on healthcare reform. In-depth interviews were conducted with representatives of the main political actors – members of the government's reform team, the World Bank (WB), the Turkish Medical Association (*Türk Tabipleri*

Birliği, TTB), private healthcare provider organisations and state institutions, specifically the Social Security Institution (*Sosyal Güvenlik Kurumu, SGK*) and the Ministry of Health (MoH) – in order to gain insights into the power struggle on particular junctures and issues. The research did not make use of original qualitative data collected from patients. Findings from public opinion surveys that investigate the above-mentioned themes were used instead.

1.5 Fieldwork

I conducted 33 face-to-face in-depth interviews, most of which were in Ankara and Istanbul, with a few in Adana, Izmir and Samsun. The majority were conducted between August 2011 and December 2011. Interviewees included members of the reform team, key bureaucrats in the MoH and the SGK, WB experts, executives from private healthcare provider organisations, the leadership cadre of the TTB and the trade unions organised in the domain of healthcare services and politically engaged experts on healthcare policies.

Arranging face-to-face interviews with people who hold key positions is not always an easy task. For those who could not be reached easily, I employed an alternative strategy of organising academic workshops on healthcare reform in Turkey and inviting key people (with whom I might not otherwise succeed in securing an interview) to give public speeches at these workshops. In doing so, I organised a workshop[2] and co-organised two panels.[3] This strategy proved to be successful, as I managed to get the accounts of three people holding key positions in the first workshop and an additional three people in the panels via their presentations and their comments during Q&A sessions. I collected additional information by attending conferences and workshops of medical associations and exchanging ideas with medical doctors and activists at those conferences.[4]

Scholars call for explicit discussion on researcher positionality in healthcare policy research (Walt et al. 2008). Throughout the research, I did not engage in policy communities that supported or opposed the HTP. I did not belong to any of the parties involved in the HTP, which made me an outsider researcher. This outsider position helped me to maintain impartiality during the interviews. Yet as a researcher working on the case of his own country, I was also an insider to the political structure and healthcare system in Turkey. Being an insider eased my access to textual material in Turkish, facilitated my contextualising the information that I got and helped me better understand the political positions of the actors I interviewed.

1.6 The Content of Chapters

This book is organised into nine chapters. After this introductory chapter on the methodological premises upon which the research was based, Chapter 2 reviews different perspectives on the study of healthcare politics, offering answers to the following questions: How can we understand healthcare politics today? What is at stake and for whom? With the objective of providing a sound approach to examining these questions, Chapter 2 presents the historical foundations of healthcare policy (Section 2.2), while Section 2.3 presents the main characteristics of modern healthcare systems before the emergence of a worldwide pro-market reform trend in the early 1980s. Section 2.4 lays out the main features of contesting scholarly approaches to healthcare politics. The aim here is to demonstrate the content of the political nature of debates surrounding healthcare by introducing different theoretical takes on the question of how healthcare should be treated in today's societies. Drawing on theoretical debates with respect to the status of healthcare in contemporary societies, Section 2.5 discusses the context within which healthcare reforms have come onto the political agenda in different countries after the 1970s. The main objective of this section is to set the political-economic scene within which the healthcare reforms emerged and to introduce the main concepts that are widely used in explaining reform-led changes in healthcare systems.

Chapter 3 describes the historical legacy of the healthcare system upon which Turkey's healthcare reform was introduced, situating it against the background of Turkish politics. This chapter provides an overview of the historical development of Turkey's healthcare system by linking the historical process to the history of Turkish politics. In doing so, the main objective is to provide a historical background to the analysis of the political contestations on contemporary healthcare reform in Turkey. After an introduction in Section 3.1, Section 3.2 outlines the history of healthcare system development and the politics of healthcare in Turkey. Section 3.3 reviews the main tenets of Turkey's healthcare system before the reform and locates the reform within a comparative framework. Section 3.4 links the politics of healthcare before the rise of the AK

Party and the main parameters of healthcare system development until the introduction of the HTP in Turkey.

Chapter 4 examines the HTP within the context of healthcare reforms in selected emerging market economies. Its major objective is to describe the HTP and to situate it within the context of post-1980s' healthcare reforms in other emerging market economies. The chapter has four main sections. After an introduction, Section 4.2 describes the main parameters of the HTP. Section 4.3 provides an overview of the post-1980s' healthcare reforms in other emerging market economies, with a special focus on Latin America, Southern Europe and East Asia. The conclusion (Section 4.4) compares the HTP and reforms that were carried out in Latin American, Southern European and East Asian countries.

Chapter 5 addresses the role of the WB in Turkey's healthcare reform in order to understand how and to what extent the global healthcare reform agenda was able to make its way into healthcare policy circles in Turkey. It examines the question of how and to what extent the WB has been influential in the healthcare reform process in Turkey. It particularly investigates the interaction between the WB and successive AK Party governments in the domain of healthcare policy, along with the historical and ongoing institutional ties established between the WB and successive Turkish governments that have fed into the establishment of contemporary partnership between these two actors. The chapter draws on a qualitative content analysis of WB documents as well as interviews conducted with WB experts who played a role in the partnership with the Turkish government and the members of the government's reform team. After an introductory section (Section 5.1), Section 5.2 discusses the WB approach to healthcare policies and healthcare reforms in emerging market economies. It explores whether the WB has a blueprint in healthcare reforms or not, and if it does, what the main components are. Section 5.3 provides an overview of the history of the partnership between the WB and Turkey in healthcare. Section 5.4 examines the partnership between the WB and the AK Party government during the preparation and implementation of the HTP. Section 5.5 investigates the effectiveness of WB loans in providing the WB with political leverage to further its policy advices in the Turkish case. Section 5.6 examines the influence of the WB's know-how and policy advices on the reform. Section 5.7 analyses WB experts' insights about the design of the reform process and discusses the elective affinity of undemocratic policy processes and the WB's technocratic approach to policy-making. Section 5.8 examines the causes of tensions between the WB and the Turkish government throughout the reform process and discusses if and how these tensions have been defused. The last section (Section 5.9) analyses the overall impact of the WB on Turkey's healthcare reform.

Chapter 6 investigates the AK Party's impact on the healthcare reform. It examines how and to what extent the AK Party exerted its influence on the content of the reform, tackled the political conflicts throughout the reform process, rendered the reform politically possible and benefited politically from the outcomes of the reform. This chapter explores the compatibility between the HTP and the AK Party ideology. After an introduction in Section 6.1, Section 6.2 discusses the literature on the relationship between society and political parties in the domain of welfare politics. Section 6.3 explores the influence of the AK Party's political ideology on the design of the reform. Section 6.4 examines how the HTP became a factor in the consolidation of the AK Party rule by rendering its legitimacy in the society. Section 6.5 explores the origins of the AK Party's dual alliance with the poor and the new private healthcare providers and the tensions this alliance may create in the future. In the concluding section (Section 6.6), the AK Party's discursive and practical strategies in making the HTP possible are analysed so as to provide a holistic account of its role.

Chapter 7 examines the role of the Turkish Medical Association (TTB) in the reform. It is organised into five sections, including the introductory one (Section 7.1). Section 7.2 provides an assessment of the literature on the role of medical doctors in healthcare reforms and their professional organisations. Following this assessment, Section 7.3 introduces a brief political history of the TTB and situates this organisation within Turkey's political system. Section 7.4 examines the origins and modes of contestations between the TTB and the government especially over the employment status of medical doctors during the reform. Section 7.5 provides an analysis of the role of the TTB as an actor in the politics of healthcare in the light of the literature on the role of medical doctors in healthcare reforms and their professional organisations.

Chapter 8 investigates the emergence and subsequent role of private healthcare provider organisations during the reform process. It examines the discourse these organisations employed to influence the reform, the content of their demands and concerns about the reform and the strategies they used to pursue their interests. The chapter is organised into eight sections, including an introduction (Section 8.1). Section 8.2 reviews the literature on the relationship between the state and business organisations. Section 8.3 provides a review of the literature on state-business relations in Turkey. Section 8.4 offers a historical overview of the role of private healthcare providers in Turkey's healthcare system before the launch of the HTP and explains the new direction their role has taken with the reform. Section 8.5 offers an empirical analysis of the impact of the reform on private healthcare provision. Against this background, Section 8.6 explores the emergence and organisational structure of private healthcare provider organisations as new actors in healthcare politics. Section 8.7 examines the discourse and strategies that private healthcare provider organisations used in order to influence the future direction of Turkey's healthcare system. Section 8.8 provides an analysis of the impact of the HTP on the landscape of healthcare politics in Turkey and explains how private healthcare provider organisations arising from the Programme influenced the reform itself.

In concluding, Chapter 9 offers insights into the interplay between healthcare politics and policy change in Turkey. It uncovers the political dynamics that made the HTP possible, the impact of these dynamics on the design and implementation of the reform and how the reform changed the power dynamics in the healthcare politics scene. The first political dynamic that paved the way for the introduction of the HTP was the electoral victory of the AK Party in the 2002 general election. An inheritor of the far-right Political Islamist National Outlook movement, the AK Party used the HTP as a tool to reach out to the masses, aspiring to become a 'catchall party.' The second political dynamic was the involvement of the WB in healthcare policy-making. The WB influence on the HTP was two-fold: the historical influence of the WB on healthcare bureaucracy in Turkey, which originated from its leadership in global healthcare policy governance and its historical partnership with the successive governments of Turkey; and the impact of the WB's hands-on involvement in the preparation and the implementation of the HTP. The third political dynamic was the involvement of the TTB in the reform process as a contending party to the government, especially with respect to controlling the labour of medical doctors. The fourth political dynamic was the birth of private healthcare provider organisations, their involvement in the reform process as an uneasy partner of the government, the tension between them and the government over the limits of capital accumulation in the healthcare delivery sector and the new dynamics of healthcare policy changes their involvement has generated.

Notes

1. Welfare state generally refers to a state 'which intervenes within the processes of economic reproduction and distribution to reallocate life chances between individuals and/or classes.' See. PIERSON, C. 1991. *Beyond the Welfare State? The New Political Economy of Welfare*, Pennsylvania, The Pennsylvania State University Press.
2. 'The Transformation of Turkey's Health System' on November 25, 2011 at Boğaziçi University, Istanbul. I would like to thank the Boğaziçi University Social Policy Forum and Friedrich Ebert Stiftung Istanbul for their support.
3. 'Turkey's Healthcare Reform and Its Critiques,' 7th National Congress of Bioethics on October 13, 2012.
4. Crisis of Capitalism and Health, organised by International Association of Health Policies and the Turkish Medical Association, Ankara, October 2011; Transformation and Changes in Healthcare, Çukurova Scholars Association, February 2013; National Congress of Turkish Thoracic Society, Antalya, April 2013.

References

Adaman, F. (2003). Study on the social protection systems in Turkey. *Entry for the report study on the social protection systems in the 13 applicant countries.* Brussels: European Commission.

Adıyok, M. (2012). Turkey's healthcare: A bad prognosis. *Turkish Review*, 2(4), 26–31.

Ağartan, T. İ. (2007). Turkish health policy in a globalizing world: The case of 'Transformation of Health' program. *ISA Research Committee 19 Annual Academic Conference.* Florence: ISA.

Ağartan, T. İ. (2008). *Turkish health system in transition: Historical background and reform experience.* Ph.D., State University of New York.

Ağartan, T. İ (2012a). Gender and health sector reform: Policies, actions and effects. In A. Y. Elveren and S. Dedeoğlu (eds.), *Gender and society in Turkey: The impact of neo-liberal policies, political Islam and EU accession* (pp. 155–173). London and New York: IB Tauris.

Ağartan, T. I. (2012b). Marketization and universalism: Crafting the right balance in the Turkish healthcare system. *Current Sociology*, 60(4), 456–471.

Ağartan, T. I. (2015a). Explaining large-scale policy change in the Turkish healthcare system: Ideas, institutions, and political actors. *Journal of Health Politics, Policy and Law*, 40(5), 971–999.

Ağartan, T. I. (2015b). Health workforce policy and Turkey's healthcare reform. *Health Policy*, 119(12), 1621–1626.

Ağartan, T. I. (2016). Learn, frame and deploy? Cross-national policy ideas and comparisons in Turkey's health reform. *Journal of Comparative Policy Analysis*, 18(1), 54–69.

Akıncı, F., Mollahaliloğlu, S., Gürsöz, H., and Öğücü, F. (2012). Assessment of the Turkish healthcare system reforms: A stakeholder analysis. *Health Policy*, 107(1), 21–30.

Alford, R. R. (1975). *Healthcare politics: Ideological and interest group barriers to reform*. Chicago and London: The University of Chicago Press.

Atun, R., Aydın, S., Chakraborty, S., Sümer, S., Aran, M., Gürol, İ, Nazlıoğlu, S., Özgülcü, Ş., Aydoğan, Ü., Ayar, B., Dilmen, U., and Akdağ, R. (2013). Universal health coverage in Turkey: Enhancement of equity. *The Lancet*, 382(9886), 65–99.

Baldwin, P. (1999). *The politics of social solidarity: Class bases of the European welfare state 1875–1975*. Cambridge and New York: Cambridge University Press.

Baris, E., Mollahaliloğlu, S., and Aydın, S. (2011). Healthcare in Turkey: From laggard to leader. *British Medical Journal*, 342, 579–582.

Barrientos, A., and Lloyd-Sherlock, P. (2000). Reforming health insurance in Argentina and Chile. *Health Policy and Planning*, 15(4), 417–423.

Batley, R. (2004). The politics of service delivery reform. *Development and Change*, 35(1), 31–56.

Belek, İ (2012). *Sağlıkta dönüşüm: halkın sağlığına emperyalist saldırı (Transformation in health: Imperialist attack on people's health)*. Istanbul: Yazılama Yayınları.

Berman, P. A., and Bossert, T. J. (2000). Decade of health sector reform in developing countries: What have we learned?. In *Data for decision making project-Appraising a decade of health sector reform in developing countries*. Washington DC: Harvard School of Public Health.

Çalıkoğlu, Ş. (2008). *Influence of partisan politics on national healthcare expenditures from public and private sources of finance in OECD Countries*. Ph.D. Johns Hopkins University.

Çarkoğlu, A., and Kalaycıoğlu, E. (2012). *Türkiye'de sağlık: toplumbilimsel bir değerlendirme (Health in Turkey: A sociological analysis)*. Istanbul: Koç Üniversitesi, Sabancı Üniversitesi.

Caronna, C. A. (2010). Why use qualitative methods to study healthcare organizations? Insights from multi-level case studies. In I. Bourgeault, R. Dingwall, and R. D. Vries (eds.), *The SAGE handbook of qualitative methods in health research* (pp. 71–87). London, California, New Delhi, Singapore: Sage Publications.

Dannreuther, C., and Gideon, J. (2008). Entitled to health? Social protection in Chile's Plan AUGE. *Development and Change*, 39(5), 845–864.

Demirci, B. (2012). *Transformation in the organizational and financial set-up of the healthcare system in Turkey: Its repurcussions and similarities with the English model.* Ph.D. Ankara: Middle East Technical University.

Dorlach, T. (2015). The prospects of egalitarian capitalism in the global South: Turkish social neoliberalism in comparative perspective. *Economy and Society*, 44(4), 519–544.

Easton, D. (1985). Political science in the United States: Past and present. *International Political Science Review*, 6(1), 133–152.

Elveren, A. (2008). Social security reform in Turkey: A critical perspective. *Review of Radical Political Economics*, 40(2), 212–232.

Erus, B., and Aktakke, N. (2010). *Impact of healthcare reforms on out-of-pocket health expenditures in Turkey for public insurees.* Cairo: Economic Research Forum.

Ewig, C., and Kay, S. J. (2011). Postretrenchment politics: Policy feedback in Chile's health and pension reforms. *Latin American Politics and Society*, 53(4), 67–99.

Flyvbjerg, B. (2006). Five misunderstandings about case-study research. *Qualitative Inquiry*, 12(2), 219–245.

Freeman, R. (1998). Competition in context: The politics of healthcare reform in Europe. *International Journal of Quality in Healthcare*, 10(5), 395–401.

Freeman, R. (1999). Institutions, states and cultures: Health policy and politics in Europe. In J. Clasen (ed.), *Comparative social policy: Concepts, theories and methods* (pp. 80–94). Oxford and Massachusetts: Wiley-Blackwell.

Giaimo, S. (2005). *Markets and medicine: The politics of healthcare reform in Britain, Germany, and the United States.* Ann Arbor: The University of Michigan University Press.

Giaimo, S., and Manow, P. (1999). Adapting the welfare state: The case of healthcare reform in Britain, Germany, and the United States. *Comparative Political Studies*, 32(8), 967–1000.

Gough, I. (2004). Social policy regimes in the developing world. In P. Kennett (ed.), *A Handbook of comparative social policy* (pp. 205–226). Cheltenham Northampton: Edward Elgar.

Guillén, A. M., and Palier, B. (2004). Introduction: Does Europe matter? Accession to EU and social policy developments in recent and new member states. *Journal of European Social Policy*, 14(3), 203–209.

Hall, P. A., and Taylor, R. C. (1996). Political science and the three new institutionalisms. *Political Studies*, 44(5), 936–957.

Hall, P. A., and Thelen, K. (2009). Institutional change in varieties of capitalism. *Socio-Economic Review*, 7(1), 7–34.

Ham, C. (2009). *Health policy in Britain*. Hampshire and New York: Palgrave MacMillan.

Harrison, S., and McDonald, R. (2008). *The politics of healthcare in Britain*. London: SAGE Publications.

Hassenteufel, P., and Palier, B. (2007). Towards neo-Bismarckian healthcare states? Comparing health insurance reforms in Bismarckian welfare systems. *Social Policy & Administration*, 41(6), 574–596.

Hazama, Y. (2013). *Health reform and service satisfaction in the poor: Turkey*. Chiba: Institute of Developing Economies (IDE).

Homedes, N., and Ugalde, A. (2005). Why neoliberal health reforms have failed in Latin America. *Health Policy*, 71(1), 83–96.

Horton, R., and Lo, S. (2013). Turkey's democratic transition to universal health coverage. *The Lancet*, 382(9886), 3.

Immergut, E. M. (1992). *Health politics: Interests and institutions in Western Europe*. Cambridge, New York and Melbourne: Cambridge University Press.

Jacobs, L. R., and Skocpol, T. (2010). *Healthcare reform and American politics: What everyone needs to know*. Oxford and New York: Oxford University Press.

Kasza, G. J. (2002). The illusion of welfare 'regimes'. *Journal of Social Policy*, 31(2), 271–287.

Keyder, Ç. (2007a). Giriş (Introduction). In Ç. Keyder, N. Üstündağ, T. Ağartan, and Ç. Yoltar (eds.), *Avrupa'da ve Türkiye'de sağlık politikaları (Health Policies in Europe and in Turkey)*. Istanbul: İletişim.

Kılıç, A. (2008). The gender dimension of social policy reform in Turkey: Towards equal citizenship?. *Social Policy & Administration*, 42(5), 487–503.

Klein, R. (2010). *The new politics of the NHS: From creation to reinvention*. Oxon: Radcliffe Publishing.

Korpi, W. (1980). Social policy and distributional conflict in the capitalist democracies. A preliminary comparative framework. *West European Politics*, 3(3), 296–316.

Korpi, W. (1989). Power, politics, and state autonomy in the development of social citizenship: Social rights during sickness in eighteen OECD countries since 1930. *American Sociological Review*, 54, 309–328.

Korpi, W., Palme, J. (2003). New politics and class politics in the context of austerity and globalization: welfare state regress in 18 countries, 1975–95. *The American Political Science Review*, 97(3), 425–446.

Lasswell, H. D. (1936). *Politics: Who gets what, when, how*. Michigan: Whittlesey house, McGraw-Hill book Company, Incorporated.

Laurell, A. C. (2001). Health reform in Mexico: The promotion of inequality. *International Journal of Health Services*, 31(2), 291–321.

Lister, J. (2005). *Health policy eeform: Driving the wrong way?*. Middlesex: Middlesex University Press.
Lloyd-Sherlock, P. (2005). Health sector reform in Argentina: A cautionary tale. *Social Science & Medicine*, 60(8), 1893–1903.
Lloyd-Sherlock, P. (2006). When social health insurance goes wrong: Lessons from Argentina and Mexico. *Social Policy & Administration*, 40(4), 353–368.
Marmor, T. R. (1999). *The politics of medicare*. New York: Aldine De Gruyter.
Moran, M. (1992). The health-care state in Europe: Convergence or divergence?. *Environment and Planning C: Government and Policy*, 10(1), 77–90.
Moran, M. (1999). *Governing the healthcare state: A comparative study of the United Kingdom, the United States and Germany*. Manchester and New York: Manchester University Press.
Moran, M. (2000). Understanding the welfare state: The case of healthcare. *British Journal of Politics and International Relations*, 2(2), 135–160.
Muntaner, C., Salazar, R. M. G., Benach, J., and Armada, F. (2006). Venezuela's Barrio Adentro: An alternative to neoliberalism in healthcare. *International Journal of Health Services*, 36(4), 803–811.
Navarro, V. (1994). *The politics of health policy: The US reforms, 1980–1984*. Oxford & Cambridge: Blackwell.
OECD. (2012). *OECD health data 2012: How does Turkey compare?*.
Ökem, Z. G., and Çakar, M. (2015). What have health care reforms achieved in Turkey? An appraisal of the 'Health Transformation Programme'. *Health Policy*, 119(9), 1153–1163.
Oxley, H., and Macfarlan, M. (1995). Healthcare reform: Controlling spending and increasing efficiency. *OECD Economic Studies*, 24, 8–55.
Pala, K. (2007). Türkiye sağlık sistemi nereye gidiyor? (Where is Turkey's health system heading?). *Toplum ve Hekim*, 22(1–2), 62–69.
Petmesidou, M., and Guillén, A. M. (2008). 'Southern-style' National Health Services? Recent reforms and trends in Spain and Greece. *Social Policy & Administration*, 42(2), 106–124.
Pierson, P. (1996). The new politics of the welfare state. *World Politics*, 48(2), 143–179.
Reich, M. R. (1995). The politics of health sector reform in developing countries: Three cases of pharmaceutical policy. *Health Policy*, 32(1), 47–77.
Rosetti, A. G. (2004). *Strategic options for the implementation of the health sector transformation in Turkey*. Ankara: Ministry of Health and the World Bank.
Rothgang, H., Cacace, M., Grimmeisen, S., and Wendt, C. (2005). The changing role of the state in healthcare systems. *European Review*, 13(Suppl. 1), 187–212.
Rothstein, B., and Steinmo, S. (2002). Restructuring politics: Institutional analysis and the challenges of modern welfare states. In B. Rothstein and S. Steinmo

(eds.), *Restructuring the welfare state: Political institutions and policy change* (pp. 1–19). New York and Hampshire: Palgrave Macmillan.

Schieber, G., and Maeda, A. (1999). Healthcare financing and delivery in developing countries. *Health Affairs*, 18(3), 193–205.

Sen, K., and Koivusalo, M. (1998). Healthcare reforms and developing countries: A critical overview. *International Journal of Health Planning and Management*, 13(3), 199–215.

Skocpol, T. (1992). *Protecting soldiers and mothers: The political origins of social policy in the United States*. Cambridge and London: The Belknap Press of Harvard University Press.

Skocpol, T. (1997). *Boomerang: healthcare reform and the turn against government*. New York and London: W. W. Norton & Company.

Sönmez, M. (2011). *Paran kadar sağlık: Türkiye'de sağlığın ticarileşmesi (Healthcare as much as you have money: The commercialisation of health in Turkey)*. Istanbul: Yordam Kitap.

Soyer, A. (2004). *Sanayi Devriminden küreselleşmeye darbeden AK Partiye sağlığın öyküsü (The history of health: From the Industrial Revolution to globalisation; from the military coup to the AK Party)*. Istanbul: Sorun Yayınları.

Soyer, A. (2007). *AKP'nin sağlık raporu (Health report of the AKP)*. Istanbul: Evrensel Basım Yayın.

Sparkes, S. P., Bump, J. B., and Reich, M. R. (2015). Political strategies for health reform in Turkey: Extending veto point theory. *Health Systems & Reform*, 1(4), 263–275.

Teksöz, T., Kaya, Y., and Helvacıoğlu, K. (2009). *Sağlık reformunun sonuçları itibariyle değerlendirmesi (Analysis of health reform by examining its results)*. Istanbul: Türkiye Ekonomi Politikaları Araştırma Vakfi (Economic Policy Research Foundation of Turkey.

The Ministry of Health. (2003). *Transformation in health*. Ankara: The Ministry of Health.

Ucku, R., and Elçi, O. C. (2010). Turkey. In J. A. Johnson and C. H. Stoskopf (eds.), *Comparative health systems: Global perspectives* (pp. 273–286). Boston, Toronto, London and Singapore: Johns and Bartlett Publishers.

Üstündağ, N., and Yoltar, Ç. (2007). Türkiye'de sağlık sisteminin dönüşümü: bir devlet etnografisi (Transformation of Turkey's healthcare system: A state ethnography). In Ç. Keyder, N. Üstündağ, T. Ağartan, and Ç. Yoltar (eds.), *Avrupa'da ve Türkiye'de sağlık politikaları* (pp. 55–95). Istanbul: İletişim.

Vromen, A. (2010). Debating methods: Rediscovering qualitative approaches. In D. Marsh and G. Stoker (eds.), *Theory and methods in political science* (pp. 249–257). Hamphsire and New York: Palgrave Macmillan.

Walt, G., Shiffman, J., Schneider, H., Murray, S.F., and Brugha, R. (2008). 'Doing' health policy analysis: Methodological and conceptual reflections and challenges. *Health Policy and Planning*, 23(5), 308–317.

Wessen, A. F. (1999). Structural differences and healthcare reform. In F. D. S. Powell and A. F. Wessen (eds.), *Healthcare systems in transition: An international perspective* (pp. 369–392). Thousand Oaks, London and New Delhi: Sage Publications.

WHO. (2000). *The World Health Report.* Geneva: World Health Organization.

World Bank. (2008). *Country partnership strategy with the Republic of Turkey for the period 2008–2011.* Turkey Country Management Unit-Europe and Central Asia Region, International Finance Cooperation-Central and Eastern Europe Department, Multilateral Investment Guarantee Agency: The World Bank.

Yanow, D., Schwartz-Shea, P., and Freitas, M. J. (2010). Case study research in political science. In A. J. Mills, G. Eurepos, and E. Wiebe (eds.), *Encyclopedia of case study research* (pp. 108–113). California, London, New Delhi and Singapore: Sage Publications.

Yaşar, G. Y. (2011). Review: 'Health transformation programme' in Turkey: An assessment. *International Journal of Health Planning and Management*, 26(2), 110–133.

Yaşar, G. Y., and Uğurluoğlu, E. (2011). Can Turkey's general health insurance system achieve universal coverage?. *International Journal of Health Planning and Management*, 26(3), 282–295.

Yılmaz, V. (2013). Changing origins of inequalities in access to healthcare in Turkey: From occupational status to income?. *New Perspectives on Turkey*, 48, 53–75.

CHAPTER 2

The Politics of Healthcare: A Critical Review of the Literature

2.1 Introduction

Healthcare reform in Turkey has been a platform for critical contestations as well as alliances among different actors. Contestation between competing perspectives towards the general philosophy of the HTP and its outcomes were manifested in internationally acclaimed scholarly journals. For instance, the *British Medical Journal* published an article entitled 'Healthcare in Turkey: From Laggard to Leader', which presented the HTP as a successful reform that guaranteed universal health coverage for essential services and improved health outcomes (Baris et al. 2011). Two of the authors were healthcare bureaucrats. A number of responses appeared in the same journal, painting a pessimistic picture of Turkey's post-reform healthcare system (e.g. Civaner 2011). Such a debate, visible in the *British Medical Journal* alone, is just one manifestation of the heated political conflicts that have arisen since the introduction of the HTP in 2003. Turkey's healthcare reform has not been the only one to cause significant political conflicts. Both Obamacare in the United States and the reform of the National Health Service (NHS) in Britain generated similar political conflicts that still persist today.

How can we understand these political conflicts in healthcare today? What is at stake and for whom? With the objective of providing a sound approach to examining these questions, this chapter proceeds with a presentation of the historical foundations of healthcare policy.

V. Yılmaz, *The Politics of Healthcare Reform in Turkey*,
DOI 10.1007/978-3-319-53667-5_2

2.2 A Short History of Healthcare Policy

Public health measures are considered to be the first form of health policy. Modern states initially developed such measures in the eighteenth and nineteenth centuries to combat communicable diseases, which were then the major cause of death in societies during the advent of industrial capitalism (Rosen 1993).

Three divergent explanations appear in the literature to account for the political dynamics that have contributed to the development of public health measures and the relationship between public health and capitalism. The first suggests that public health measures came about in order to ensure the well-being of labourers, as they were considered an important infrastructure of capitalist production (Navarro 1976, p. 197). The second explanation identifies public health measures with the genesis of a new logic of government, or 'governmentality', which centres its power base on the regulation of the lives of the population at large, or biopower (Foucault 1991). The third explanation suggests that public health measures were developed, thanks to the political reaction of organised labour against the social costs of capitalism (Leys 2010, p. 5). Leys argues that public health measures emerged 'in spite of capitalism as much as because of it' (2010, p. 2).

The public health approach introduced after the rise of industrial capitalism was much broader than contemporary approaches used in the healthcare policy scholarship. Rather than reducing health to individuals' access to healthcare services, the public health approach aims to transform social, economic and ecological configurations that lead to ill health. Public health measures, in fact, proved their effectiveness by increasing life expectancy and eliminating communicable diseases in most countries during the nineteenth and twentieth centuries. In those countries, non-communicable diseases replaced communicable diseases as the prominent cause of health problems and death, which is commonly referred to as 'epidemiological transition' (Leys 2010, p. 2). The epidemiological transition resulted in longer life expectancy and increased the need for curative healthcare services, especially the treatment of chronic diseases.

In contemporary societies, the role of preventive healthcare has been restricted to a marginal subsector within healthcare services,[1] and its approach has been transformed into an individualistic behaviouralist one. Preventive healthcare today is commonly associated with primary healthcare services such as ambulatory care, visits to general practitioners and/or health posts and centres. Healthcare services today have mainly taken the form of curative healthcare and are associated with large hospital complexes, specialists, health technology and medications (Blank and Burau 2010, p. 18).[2] In this context, healthcare policy refers to the courses of action pursued by governments with respect to the financing, regulation and provision of preventive and curative healthcare services in a given country (Blank and Burau 2010, p. 2).[3]

The widespread production and consumption of curative health services date back to the 'therapeutic revolution' in Western medicine and the emergence of health insurance in nineteenth-century Germany, when Chancellor Bismarck introduced pensions and health insurance programmes in order to appease workers who were mobilised by socialist ideas.

In line with T. H. Marshall's expectation of the extension of citizenship rights to cover social rights that might work against class inequality in capitalist societies (2008), after the Second World War, access to healthcare services came to be associated with citizenship rights. The welfare states of Western Europe and some developing countries (including former socialist bloc countries under the Union of Soviet Socialist Republics) played a critical role in giving shape to healthcare policies as we know them today. The consolidation of welfare states affected healthcare policy in two fundamental ways. First, welfare states had been committed to make curative medicine accessible to society at large. Indeed, all member states of the Organisation for Economic Cooperation and Development (OECD), with the exception of the United States, succeeded in providing nearly universal access to virtually free healthcare for their citizens.[4] Welfare states also opened up a pathway for greater employment especially in healthcare delivery in the public sector (Leys 2010, p. 11).

Secondly, welfare states contributed to the creation of an immense healthcare industry, including the pharmaceutical sector and health technology controlled mostly by the private sector (Moran 1999, pp. 177–8). Through these mechanisms, welfare states acted as the primary engine behind the dramatic growth in the healthcare economy after the Second World War (Moran 1999, pp. 2–3), which has now become one of the largest sectors of the global economy (Tulenko 2016).

2.3 Is Healthcare a Commodity?

As in all other cases of institutional change (Hall and Thelen 2009, p. 21), distributional concerns, or the classic 'who gets what' question, lie at the heart of healthcare politics with respect to access to healthcare services and medications. Here we look at the common assumptions that feed into the political debates around healthcare and introduce different theoretical takes on the question of how healthcare should be treated in today's societies.

Is healthcare a commodity today? Commodity is defined here as a product that is being bought and sold by means of exchange which satisfies human want in one way or another (Marx 2008, pp. 13–50).[5] From one perspective, the products of the healthcare industry, including health technologies and medications, have long been global commodities. Rising medical tourism and increasing foreign direct investment in healthcare services, along with a greater movement of medical doctors across borders, would suggest that healthcare service provision is also becoming a global commodity. The transnationalisation of healthcare services accelerated after the ratification of the World Trade Organisation's General Agreement on Trade in Services (GATS) and other regional conventions (Blank and Burau 2010, p. 8; Sexton 2003, pp. 39–40). The failed Transatlantic Trade and Investment Partnership (TTIP) that the European Commission negotiated with the United States posed a threat to the future sustainability of the UK's NHS, as it would open up the healthcare market to transnational companies without leaving any room for national governments to put restrictions on the commodification of healthcare services (PATIENTS4NHS 2014). In this regard, it could be suggested that the ratification of the TTIP, if it had happened, would have increased the commodification of healthcare delivery. Despite the recent negative political environment for the expansion of international trade, the incorporation of healthcare services into the global free trade regime is always on the table.

The establishment of healthcare as a right refers to the legal codification and implementation of the 'decommodification of healthcare', that is, the extent to which an individual's access to healthcare is not dependent upon their market position and 'the extent to which a country's provision of health is independent from the market' (Bambra 2005b, p. 33). In fact, healthcare systems in various countries substantively restrict the commodification of healthcare by undertaking or regulating the financing, production and consumption of healthcare services.

Although healthcare remains both a commodity and a right in the majority of countries today, neither notion is complete. On the one hand, healthcare is associated with citizenship rights, but it is mostly stripped of the previous holistic approach that manifested itself in the public health approach (Bambra et al. 2005, pp. 189–90). On the other hand, the very reduction of the right to health to healthcare only, including individuals' access to medications, specialist medical services and health technologies, enabled its marketisation. In order to keep the healthcare as a right of citizenship, the fundamentals of the public health approach that demonstrates the social determinants of health has to be revisited. Otherwise, the individualisation of health and its marketisation is hard to resist.

While many countries have been taking a pro-market route in their healthcare policies, there seems to be a consensus in the literature on the inappropriateness of pure market solutions in healthcare. Blank and Burau argue that markets in healthcare are prone to failure, as perfect knowledge is not available to the consumer of healthcare services. Therefore, consumers make their decisions with limited knowledge and rely mainly on the expertise of medical doctors. Secondly, consumers of healthcare services do not know the value and costs of the goods and services that they consider purchasing. This lack of price knowledge disempowers them as consumers. Last, consumers may not be able to receive the full value of goods and services that they buy due to the unpredictability of the efficacy of medical treatment (Blank and Burau 2010, pp. 107–8). Others claim that the exchange value of healthcare becomes unaffordable at times when it is urgently needed and when its use value is the greatest (Lister 2005, p. 98; Skocpol 1997, p. 17). These assertions are especially valid, as only the very rich can purchase high-technology healthcare on the spot (Moran 2000, p. 141).

The health economics approach is important to explore, as it pioneered the use of economics discourse in the healthcare domain and contributed to the understanding and development of healthcare as a commodity. The question of whether healthcare is a public or a private good is still an open question. Health – if understood as healthcare – may cease to be a public good, as there is rivalry and excludability in consumption.

Fuchs succinctly summarises universal assumptions of a health economics approach (1996, p. 3). According to Fuchs, health economics has three main assumptions: scarcity, substitutability and heterogeneity. Scarcity here refers to the scarcity of resources. In other words, health economics treats healthcare as a scarce resource over which individuals compete to access. Substitutability refers to the idea that investing in healthcare has an opportunity cost of not investing in another domain. By heterogeneity,

Fuchs emphasises the availability of alternative medical interventions for any health problem (1996, p. 4).

The health economics approach also concludes that pure market solutions will not work in healthcare and suggests that the uncertainty of demand for healthcare makes it a candidate for an insurance market (Appleby 1998, p. 39; Ranade 1998, p. 3). For health economists, a tax-financed healthcare system that provides free healthcare at the point of service is doomed to suffer from the problem of moral hazard (Arrow 1963, pp. 961–2). The problem of moral hazard refers to the tendency of individuals to consume goods or services more frequently than necessary when they are not paying for the service themselves (Appleby 1998, p. 39). From the perspective of health economists, moral hazard becomes much more acute in the case of state-organised health insurance; the system removes all incentives to economise, not only for patients, but also for medical doctors. According to health economics, the best model for allocating healthcare services is through the insurance model of financing. In doing so, health economics excludes the tax-based financing option. In addition, it leaves question of which configuration of insurance-based healthcare financing has better social outcomes unanswered, as it is largely blind to distributional questions in healthcare policy (Evans 1997, p. 463).

The health economics approach has become the dominant paradigm in global healthcare policy circles since the late 1970s. International organisations such as the WB and the OECD popularised the health economics approach in emerging market economies (Freeman 1998, p. 398). Part of an international 'epistemic community', health economists have been in charge of preparing most healthcare reform projects and therefore their assumptions have constituted the bedrock of these projects (Appleby 1998, p. 35). More importantly, health economics engendered a new 'policy paradigm', defined as an ideational framework that identifies problems, policy objectives and policy tools as well as outcomes to be assessed (Hall 1993, p. 279). In this paradigm, the terminology changes significantly: patients become consumers, managers become necessary actors whose intention is to ensure consumer satisfaction and service efficiency and medical doctors become unreliable providers whose practice should be closely regulated (Irvine 2002, pp. 31–8). The new policy paradigm promoted the insurance-based financing model – first in its private sector-dominated form, and then included public health insurance as a viable policy alternative – at the expense of the tax-based financing model. Meanwhile, universal healthcare systems in Western Europe have been undermined ideologically; these were the models for reform in developing countries and in the United States before the rise of neoliberalism. Instead of universal healthcare systems, the US modified market model has emerged as the preferred source of inspiration in healthcare policy with the rise of neoliberalism (Moran 1998, pp. 18–19).

2.4 Healthcare Reform Under Neoliberalism

The increasing popularity of health economics since the early 1970s and the rise of pro-market healthcare reform in the political agenda was not a coincidence. Neoliberalism, a new powerful political project, emerged as a response to save advanced capitalist economies from the contraction that followed the oil crises in the early 1970s and the decrease of profit margins worldwide. As a political project, neoliberalism is characterised by strong private property rights, free financial markets and free trade, which are believed to enable individual entrepreneurship and freedom to flourish (Harvey 2005, p. 2). With respect to its implications for social policies, neoliberalism promotes five key ideas: confidence in the market as the most efficient way of allocating resources, the necessity of establishing a global free trade regime, the desirability of a state as a facilitator rather than as a substitute or alternative to the market, the need to subordinate fiscal to monetary policy to introduce budget discipline and the necessity to institute flexible labour markets by lowering labour costs, and the necessity of eliminating social policy disincentives to market participation (Hay 2004, pp. 507–8).

Ideologically, neoliberalism is based upon a critique of all forms of institutionalised solidarity between citizens. For example, Hayek argues that 'general altruism' is a groundless conception. This is because individuals can only assume particular responsibilities and effectively care for a specific group of people. Individuals should left free to decide 'what and whose needs appear to him most important' (Hayek 1978, pp. 78–9). This idea undermines the ideational basis of welfare programmes including state and societal healthcare systems and promotes philanthropy as the main alternative for these programmes.

Transforming ideas into policy actions is messy. As a political project, neoliberalism is an open-ended one that manifests itself in different socio-spatial contexts in variegated and sometimes contradictory ways (Brenner and Theodore 2002, p. 353). In fact, scholars proposed two phases of neoliberalism: roll-back and roll-out neoliberalism (Peck and Tickell 2002, p. 384). In its roll-back phase, neoliberalism implied deregulation and dismantlement of previous political and economic institutional structures, whereas in its roll-out phase, it signified active institutional building and regulation (Peck and Tickell 2002, p. 384). Parallel to this periodisation, neoliberalism in its early phase appeared as an overtly ideological project; over time, neoliberalism gradually became a technocratic and seemingly apolitical modus operandi (Hay 2004, pp. 511–18).

What does neoliberalism mean for healthcare policy? What are the common dynamics that neoliberal healthcare reforms generate? In line with its premises summarised above, the neoliberal project aimed to deepen healthcare markets where they already existed and to establish new healthcare markets where there were none before. It could be argued that neoliberal healthcare reforms generally rely upon a combination of four dynamics that are not mutually exclusive, and are explained later. These dynamics are privatisation, marketisation, commercialisation and economisation.

Privatisation refers to a policy direction that promotes more reliance on the private sector and the non-profit sector to a certain extent, and less on the state in any domain of the economy. Privatisation can appear in three forms. The first is characterised by a reduced role for the state in producing goods and services and/or state ownership and the transfer of this role and ownership to private hands. Secondly, privatisation can be put into practice by allowing the private sector to increase its share in the production of goods and services and in the ownership of property (Savas 2000, pp. 3–4), which can be conceptualised as passive privatisation. The first route for privatisation is politically contentious and generally associated with the roll-back phase of neoliberalism, especially in welfare domains such as healthcare policy. In the roll-out phase of neoliberalism, governments increasingly prefer pursuing the second route to privatisation as a long-term agenda in order to avoid political conflicts. In addition to these forms of privatisation, public-private partnerships can also be considered a form of privatisation. Public-private partnerships refer broadly to arrangements between the state and the private sector that delegate formerly public responsibilities to the private sector (Savas 2000, p. 4).

Another common pillar of contemporary healthcare reforms is marketisation. Marketisation can be defined as a policy paradigm aimed at redesigning a policy domain in the image of a market. In the domain of healthcare, the main objective of marketisation is to establish a competitive healthcare market where the demand for and the supply of services belong to different parties (Ewert 2009, pp. 23–4). Ideologically, the discourse on the marketisation of healthcare services prioritises consumer choice, innovation in health technologies, 'value for money' and diversification of healthcare services instead of the provision of equal benefit packages of healthcare services for all citizens. According to the marketisation paradigm, the role of the state should be limited to the regulation of markets.

However, the retrenchment of the role of the state in regulation is not an easy task in the short run, especially in state-dominated healthcare systems. Therefore, the marketisation paradigm is generally put into practice through the introduction of 'quasi-markets' in the various domains of welfare services. Quasi-markets broadly refer to the policy arrangements in which the state ceases to be a provider of welfare services and starts purchasing these services from a competitive market through mechanisms such as bidding (Le Grand 1991, p. 1257). Quasi-markets are labelled as 'quasi' due to their two distinct features: first, service providers in quasi-markets may include private actors as well as non-profit third sector and public actors who compete with each other for stimulating consumer demand. A second feature of quasi-markets is that consumers are not always free individuals who are authorised to make autonomous consumption decisions. They are either represented by a third-party actor or a 'sponsor' who purchases services on their behalf or selects services from a predetermined portfolio of providers (Enthoven 1993, pp. 29–30; Le Grand 1991, pp. 1259–60). For example, in line with Enthoven's policy suggestions for the UK (1993), quasi-markets in healthcare were established in the NHS in 1991 (Ranade 1994, p. 63) to boost efficiency and promote consumer choice (Appleby 1998, p. 34).

A third dynamic that neoliberal healthcare reforms generate is commercialisation, which is defined as increasing the use of market relations in healthcare finance and provision (Mackintosh and Koivusalo 2005, pp. 3–4). Mackintosh and Koivusalo suggest that the concept of commercialisation can have a wider meaning that encompasses the processes of privatisation and marketisation but is not limited to them. In their approach, the commercialisation of healthcare services represents the commodification of healthcare in general.

Neoliberal healthcare reforms can also lead to economisation, which can be defined as a policy approach that aims to establish efficient distribution of limited resources; however, it does not automatically imply the processes of privatisation, marketisation and commercialisation. Economisation emphasises that state's financial and other resources for healthcare services is always limited and should be used efficiently. On the basis of these assumptions, economisation in the domain of healthcare generally refers to the introduction of private sector mechanisms targeting cost-containment and/or better allocation of healthcare resources. These policies involve the restructuring of public healthcare services in order to ensure efficiency and value for money (Ewert 2009, pp. 23–4).

The need for cost containment has made priority-setting in healthcare a critical issue (Blank and Burau 2010, p. 111) and is commonly known as healthcare rationing. Rationing, part of the economisation dynamic, refers to various sets of restrictions on eligibility, delay, deterrence and deflection (Wall 1996, p. 192). While rationing has always been part of healthcare systems – even before the age of neoliberalism – the distinctiveness of neoliberal-inspired rationing lies in its reliance on market mechanisms that are considered to be the best form of rationing.

Economisation generally has manifested itself in the form of 'New Public Management' (NPM) reforms. The UK was the first country to initiate NPM measures, and this paradigm then spread to other countries (Lane 2000, p. 3). Inspired by strong public sector criticism from the public choice school and the Chicago school of economics, NPM reforms call for the import of management techniques from the private sector (Ferlie et al. 1996, p. 9). This idea originated from the belief that management tasks in the public and private sectors are similar and that private sector managerial expertise is superior to public administration (Ranade 1994, p. 90). Some of the best known examples of NPM mechanisms are total quality management applications, the establishment of autonomous expert bodies in various domains of public policy, decentralised budgeting and management, managerial control and accountability tools, assessment of organisational efficiency based on input-output comparisons and productivity-linked rewards and financing applications (Harrison 2004, pp. 173–4).

Neoliberal healthcare reforms generally introduce a combination of the dynamics explained above. However, in the light of Brenner and Theodore's conceptualisation of 'actually existing neoliberalism' (2002), it should be noted that these reforms can be subjected to significant modifications as a result of contestations and negotiations between different political actors in countries undertaking these reforms. Different approaches to the politics of healthcare are explained below, and these contestations and negotiations about healthcare reforms are examined.

2.5 The Politics of Healthcare: Different Approaches

Whether politics is the leading factor for the emergence of modern healthcare systems and contemporary healthcare reforms remains a contested issue. As noted earlier, several factors were important in providing the necessary conditions for the emergence of neoliberal healthcare reforms, including the budgetary crisis of the modern state, a drastic rise in the cost of healthcare services, and a dramatic increase in demand for healthcare services due to factors including but not limited to ageing populations. However, studies increasingly demonstrate that politics constitutes at least one important factor that affects the possibilities of the enactment, implementation and content of healthcare reforms (i.e. Millar et al. 2013; Bhatia and Coleman 2003; Chinitz 1995).

Baldwin, for instance, suggests that broader economic dynamics might create a need for the development of social policies that have to perform various social functions. However, he emphasises that social policies generally go beyond this minimal function. In addition, countries formulate different social policies to deal with common social problems (Baldwin 1999, p. 5). Skocpol also agrees with the idea that long-term or structural factors such as the level of industrialisation or the budgetary crisis of the modern state might constitute necessary yet insufficient conditions or the emergence of the welfare state and/or different sorts of social policies. While long-term or structural factors might induce new social risks and give birth to new social groups, Skocpol underlines that they determine neither the patterns of politics nor the policy outcomes (1992, pp. 13–14). Korpi's power resources approach also suggests that, while industrialisation led to the emergence of organised labour, without the political attempts of organised labour, there would be no welfare state (Korpi 1980, pp. 296–7).

Therefore, both the genesis and alteration of social policies have a significant political component to them. How are we going to understand the role of politics in healthcare policy reforms? There are as many approaches to the politics of healthcare as there are to politics in general. For the purpose of this book, I would like to review the most dominant approaches to the politics of healthcare, as they have inspired seminal works on the issue. The four major approaches include the pluralist, the power resources, the institutionalist and the new politics approaches.

2.6 The Pluralist Approach

The pluralist approach to the politics of healthcare might be considered the application of a classical liberal perspective on healthcare politics. Schmitter defines pluralism, in direct contrast to corporatism, as an interest representation model that relies on a perfectly competitive market of ideas and interests (1974, p. 96).

The pluralist approach relies upon three general assumptions. First, it presents the political domain and the economic domain as separate and limits the political domain to activities within formal political institutions. Secondly, it suggests that all actors, including political actors, are self-interested; however, the self-interest of political actors is defined within the scope of politics. Therefore, in the pluralist approach, politics is mainly interest-group politics. The third assumption of the pluralist approach is that society can be understood as a free marketplace of ideas: individuals can express their preferences in general elections or they can organise in line with their own interests and lobby those in power, without any interference from authorities.

Chinitz provides an example of the application of the pluralist approach in the analysis of healthcare politics in Israel. He suggests that the pluralist democratic system of Israel made the rise of a powerful government possible, which led to a non-incremental change in the healthcare financing policy of the country in spite of the traditional opposition of the labour federation and the Labour Party (Chinitz 1995, p. 923).

According to critiques, the main problem with this approach lies in its conflation of normative and empirical claims. In fact, political groups have different capacities, and these differences in capacity determine their ability to influence the political outcomes (Giaimo 2005, p. 196). As Navarro's study on the inability of the United States to introduce universal health insurance indicates, what the majority of people think on a particular topic might not be sufficient to change policies accordingly. Navarro argues that the United States has long been a place where public opinion on healthcare policy was not in favour of the status quo in healthcare policies, yet the popular idea did not resonate at the political level (1994, p. 173). In addition, as Alford discovers, there might also be 'repressed structural interests', which refer to the interests of sectors of society that have not been served by any social institution or political mechanism (Alford 1975, p. 15). Therefore, these critiques suggest that the pluralist approach to politics fails to grasp how politics operates within the context of unequal power relations.

Despite the theoretical strength of the critiques, it can be argued that it is not easy for researchers to avoid the pluralist approach to politics when analysing healthcare politics. Empirical research generally involves investigating visible political conflicts between particular actors. If scholars fail to link these observations of healthcare politics to political, economic and historical contexts and to the positions of political actors in unequal power dynamics, the resulting analysis will most likely echo the pluralist approach. A structural investigation is therefore a must for researchers aiming to escape the naiveté of pluralist findings.

The pluralist approach to politics might be suitable for the analysis of small-scale political processes. After the most powerful actors set the general parameters of a political debate, Walt argues that 'bounded pluralism' might apply to sub-decisions (1994, p. 202). Applied to healthcare politics, it can be argued that powerful political actors determine issues of systemic importance in the high politics of healthcare. The high politics of healthcare here refers to issues that are closely interlinked with wider economic and political decisions. Alternatively, a wide range of groups may have a say and even influence a final decision in the low politics of healthcare (Walt 1994, p. 10). However, Walt adds a word of caution to his promotion of the bounded pluralist approach for issues of the low politics of healthcare; he notes that even the bounded form of pluralism may not be appropriate for countries that are under the total hegemony of market ideology (Walt 1994, p. 203).

2.7 The Power Resources Approach

The power resources approach can be regarded as the application of social democratic theory to the studies of welfare politics and policies. Korpi, the pioneering scholar of the power resources approach, suggests that there are basically two power resources in capitalist democracies. The first derives from control over the means of production, and the second originates from universal suffrage and democratic political organisations (1980, p. 298). While the power resources approach also represents politics and the economy as separate domains as the pluralist approach does, it identifies the broader system as capitalist, which distinguishes it from the pluralist approach. And unlike the pluralist approach, the power resources approach assumes that power is not evenly distributed in capitalist democracies. For Korpi, the capitalist system is based on a class structure (1989; 1980). Similar to Korpi, Navarro suggests that interest groups are part of broader class politics (1994, pp. 174–5).

Classes can manifest their power in political struggles through diverse forms of political organisations. According to the power resources approach, class power can be observed in organisational power (Korpi 1989, p. 312). More specifically, Korpi evaluates the scope of a working class organisation based on the proportion of unionised workers in the labour force and the proportion of the constituency that supports political parties on the left end of the spectrum (1980, p. 307). Esping Andersen elaborates this approach by noting that the power of organised labour always has to be assessed in relation to the contending actors (Esping-Andersen 1990, p. 16).

For Korpi, although the working class is the less powerful party in the economic realm, it can become a significant power in the political realm, as it is the numerical majority (1989, p. 312). As a result, the power of organised labour can infuse state intervention into distributive issues to the benefit of its members (Korpi 1980, p. 298). In other words, left-wing parties and trade unions can institute social rights by assuming the power of the state, or they might act as powerful political alternatives that push governments to adopt (at least partly) their social agendas (Korpi 1989, p. 316). As the power resources approach assumes that the state is a relatively autonomous entity, it suggests that organised labour can grab state power through democratic means and use it for their own interests. Once organised labour starts to use the legislative power to introduce pro-welfare policies, the introduction of these policies can further strengthen organised labour in return (Esping Andersen 1990, p. 16).

Critics of the power resources approach include representatives of the institutionalist school (Immergut 1992; Skocpol 1992, 1980) and scholars who argue that Christian democracy, not social democracy, has been decisive in the establishment of welfare states in most countries (Manow and Kersbergen 2009; Van Kersbergen 1995).

The main criticisms of the power resources approach are as follows: The first is that the power resources approach imposes one form of political organisation (left-wing parties and trade unions) on the politics of welfare while disregarding all other forms of political organisation. However, the significant influence of trade unions and left-wing parties on the development of welfare states is due to the particular historical experience of certain countries, leaving a significant group of others as outliers to the norm. The second criticism questions the portrayal of welfare politics as a class struggle between two broad categories of classes, namely, the working class and the bourgeoisie. Alternatively, many scholars underline the importance of the middle class in the development of welfare states (Baldwin 1999, p. 9) and in the transformation of healthcare systems (Leys 2010, p. 19; Evans 1997, p. 453). Skocpol too underlines the significance of cross-class coalitions as a driver of social policy expansion (1992, p. 25).

In another criticism, Van Kersbergen questions the empirical validity of the power resources approach. He suggests that religiously motivated political actors, specifically Christian democratic parties, played a key role in the creation of welfare states and policies in most European countries, not social democrats and trade unions. Van Kersbergen argues that the particular ideologies of the Christian democratic parties created a distinctive welfare state regime (1995, pp. 239–40). More generally, Manow and Van Kersbergen suggest that the state-church conflict and the conflict between different sects of Christianity had an immense effect on the development of social policies (2009, p. 4).

2.8 The Institutionalist Approach

The institutionalist approach asserts that political systems frame politics by defining the terms within which political conflicts take place (Rothstein and Steinmo 2002; Hall and Taylor 1996; Immergut 1992). Institutionalism has several variants, including sociological, historical, rational and ideational. Here the focus is on historical and ideational versions in particular, as they are well-established approaches to the study of welfare and healthcare politics.

Institutionalist arguments on welfare state development and reform can differ on the basis of the intensity they attribute to the agency of institutions. While some scholars point to the key role of political systems in framing welfare politics without eliminating the agency of actors involved, others give political systems a decisive agency over policy decisions. Immergut, who exemplifies the latter trend, argues that the political system in a country has much more influence on policy decisions than the initial ideas and organisational strengths of political actors involved in the decision-making process (1992, p. xiii). Similarly, Skocpol argues that political systems shape the demands of both the capital and the labour. They have no a priori demands (Skocpol 1992, pp. 25–30). The political system here refers to what extent an executive body can act independently from the legislature, the courts, or the electorate (Immergut 1992, p. 26); what is politically feasible (Immergut 1992 p. xiii); where 'veto points' in the political system lie (Immergut 1992, p. 7); and which actors are excluded from the political process (Immergut 1992, p. 21).

For institutionalists, political institutions may affect political processes and policy outcomes by reproducing themselves; in other words, 'institutional inertia' affects policy outcomes. In this regard, the state bureaucracy is one of the most crucial yet most neglected political institutions in the politics of welfare. For instance, Asiskovitch proposes that all democracies allocate power to the bureaucracy (Asiskovitch 2010, p. 548). In addition, relatively specialised policy communities within a bureaucracy may also emerge as important actors (Walt 1994, p. 86). Asiskovitch notes, however, that the power of bureaucracies varies according to the political importance of the issue at hand: if the issue can affect the electoral prospects of the government, the power of the bureaucracy over that issue is limited (2010, p. 550). Moreover, the leverage of the bureaucracy varies according to the political system in a particular country. As evidenced in the case of the United States, the impact of the expert-run Central Budget Office on the design of healthcare reform was greater than that of the contending different political factions at the time (Skocpol 1997, p. 67).

Finally, ideational institutionalism is one of the dominant approaches to policy change and healthcare politics. One of its prominent scholars, Béland, argues that taking ideas seriously in researching policy change and healthcare politics can enable institutionalism to look beyond path dependency and incremental change. It can do so by linking the politics of ideas with the mobilisation of political actors without underestimating the impact of unequal power distribution and the limits that existing policy structures on policy change (Béland 2010, p. 626). In their study on Canadian and German health systems, for instance, Bhatia and Coleman exemplify the explanatory power of the ideational institutionalism in the domain of healthcare politics (for a similar case study see Millar et al. 2013). They argue that the presence of a challenging discourse and a consensus among different political actors over that discourse contributed to the emergence of significant policy change in Germany, the absence of which left Canada with minor policy changes (Bhatia and Coleman 2003, p. 717).

The main benefit of the institutionalist approach is that it allows room for understanding how different configurations of politics and political systems in different geographies shape the impact of political actors on reforms and policy outcomes. Bringing history, political systems and ideas into the analysis, the institutionalist approach draws the attention of scholars to the importance of the contextualisation of the subject matter.

2.9 The New Politics Approach

The new politics approach, which is part of the institutionalist tradition, emerged as a reaction to once-popular arguments that claimed welfare states have been in decline since the late 1970s (e.g. Clayton and Pontusson 1998, p. 1131). To counter this claim, the new politics approach proposes that the extension of social rights in the golden age of capitalism reshuffled welfare politics (Pierson 1996). Despite the erosion of the political power of organised labour over time, Pierson underlines the fact that welfare programmes survive, thanks to the public support they had generated (1996, p. 175).

According to the new politics approach, the resilience of pre-established welfare programmes in the context of a disempowered labour movement can be explained in two ways. First, power-sharing in modern democracies has made radical reforms harder. Welfare policies that we inherited from the post-WWII (World War II) period significantly altered the environment in which policymakers are embedded today (Pierson 1996, p. 179). Given that welfare programmes signify the new status quo, the conservative attitude of democratic institutions guarantees the resiliency of these programmes. Secondly, major welfare policies created their own beneficiary groups (Pierson 1993, p. 628) – each with its own particular features (Pierson 1996, p. 175) – who had the power to punish politicians who might undermine the programme (Pierson 1996, pp. 174–5). Similarly, rather than limiting the analysis to one side of the equation, Skocpol also underlines the dialogical relationship between policies and politics, and suggests that changes in each significantly shape the other (1992, p. 58).

In practice, the new politics approach generally accounts for sustained levels of public spending for welfare programmes and public support for the welfare state; it also expects 'incremental policy change' in popular welfare policies. According to the new politics approach, governments can only introduce radical reforms if they are in a position to absorb negative electoral consequences (Pierson 1996, p. 176) or if they face a serious budgetary crisis (Pierson 1996, p. 177). In its current form, the new politics approach offers a rather conservative understanding of the welfare politics and fails to explain the recent enactment of harsh austerity programmes in countries like Greece and Brazil.

2.10 Conclusion

This chapter demonstrated the importance of politics as a factor contributing to policy change in the domain of healthcare and reviews leading approaches to welfare and healthcare politics in the literature. It laid out the main parameters of the political conflict within the realm of healthcare policies today, which centres on the commodity status of healthcare services as well as distributive concerns about healthcare financing and delivery. The chapter also presented the political-economic context, namely neoliberalism, within which this political conflict has taken place from the late 1970s until today.

The major approaches to examining healthcare politics outlined in this chapter are the pluralist, the power resources, the institutionalist and the new politics approaches. While insights from all these approaches are used where appropriate, in the analysis of the empirical data collected for this book, I take Béland's suggestion to examine the multiplicity of causes for policy change, including ideas, actors and institutions, while situating all into the changing social, political and economic circumstances (Béland 2010, p. 627).

Notes

1. Increasing prioritisation of curative healthcare services over preventive healthcare services in the last century has been harshly criticised in the literature e.g. Navarro 1976, pp. 19–20).
2. This dominance of curative healthcare in contemporary societies originates from the 'therapeutic revolution' in Western medicine. The therapeutic revolution is known as the transformation of the dominant paradigm in medicine due to the genesis of the germ theory of disease, which promotes the idea that 'each disease had a well-defined cause and its control could best be achieved by attacking the causative agent or if this was not possible, by focusing treatment on the affected part of the body'. See Dubos, R. J. 1987. *Mirage of Health: Utopias, Progress and Biological Change*, New Jersey, Rutgers University Press. Scholars argue that there is both an economic and ideological elective affinity between the germ theory of disease and capitalism, which together culminated in the dominance of curative healthcare. See Navarro, V. 1976. Social Class, Political Power, and the State: Their Implications in Medicine. Medicine Under Capitalism. New York and London: Prodist and Croom Helm, Doyal, L., Pennell, I. 1994. *The Political Economy of Health*, London, Pluto Press
3. Healthcare policy can be defined as a subset of health policy. See Walt, G. 1994. *Health Policy: An Introduction to Process and Power*, Johannesburg: Witwatersrand University Press, London and New Jersey: Zed Books, Moran, M. 1999. *Governing the Healthcare State: A Comparative Study of the United*

Kingdom, the United States and Germany, Manchester and New York, Manchester University Press. Health policy is a term that refers to the whole set of policies that directly or indirectly affects the well-being of individuals and the environment in which individuals live. In other words, as Blank and Burau put it, health policy can be defined as any policy action that has health implications. See Blank, R. H., Burau, V. 2010. *Comparative Health Policy*, Hampshire, Palgrave Macmillan, ibid. According to this definition, health policy includes a wide range of policy domains from urban planning to consumer protection. In line with these broad policy domains that health policy refers to, the literature on health policy addresses relationships between the well-being of societies and a wide range of other factors such as environment, demography, and social inequalities. See Wilkinson, R., Pickett, K. 2010. *The Spirit Level: Why Equality Is Better for Everyone*, London, Penguin Books.

4. The level of healthcare expenditures in countries is in positive correlation with the level of GDP per capita. The higher a country's GDP per capita, the more it spends on healthcare. See Wall, A. 1996. Conclusion. In: Wall, A. (ed.) *Healthcare Systems in Liberal Democracies.* London and New York: Routledge, Moran, M. 1999. *Governing the Healthcare State: A Comparative Study of the United Kingdom, the United States and Germany*, Manchester and New York, Manchester University Press, Blank, R. H., Burau, V. 2010. *Comparative Health Policy*, Hampshire, Palgrave Macmillan

   Comparative studies of health expenditures in countries with similar levels of GDP per capita, however, demonstrate that the levels of healthcare expenditures in these countries display a significant variation, which led to the growth of the healthcare system typologies debate that I will discuss later in this chapter. See Wall, A. 1996. Conclusion. In: Wall, A. (ed.) *Healthcare Systems in Liberal Democracies.* London and New York: Routledge, Wendt, C., Frisina, L., Rothgang, H. 2009. Healthcare System Types: A Conceptual Framework for Comparison. *Social Policy & Administration*, 43, 70–90.
5. Things gain meaning due to their use-values for human beings. These things, that are of use to human beings, start to bear an exchange-value when they stand in relation to each other. The imaginary construct that brings commodities in relation to each other is the idea of market.

References

Alford, R. R. (1975). *Healthcare politics: Ideological and interest group barriers to reform.* Chicago and London: The University of Chicago Press.

Appleby, J. (1998). Economic perspectives on markets and healthcare. In W. Ranade (ed.), *Markets and healthcare: A comparative analysis* (pp. 34–53). London and New York: Longman.

Arrow, K. J. (1963). Uncertainty and the welfare economics of medical care. *The American Economic Review*, 53(5), 941–973.

Asiskovitch, S. (2010). Bureaucratic actors in mature welfare states: The case of Israel. *Policy & Politics*, 38(4), 547–563.

Baldwin, P. (1999). *The politics of social solidarity: Class bases of the European welfare state 1875–1975.* Cambridge and New York: Cambridge University Press.

Bambra, C. (2005b). Worlds of welfare and the healthcare discrepancy. *Social Policy & Society*, 4(1), 31–41.

Bambra, C., Fox, D., and Scott-Samuel, A. (2005). Towards a politics of health. *Health Promotion International*, 20(2), 187–193.

Baris, E., Mollahaliloğlu, S., and Aydın, S. (2011). Healthcare in Turkey: From laggard to leader. *British Medical Journal*, 342, 579–582.

Béland, D. (2010). Policy change and healthcare research. *Journal of Health Politics, Policy and Law*, 35(4), 615–641.

Bhatia, V., and Coleman, W. D. (2003). Ideas and discourse: Reform and resistance in the Canadian and German health systems. *Canadian Journal of Political Science*, 36(4), 715–739.

Blank, R. H., and Burau, V. (2010). *Comparative health policy.* Hampshire: Palgrave Macmillan.

Brenner, N., and Theodore, N. (2002). Cities and the geographies of actually existing neoliberalism. *Antipode*, 34(3), 349–379.

Chinitz, D. (1995). Israel's health policy breakthrough: The politics of reform and the reform of politics. *Journal of Health Politics, Policy and Law*, 20(4), 909–932.

Civaner, M. (2011). 'Transforming' our health by privatisation-Response to Baris et. al. *British Medical Journal*, 342.

Clayton, R., and Pontusson, J. (1998). Welfare-state retrenchment revisited: Entitlement cuts, public sector restructuring, and inegalitarian trends in advanced capitalist societies. *World Politics*, 51(1), 67–98.

Doyal, L., and Pennell, I. (1994). *The Political Economy of Health.* London: Pluto Press.

Dubos, R. J. (1987). *Mirage of Health: Utopias, Progress and Biological Change.* New Jersey: Rutgers University Press.

Enthoven, A. C. (1993). The history and principles of managed competition. *Health Affairs*, 12(Suppl. 1), 24–48.

Esping Andersen, G. (1990). *The three worlds of welfare capitalism.* Cambridge and Princeton: Polity Press and Princeton University Press.

Evans, R. G. (1997). Going for the gold: The redistributive agenda behind market-based healthcare reform. *Journal of Health Politics, Policy and Law*, 22(2), 427–465.

Ewert, B. (2009). Economization and marketization in the German healthcare system: How do users respond?. *German Policy Studies*, 5(1), 21–44.

Ferlie, E., Ashburner, L., Fitzgerald, L., and Pettigrew, A. (1996). *The new public management in action.* Oxford and New York: Oxford University Press.

Foucault, M. (1991). Governmentality. In G. Burchell, C. Gordon, and P Miller (eds.), *The Foucault effect: Studies in governmentality* (pp. 87–104). Chicago: University of Chicago Press.

Freeman, R. (1998). Competition in context: The politics of healthcare reform in Europe. *International Journal of Quality in Healthcare*, 10(5), 395–401.

Fuchs, V. R. (1996). Economic, values, and healthcare reform. *The American Economic Review*, 86(1), 1–24.

Giaimo, S. (2005). *Markets and medicine: The politics of healthcare reform in Britain, Germany, and the United States.* Ann Arbor: The University of Michigan University Press.

Hall, P. (1993). Policy paradigms, social learning, and the state: The case of economic policy-making in Britain. *Comparative Politics*, 25(3), 275–296.

Hall, P. A., and Taylor, R. C. (1996). Political science and the three new institutionalisms. *Political Studies*, 44(5), 936–957.

Hall, P. A., and Thelen, K. (2009). Institutional change in varieties of capitalism. *Socio-Economic Review*, 7(1), 7–34.

Harrison, M. I. (2004). *Implementing change in health systems.* London: Sage Publications.

Harvey, D. (2005). *A brief history of neoliberalism.* Oxford and New York: Oxford University Press.

Hay, C. (2004). The normalizing role of rationalist assumptions in the institutional embedding of neoliberalism. *Economy and Society*, 33(4), 500–527.

Hayek, F. A. (1978). *The constitution of liberty.* Chicago: The University of Chicago Press.

Immergut, E. M. (1992). *Health politics: Interests and institutions in Western Europe.* Cambridge, New York and Melbourne: Cambridge University Press.

Irvine, R. (2002). Fabricating 'health consumers' in healthcare politics. In S. Henderson and A. Petersen (eds.), *Consuming Health: The Commodification of Healthcare* (pp. 31–46). London and New York: Routledge.

Korpi, W. (1980). Social policy and distributional conflict in the capitalist democracies. A preliminary comparative framework. *West European Politics*, 3(3), 296–316.

Korpi, W. (1989). Power, politics, and state autonomy in the development of social citizenship: Social rights during sickness in eighteen OECD countries since 1930. *American Sociological Review*, 54, 309–328.

Lane, J.E. (2000). *New public management.* London and New York: Routledge.

Le Grand, J. (1991). Quasi-markets and social policy. *The Economic Journal*, 101(408), 1256–1267.

Leys, C. (2010). Health, healthcare and capitalism. *Socialist Register*, 46(46), 1–28.

Lister, J. (2005). *Health policy reform: Driving the wrong way?*. Middlesex: Middlesex University Press.

Mackintosh, M., and Koivusalo, M. (2005). *Commercialization of healthcare: Global and local dynamics and policy responses.* Hampshire and New York: Palgrave Macmillan.

Manow, P., and Kersbergen, K. V. (2009). Religion and the western welfare State – The theoretical context. In K. V. Kersbergen and P. Manow (eds.), *Religion, Class Coalitions, and Welfare States* (pp. 1–38). New York: Cambridge University Press.

Marshall, T. H. (2008). Citizenship and Social Class. In S. Leibfried and S. Mau (Eds..), *Welfare States: Construction, Deconstruction, Reconstruction* Volume Vol. *I* (pp. 89–137). Cheltenham and Northampton: Edward Elgar.

Marx, K. (2008). *Capital.* Oxford: Oxford University Press.

Millar, R., Mulla, A., and Powell, M. (2013). Delivering reform in English healthcare: An ideational perspective. *Public Policy and Administration*, 28(3), 233–252.

Moran, M. (1998). Explaining the rise of the market in healthcare. In W. Ranade (ed..), *Markets and healthcare: A comparative analysis* (pp. 17–33). London and New York: Longman.

Moran, M. (1999). *Governing the healthcare state: A comparative study of the United Kingdom, the United States and Germany.* Manchester and New York: Manchester University Press.

Moran, M. (2000). Understanding the welfare state: The case of healthcare. *British Journal of Politics and International Relations*, 2(2), 135–160.

Navarro, V. (1976). *Medicine under capitalism.* New York and London: Prodist and Croom Helm.

Navarro, V. (1994). *The politics of health policy: The US reforms, 1980–1984.* Oxford & Cambridge: Blackwell.

PATIENTS4NHS. (2014). EU/US free trade agreement. http://www.patients4nhs.org.uk/eu-us-free-trade-agreement-or-ttip/. Accessed 25 November 2014.

Peck, J., and Tickell, A. (2002). Neoliberalizing space. *Antipode*, 34(3), 380–404.

Pierson, P. (1993). When effect becomes cause: Policy feedback and political change. *World Politics*, 45(4), 595–628.

Pierson, P. (1996). The new politics of the welfare state. *World Politics*, 48(2), 143–179.

Ranade, W. (1994). *A future for the NHS? Healthcare in the 1990s.* London and New York: Longman.

Ranade, W. (1998). *Markets and healthcare: A comparative analysis.* London and New York: Longman.

Rosen, G. (1993). *A history of public health.* Baltimore and London: The Johns Hopkins University Press.

Rothstein, B., and Steinmo, S. (2002). Restructuring politics: Institutional analysis and the challenges of modern welfare states. In B. Rothstein and S. Steinmo (eds.), *Restructuring the welfare state: Political institutions and policy change* (pp. 1–19). New York and Hampshire: Palgrave Macmillan.

Savas, E. S. (2000). *Privatization and public-private partnerships.* New York: Seven Bridges Press.

Schmitter, P. (1974). Still the century of corporatism? *The Review of Politics*, 36(1), 85–131.

Sexton, S. (2003). Trading healthcare away: The WTO's General Agreement on Trade in Services (GATS). In K. Sen (ed.), *Restructuring health services: Changing contexts & comparative perspectives* (pp. 33–52). London and New York: Zed Books.

Skocpol, T. (1980). Political response to capitalist crisis: Neo-Marxist theories of the state and the case of the New Deal. *Politics & Society*, 10(2), 155–201.

Skocpol, T. (1992). *Protecting soldiers and mothers: The political origins of social policy in the United States.* Cambridge and London: The Belknap Press of Harvard University Press.

Skocpol, T. (1997). *Boomerang: Healthcare reform and the turn against government.* New York and London: W. W. Norton & Company.

Tulenko, K. (2016, May 25). The world's health sector is expanding. Can it heal our economies?. *World Economic Forum.*

Van Kersbergen, K. (1995). *Social capitalism: A study of Christian Democracy and the welfare state.* London and New York: Routledge.

Wall, A. (1996). *Healthcare systems in liberal democracies.* London and New York: Routledge.

Walt, G. (1994). *Health policy: An introduction to process and power.* Johannesburg: Witwatersrand University Press, London and New Jersey: Zed Books.

Wendt, C., Frisina, L., and Rothgang, H. (2009). Healthcare system types: A conceptual framework for comparison. *Social Policy & Administration*, 43(1), 70–90.

Wilkinson, R., and Pickett, K. (2010). *The spirit level: Why equality is better for everyone.* London: Penguin Books.

CHAPTER 3

Healthcare and Politics in Turkish History

3.1 Introduction

There seems to be an implicit consensus in the healthcare politics literature that mostly domestic politics has shaped healthcare reforms in advanced capitalist societies in Western Europe and North America, while international policy trends have had a significant influence on the framing of reforms in other parts of the world (Jacobs and Skocpol 2010; Harrison and McDonald 2008; Giaimo 2005; Giaimo and Manow 1999; Navarro 1994; Immergut 1992). Moran's study is an exception as it demonstrates the impact of the US healthcare system on healthcare reforms in other advanced capitalist countries such as the United Kingdom, especially after late 1980s (2000, p. 152). Studies on healthcare reforms in emerging market economies also tend to underestimate the power of domestic healthcare politics and its interplay with global healthcare politics.

Without underestimating the global power inequalities between countries, corporate powers and international organisations, it is argued here that this assumption renders nearly invisible the impact of three factors on healthcare reforms in the context of emerging market economies: the inherited healthcare systems, the country's political history and domestic politics.

Scholars employing the historical institutionalist perspective argue that all public policy reforms interact with inherited political and economic institutions in the context in which they are carried out (Ellison 2006, p. 1; Brenner and Theodore 2002, p. 351). In other words, domestic

V. Yılmaz, *The Politics of Healthcare Reform in Turkey*,
DOI 10.1007/978-3-319-53667-5_3

political contestations over specific public policy reforms do not occur in a vacuum. On the contrary, the historical institutional context frames, inspires and provides a meaningful platform for healthcare and all other reforms. In the light of these insights, I would like to bring the history of the healthcare system and the politics of healthcare into the analysis of healthcare reform in Turkey.

3.2 The History of Healthcare Politics in Turkey Before the Reform

One of the prominent historians of social policy development in the late Ottoman Empire and the early Republican era, Özbek, suggests that this history can be split on the basis of critical developments and overall trends into three stages: the 1850s to the 1940s, the 1940s to the 1980s and the 1980s to the present. This section is organised according to Özbek's periodisation.

3.3 The History of Healthcare and Politics Until the End of WWII

In order to explain the development of social policies in Turkey, Özbek argues that scholars should look to the late Ottoman period and suggests that the rise of the modern state and the state's engagement with public health started not with the foundation of the Turkish Republic, but during the late Ottoman era (2006, p. 19). Indeed, other historical research validates this claim. For instance, Aydın reports that the late Ottoman state began to employ medical doctors as state officials to serve the public during the late nineteenth century and the early twentieth century (2002, pp. 11–25). These medical doctors were known at the time as the physicians of the fatherland (*memleket tabibi*) or the government's physicians (*hükümet tabibi*).

The political history of the late Ottoman era suggests that the medical profession played an important role in popularising Western ideals of a secular nation state. These medical doctors were graduates of Ottoman medical schools. Modern medical training within the boundaries of the Ottoman Empire dates back to the first half of the nineteenth century, with the establishment of the Military Medical School (*Tıbhane-i Amire*), which later became known as the first modern School of Medicine (*Mekteb-i Tıbbiye-i Adliye-i Şahane*).

Students and graduates of the medical school formed a well-organised sector of the late Ottoman society. In fact, the first medical association was founded in the second half of the nineteenth century. Doctors organised in ways that went beyond the usual parameters of professional medical societies, and students and graduates of the School of Medicine were among the founders of the Committee of Union and Progress (*İttihat ve Terakki Cemiyeti, or İTC*). The İTC was considered the political organisation responsible for the establishment of the Turkish Republic, and medical doctors were commonly in the higher ranks. Given their historic role in the establishment of the Republic of Turkey in the early twentieth century and the elective affinity between their secular educational backgrounds and the official ideology at the time, doctors protected their elite status in the social and political hierarchy in the Republic.

Medical doctors became part of the governing bloc in the early Republican period. Founded in 1923, the Republic was first run by the Republican People's Party (*Cumhuriyet Halk Partisi, or CHP*), with its charismatic leader and founding father, Mustafa Kemal Atatürk. The CHP ruled as a single-party government until the peaceful transition to a multiparty system in the early 1950s.

While being part of the governing bloc empowered doctors politically, it also led to the evolution of medical profession as part of the bureaucracy. Law on the practice of medicine, ratified in the early days of the Republic, established provincial medical chambers (*Etibba Odaları*) (The Republic of Turkey 1928). The first of these, the Istanbul provincial medical chamber, was established in 1929. It could be argued that the establishment of provincial medical chambers by law implied a corporatist tendency in the political structure of the early Republic. State dominance over professional bodies can be considered a reflection of the Ottoman-Turkish polity's 'bureaucratic centralist' character (Heper 1991, p. 12).

One of the defining features of the origin of social policies, according to Özbek, is that policies emerged in a context of limited industrialisation and in the absence of a politically and socially significant social category: the industrial workers. For Özbek, in the first period of this history, the Turkish state mainly introduced social assistance measures and was heavily involved in pro-natalist policies (2006, pp. 20–1).

In addition to the social assistance and population policies that Özbek mentions, one of the critical developments in the first period was the promulgation of the Public Health Law. With this law, the state openly declared itself responsible for protecting the health of its population against communicable diseases (The Republic of Turkey 1930). Günal notes that this was a necessary step at the time, as communicable diseases such as malaria, tuberculosis, trachoma, syphilis and leprosy were prevalent in the early days of the Republic (2008, p. 22).

In the first period, curative healthcare services were left to the resource-deficit municipalities and the state financed only preventive healthcare services. Financing curative healthcare services therefore constituted a significant policy problem at the time. Although social insurance and taxation had both been considered as possible sources of healthcare financing during the National Economy Congress in 1923 (Talas 1992, pp. 94–5), the state assumed no responsibility for establishing public insurance funds until the end of WWII.

While the state did not establish modern social security measures in this period, some scholars emphasise that it did pioneer significant legislative developments that began to regulate the labour market, including attempts to enhance workers' health. One such example was the establishment of health insurance funds and the provision of healthcare services in the mining sector, which employed the largest portion of industrial workers in the country at the time. The Turkish parliament passed legislation to regulate the working conditions of coal miners in Zonguldak and the Ereğli basin (The Republic of Turkey 1921). This law required the owners of coal mines to contribute to health insurance funds for their workers and to provide free healthcare services. Talas argues that this legislation was the first social policy legislation of the Republic, which symbolised the emergence of a new policy paradigm that portrayed the state as the regulating party in relations between workers and employers (1992, p. 85–86). Although the state was involved in regulating labour relations in the mining sector, it is important to note that it did not make financial contributions to the health fund for the workers. The revenues for the fund were collected from workers and their employers (Talas 1992, p. 119). The state's non-contribution to the workers' social security funds became the norm in the second period.

In the domain of healthcare provision, the state lacked sufficient human, technical and institutional capacities to meet the health needs of the general population during this period. Buğra reports that all international observers in Turkey at the time declared that human resources and the institutional capacity of Turkey's healthcare system were insufficient (2008, pp. 120–1).

The major development in this period was the state's involvement in public health, which aimed to protect the population from communicable diseases but left curative healthcare services out of the political agenda. Medical doctors became part of the bureaucracy, and the basic features of the nascent social security system started to emerge in the mining sector.

3.4 The History of Healthcare and Politics Between the End of WWII and the Military Coup d'État in 1980

In line with international trends, the end of WWII marked the start of the second period in the history of social policy development in Turkey. In this period, social policies in Turkey developed in accordance with national developmentalist economic policies. In this regard, it is suggested here that Turkey's welfare system was an example of a 'protective welfare state', defined as a system that makes social rights contingent on labour market attachment, which makes these rights available to only a limited stratum of the society (Rudra 2007, p. 384). Parallel to social policy developments in Western European countries, Turkey began to initiate modern social security measures and to invest in expanding public capacity for providing healthcare services. According to Özbek, this period witnessed the strongest developments in the history of social policies in Turkey (2006, pp. 22–3).

3.4.1 The Transition to Electoral Democracy and Its Impact on Healthcare Politics

The second period commenced with the introduction of two consecutive national health plans. Mr Refik Saydam, the first Minister of Health, introduced the first plan in the late 1940s. It called for the extension of preventive healthcare services, better organisation of healthcare delivery and the establishment of health chests or social insurance funds to finance these services (Aydın 2002, pp. 53–4).

The CHP had ruled the country as a single-party government since the founding of the Republic in 1923. General elections in 1950, however, marked Turkey's transition to a multi-party parliamentary democracy. The Democratic Party (*Demokrat Parti, or DP*), established by former CHP members, won more than half of the national votes, which led to a peaceful transition of power from the CHP to the DP. Later, Mr Behçet Uz, the

DP Minister of Health, launched a second health plan. Similar to Saydam's plan, the major objectives of the second plan were to improve the organisation of healthcare services and to extend healthcare services to all parts of the country (Aydın 2002, pp. 53–4).

Keyder makes it clear that populism became a powerful political tool only after the ruling bloc in Turkey divided into two political parties, the CHP and DP (Keyder 2007b, p. 147). Toprak argues that this form of populism, blended with nationalism, was based on the ideal that the social policies of the state might abolish class differences and create a 'classless' nation (Toprak 1982, p. 350). As T. H. Marshall's seminal work on citizenship and social class exemplifies (2008), this ideal was not unique to Turkish policymakers at the time but it manifested the spirit of the time.

The emergence of the healthcare service provision as a democratic imperative yielded fruit in the DP period. Günal reports that the share of the Ministry of Health (MoH) budget increased substantially, and public capacity of healthcare provision also made significant progress during this period (2008, p. 23). Günal further notes that investment in the development of curative healthcare services had started (2008, p. 145).

In line with the national developmentalist policy paradigm, the governments in this period were also active in supporting the making of a national bourgeoisie. Toprak suggests that the state's investment in the creation of a national bourgeoisie also dated back to the late Ottoman era (Toprak 1982, p. 348). Boratav argues that the Republic was no different; it had always been committed to nurturing a national bourgeoisie (Boratav 2010, p. 40). However, the state's involvement in the creation of a national bourgeoisie did not resonate in the domain of healthcare, as healthcare delivery and insurance were not considered market commodities at the time. Healthcare services emerged and began to grow as part of the public sector.

3.4.2 *The 1961 Constitution and the Socialisation of Healthcare Services*

The first military coup d'état in the history of the Republic overthrew the DP government on 27 May 1960 and sentenced the prime minister to death. The National Unity Committee (*Milli Birlik Komitesi*) then ruled the country for over a year and ratified a new constitution in 1961 before transferring power back to civilians. Many professionals, including academics and other leading civil servants, took up positions in the political cadre in the establishment of the new regime.

Despite the fact that the new constitution was the product of a military junta, many scholars consider it to be the most democratic and progressive constitution that Turkey had had until then. Talas, one of the pioneering scholars of social policy in Turkey, argues that the 1961 constitution was a progressive development, as it included clauses guaranteeing the right to unionise, the right to collective bargaining and the right to industrial action for the first time in Turkish history (1992, p. 70). Similarly, Boratav argues that the 1961 constitution paved the way for the emergence of populist redistributive policies between 1962 and 1976 (2010, p. 123).

Indeed, the 1961 constitution strengthened the social state components of the Republic and included a special 'right to health' clause that made the state responsible for universal healthcare provision. In this context, a 15-year-long government project called 'the Socialisation of Health Services Programme' or 'the Socialisation Programme' (The Republic of Turkey 1961) was launched. Mr Nusret Fişek, a distinguished professor of public health, was the leading figure during the reform process. The main objective of this Programme was to establish a vertically organised healthcare delivery system to serve the country as a whole, from the smallest villages to the largest cities. In line with this objective, the Programme aimed to establish public healthcare service provider institutions on different geographical scales: health posts, health stations and health centres. These would operate on a referral system and integrate all healthcare delivery units in the country under the purview of the MoH (Günal 2008, pp. 380–1).

The Programme contributed to the dissemination of primary care services to rural areas and socially and economically deprived neighbourhoods. While the Programme was initiated first in one of the most deprived cities of Turkey – namely, Muş – it reached only 26 cities in 14 years, which left 41 cities, including three metropolitan areas, out of the Programme (Günal 2008, p. 25). The main reasons for this failure were threefold: one, the Programme lacked sustainable financing from the public budget; two, the SSK started organising separate healthcare services for workers in urban areas; and three, the majority of medical doctors were unwilling to work in deprived areas of the country.

In the eyes of the leadership cadre of the TTB and among left-wing intellectuals, the introduction of the Socialisation Programme was considered one of the most significant historical events in the history of the Republic, as the state attempted to strengthen its 'social' side by providing preventive healthcare services. This Programme was believed to have initiated a new policy paradigm aiming at the development of a tax-based universal national healthcare system with a strong public health approach. Indeed, the Programme extended the scope of primary healthcare services, which were provided free of charge at the point of delivery. In addition, the Socialisation Programme strengthened citizens' perception that healthcare provision is the responsibility of the state.

Günal, however, argues that the Socialisation Programme failed to establish a universal national healthcare system, especially in the area of healthcare financing (2008, p. 26). Aydın argued that Mr Nusret Fişek, the pioneer of the Socialisation Programme, had supported the establishment of health insurance funds rather than supporting a tax-based healthcare financing model (2002, p. 90). He goes on to suggest that the Socialisation Programme did not call for the establishment of a full-fledged state healthcare system (2002, pp. 82–3). Despite the controversy about its limits, the Socialisation Programme maintains its position as a reference point in debates on healthcare politics in Turkey.

3.4.3 The Developments in Social Security

In this period of the history of social policies in Turkey, the main parameters of the healthcare financing slowly consolidated (e.g. The Republic of Turkey 1950). Healthcare financing was in fact not separated from pensions at the time; all social insurance funds offered both to their beneficiaries.

The Social Insurance Institution (*Sosyal Sigortalar Kurumu, or SSK*), formerly known as the Workers' Insurances Institution, was founded in 1946 as Turkey's first social insurance institution. The active labour force numbered around 14.5 million in the early 1950s, but the SSK provided insurance coverage to only half a million workers (Buğra 2008, p. 161). The number of insured workers substantially increased, however, throughout the 1960s. In the meantime, the SSK extended insurance coverage to workers' family members (Buğra 2008, p. 178), which facilitated access to healthcare services for an even greater number of citizens.

Shortly after the SSK was created, the Retirement Fund for Civil Servants (*Emekli Sandığı, or ES*) was established in 1954 (The Republic of Turkey 1949). Only in 1971 did Turkey's social security system begin to provide insurance coverage for the self-employed, including farmers, with the establishment of the Pension Fund for the Self Employed (*Esnaf, Sanatkarlar ve Diğer Bağımsız Çalışanlar Sigorta Kurumu, or BAĞ-KUR*) (The Republic of Turkey 1971).

While the healthcare financing model in Turkey started to take shape as a social security-based model, the structure of the country's labour market posed serious challenges to the model's ability to provide universal coverage. For instance, in 1927, only one-fourth of the population resided in cities. It was only in 1985 that the urban population exceeded the rural population. Given the delayed establishment of a social security fund for farmers, it is not surprising that the social security schemes (especially before the establishment of BAĞ-KUR) failed to reach the large majority of the population working in agriculture until early 1970s.

In order to compensate for this failure to provide universal coverage, the Hospitals Ordinance of 1955 included a special clause that would provide free medical examinations in public hospitals for civil servants, medical professionals, pregnant women, people with infectious diseases, emergency patients and people who were able to provide official documents from local authorities called *muhtars*, proving that they were indigent (The Republic of Turkey 1955). Buğra suggests that by dealing with the failure to provide universal coverage in this way, social policies emerged not in the form of formal social rights for all but rather through reciprocity relations between individuals left outside the formal social security system and the state (2008, p. 183). This practice was just one example of how the shortcomings of the social security system opened up a space for informality and patronage relationships. Outsiders to the social security system therefore had to find a way to navigate around the special relationships in order to access their citizenship entitlements (Buğra 2008, p. 183).[1]

Like Buğra, Günal views these features of the Ordinance as an indication of the emergent stratified character of the social security system. Civil servants were in a favourable position at the top, while those working in informal sectors and the agricultural sector were at the bottom (Günal 2008, p. 185). In addition to these inequalities in health insurance coverage, the Ordinance also allowed public hospitals to offer private, first-class, second-class and third-class rooms to their patients. Therefore, Günal argues, the objective of healthcare policy at the time was not to institute equality in access to healthcare but rather to first create public capacity and then facilitate access to services in line with one's socio-economic and occupational position within the social stratification.

3.4.4 *The Politics of Healthcare in the Second Period*

During this period of the history of social policies, Turkey also witnessed the establishment of organisations representing employers, workers and medical doctors. Chambers of Commerce were established in 1950, and membership was compulsory. The Confederation of Turkish Trade Unions (*Türkiye İşçi Sendikaları Konfederasyonu, or TÜRK-İŞ*) was founded in 1951 as the only trade union representing workers. Both of these institutions had limited ability to mobilise constituencies, operated within the political boundaries that the government set and remained extensions of state institutions until the late 1960s. The Turkish Medical Association (*Türk Tabipleri Birliği, or TTB*) was founded in 1953 as a corporatist professional body and functioned as such in its early years. From the end of WWII until the transfer of power to civilians after the 1960 military coup d'état, it can be argued that neither the TTB nor the TÜRK-İŞ had a significant impact on the politics of social policies and healthcare in particular.

Class-based political divisions in Turkey became visible only after the 1960s. After the ratification of the 1961 constitution, labour and capital organisations based on voluntary membership began to appear (Buğra 1997, pp. 333–6). In 1961, the Turkish Confederation of Employer Associations (*Türkiye İşveren Sendikaları Konfederasyonu, or TİSK*) was founded and became the political voice of the employers. In 1967, the Confederation of the Progressive Trade Unions of Turkey (*Devrimci İşçi Sendikaları Konfederasyonu, or DİSK*) was established and became one of the most influential actors of the workers movement. In the late 1960s, 12 leading businessmen established the Turkish Industrialists' and Businessmen's Association (*Türk Sanayicileri ve İşadamları Derneği, or TÜSİAD*) to act independent of the state with the objective of formulating their class interest and influencing political decisions accordingly. TÜSİAD was soon the strongest representative of the employers.

3.5 The Political Contestations Over the Socialisation Programme

Two key parts of the Socialisation Programme sparked political debates. The first was the government's proposal to require medical doctors to work full-time for public hospitals, which reappeared during the implementation of the HTP under different political and economic circumstances. Ersoy reports that a significant number of medical doctors at the time strongly opposed these full-time work proposals (1998, p. 11). Their opposition was motived mainly by their economic self-interest. The number of private clinics operated by medical doctors proliferated in Istanbul throughout the 1950s, and newspapers were filled with private clinic advertisements (Günal 2008, p. 185), which might evidence why a considerable percentage of medical doctors opposed the full-time work requirement at the time. Their strong opposition eventually led to the dismissal of the proposal. Despite the fact that the TTB lacked veto power in the political system, the ability of medical doctors to cause the government to abandon the full-time work proposal demonstrated their political power as a professional group.

The second contested feature of the Programme was its ambition to unite all public health facilities under the MoH. Public healthcare facilities included public hospitals (affiliated with the MoH), the SSK hospitals and public university hospitals. The MoH proposal to control all public facilities was not welcomed by either the SSK bureaucrats or university hospital academics. In a meeting organised by the Ministry, the Head of Health Affairs in the SSK, Dr Refik Erer, argued that SSK hospitals had been established thanks to 'the labour of workers' and thus workers should be in charge of their hospitals. Erer concluded that a transfer of SSK hospitals to the MoH was simply legally impossible (The Ministry of Health and Social Assistance 1966). Representatives of university hospitals also opposed the proposed transfer of public university hospitals to the MoH. The firm stance taken by SSK bureaucrats and academics on this issue reflects their quest to retain their autonomy, as well as their distrust of the government. Their success in keeping the segregated public healthcare delivery structure intact also prevented a different form of universalisation that might occur as part of the Socialisation Programme.

3.6 The Power of Trade Unions and Employer Organisations in the Social Insurances Institution

Although Turkey's healthcare system was based on a social insurance model, its governance model did not resemble the social insurance-based systems of Western Europe that gave trade unions (and sometimes employer organisations as well) exclusive power to administer funds. The Turkish social security system did not allow power sharing between governments and trade unions. In fact, the composition of the executive board of the SSK reflected the bureaucratic dominance over the SSK's decision-making process. According to the constituent legislation of the SSK, five of the seven members of the executive board had to be state officials (The Republic of Turkey 1964, Article 10). One member was the representative of the employers, while another was the representative of the workers. Therefore, it can be argued that the administration of Turkey's welfare system was corporatist, yet the governance of this system was not based upon a corporatist pact between the state and other social actors. It was instead state-dominated and can be characterised as 'state corporatism', as Schmitter defines it (Schmitter 1974, pp. 103–4).

3.7 The Impact of the Left on the Politics of Healthcare

Keyder suggests that the dissolution of the world system induced by the Great Depression enabled the Turkish bureaucracy to introduce a state-directed national economy model after the end of WWII (2007b, pp. 11–12). For Yeldan, this model lent itself to the consolidation of the industrial bourgeoisie in the 1960s and 1970s as the state transferred significant amounts of profits to the Turkish bourgeoisie in this period (2001, p. 38).

In general, the late 1960s and 1970s were the most successful years for the left in Turkey, both in terms of electoral success and their ability to mobilise public support (Boratav 2010, p. 221). Even though this period marked the strongest period for Turkey's left, Keyder argues that neither workers nor farmers enjoyed enough power or organisation to have a decisive impact on policy outcomes (2007b, p. 13). For Keyder, the major influential political actors in Turkish politics were various groups within the bureaucracy and the nascent bourgeoisie (2007b, p. 13). Indeed, Keyder's argument is validated to an extent, as the institutional setting in social security also empowered the bureaucracy and made it a showpiece for trade union representatives.

Despite their limited role in the decision-making structure of the social security system, trade unions gained popularity among workers in this period, which had a discursive impact on Turkish politics. Increasing popularity of unionism was a result of a relatively favourable legal context. The second law on trade unions repealed the first legislation (The Republic of Turkey 1947) and relaxed the restrictions on the organisation of trade unions (The Republic of Turkey 1963a, 1963b).

In this context, DİSK was established in 1967 as an alternative to TÜRK-İŞ. Unlike TÜRK-İŞ, with its 'embedded' unionism and whose bureaucratic structure failed to mobilise workers' demands, DİSK emerged as the most significant political actor of the workers' movement and was able to organise massive, effective rallies. In addition, trade unions were not the sole representatives of left politics at the time. A number of university student movements – generally linked to leftist organisations – were also active in setting the political agenda in the country.

The rise of the left in Turkish politics during the 1960s found only a limited space in parliamentary politics for a number of reasons: the judiciary tended to close down socialist parties, there was an atmosphere of pro-Americanism and strong US supported anti-communism, and the most left-wing actors was ideologically averse to a parliamentary route to socialism.

The most significant initiative that the left pursued through parliamentary politics was the establishment of the Labour Party of Turkey (*Türkiye İşçi Partisi, or TİP*), founded by trade unionists and intellectuals in 1961. The first electoral success of the TİP came with the 1965 elections, in which the party received roughly 2.5 per cent of the votes nationally and won 14 of 450 seats in the Parliament. The TİP programme did not address healthcare policies specifically, which was not unusual in left-wing politics in Turkey at the time, but it did declare that workers' participation in government would make social and economic rights in the constitution 'lived realities' rather than mere clauses on paper (TİP 1964). However, the TİP experience was short-lived due to tensions among their own leadership cadre that were related to the invasion of Czechoslovakia by the Soviet Union, changes made in the election law that decreased the representative power of the party and the closure of the party by the military coup on 12 March 1971.

In response to the increasing mobilisation of workers and their growing impact on politics, and then a coup attempt by a group within the military, Mr Memduh Tağmaç, Commander of the Turkish Armed Forces (TSK), issued a memorandum that forced the centre-right AP to resign on 12 March 1971. He argued that 'social awakening went beyond economic development' (Günal 2014). The new government that followed the AP government was not a military junta, but rather a civilian, technocratic government.

The discursive power of the left-wing actors in this period constituted a moral reference point for centrist political parties to shape their policies.

For example, the power of the left-wing actors including DİSK paved the way for the transformation of the CHP into a social democratic party in the early 1970s, though not fully a Western European type (Emre 2015). Before the general elections in 1973, the CHP went through a discursive change. This discursive change started with the endeavours of Mr İsmet İnönü, one of the founding fathers of the Republic, to appeal to the newly emerging left-wing youth by declaring that the CHP was located at the 'centre left' (*ortanın solu*) of the political spectrum.

However, the success of this discursive change was only possible with the new CHP leader, Mr Bülent Ecevit, who was elected chairman of the CHP in 1972. Unlike İnönü, Ecevit brought together different variants of the left under the umbrella of the CHP and succeeded in presenting himself as the child of the people. The CHP's election promises started to resemble the platforms of social democratic parties of Western Europe. In the 1973 elections, when Turkish political life once again started resembling an electoral democracy, the CHP criticised the centre-right AP for 'undermining the social character of the state' (CHP 1973, p. 7) and declared that the prospective CHP government would make the healthcare system 'work for citizens' (CHP 1973, p. 17). They promised, in the process, to abolish inequalities between the SSK, ES and BAĞ-KUR (CHP 1973, p. 133) and to establish a new governance mechanism for social insurances that would put premium payers in charge (CHP 1973, p. 134). CHP's proposed healthcare reform was sweeping not only because it included equalisation of benefit packages for all, but also because it would increase trade union role in the governance of the social security system. The CHP won the general elections in 1973. Ecevit's CHP succeeded in repeating its victory in the 1977 election, which marked the highest share of votes ever (roughly 41 per cent) cast for a left-wing party in the history of the Republic.[2]

The rise to power of Ecevit's CHP brought hope for the realisation of the ideal of a universal healthcare system. Indeed, the CHP government tried to take critical steps to consolidate such a system. For instance, they re-introduced the proposal for a full-time work requirement for medical doctors (The Republic of Turkey 1978), which had been shelved after medical doctors opposed it during the implementation of the Socialisation Programme. However, due to political and social instability in the country, the CHP government was short-lived. Throughout the 1970s, unstable coalition governments ran the country, and armed conflicts between left-wing and the anti-Communist nationalist groups contributed to serious political instability. In these circumstances, governments were not in a position to carry out comprehensive long-term reforms, which led to the deepening of problems in Turkey's healthcare system.

The only noteworthy political development in the 1970s healthcare politics whose impact on healthcare politics is still evident today was an ideological shift in the leadership cadre of the TTB. The rising popularity of the left-wing ideas in Turkish politics during the 1960s and 1970s found its voice among medical doctors and medical students. Organised socialist groups nominated their representatives for election to the General Council of the TTB in 1977 and succeeded in electing Dr Erdal Atabek to head the TTB. This election signalled a historic change in the political positioning of the TTB. Once established as a corporatist professional body, the TTB originally took its legitimacy from the state. The rise to power of socialist medical doctors in the TTB resulted in the recalibration of the source of legitimacy for the TTB. Socialist medical doctors in charge of the TTB turned their faces to 'the people' and declared that they would search for legitimacy from the people rather than from the state. As a result, the TTB emerged as the defender of the socialist perspective on healthcare services in healthcare politics.

3.8 The History of Healthcare and Politics Since the 1980 Military Coup d'État

The military coup in 1980 marked the start of the third period in the history of social policies in Turkey. Following the junta, the pro-market Motherland Party (*Anavatan Partisi, or ANAP*) emerged as a single-party government and ruled the country throughout the 1980s. After ANAP failed to form a government in 1991, the country was ruled by a coalition of social democratic SHP (*Sosyal Demokrat Halkçı Parti, SHP*) and centre-right True Path Party (*Doğru Yol Partisi, DYP*).

The general healthcare policy environment from the 1980s until the introduction of the HTP can be broadly conceptualised as 'policy drift'. Policy drift is defined as the lack of formal reforms in welfare policies while the social risks these policies aim at mitigating are increasing (Hacker 2004, p. 246). No large-scale reform in healthcare policies was undertaken in this period, while the healthcare system faced new challenges, including but not limited to the rising number of people who were not covered in the social security system, increasing demand for curative healthcare services and the decreasing salaries of medical doctors. The lack of reform in the context of changing social and economic circumstances significantly altered the role and function of the healthcare system. While the general situation in healthcare policy was seen as policy drift, several changes in healthcare delivery and financing – the introduction of revolving funds in public hospitals, incentives for the private sector in healthcare delivery and the introduction of a Green Card scheme that granted access to inpatient services for uninsured poor – signalled a trend towards policy layering. Policy layering refers to the introduction of new (and mostly conflictual or rival) elements into an ongoing policy framework without altering the latter (Thelen 2004, p. 35). While changes in healthcare delivery signalled passive privatisation, the introduction of a Green Card scheme signified an increase in health coverage.

3.8.1 The Junta: Suppression of the Left

The military coup of 12 September 1980 was a historic moment in Turkish politics and had a substantial impact on the country's political and economic trajectory. The junta closed down all political parties, trade unions and civil society organisations. A new constitution for the country, once again, was prepared under the purview of the junta. The new constitution, ratified through national referendum in 1982, instituted a clearly authoritarian regime that introduced severe restrictions on individual and collective rights and freedoms (i.e. The Republic of Turkey 1983a, 1983b).

One of the major changes that the junta introduced was the alteration of the development strategy from import-substitution industrialisation to export-oriented growth, thus initiating a neoliberalisation process in Turkey. The junta started the integration of the Turkish economy into the emergent neoliberal global economy. Turkey's economy was transformed into a proper open market economy in the 1990s (Yeldan 2001, p. 25). In line with an export-oriented growth strategy, the junta initiated the privatisation of state economic enterprises and boosted the role of the private sector in the economy.

This top-down change in the development strategy of the country was not carried out at the expense of employers. While trade unions and the left in general were under pressure, Şenses notes that employer organisations succeeded in promoting their demands under the military rule. This was evident, as their pre-coup demands with respect to labour regulations were implemented after the military coup (Şenses 1993, p. 105).

The impact of the 1980 military coup on Turkish political life was deep and devastating. The military junta closed all active political organisations in the country; arrested activists, intellectuals, academics, journalists; and silenced all forms of political opposition. This devastating impact was skewed towards the left end of the political spectrum. Heper argues that one of the aims of the coup was to silence and exclude trade unions from political life (1991, p. 17). The attitude towards the organisation of labour was clearly much harsher: the state actively restricted, prohibited and even abolished some labour organisations. While the state's discriminatory attitude towards trade unions was part of the modus operandi much before the 1980 military coup, this attitude clearly solidified with the coup. Business organisations were allowed to continue their activities, while trade unions were not (Buğra 1997, p. 59). Therefore, it would not be erroneous to conclude that the 1980 military coup symbolised a victory of business interests over labour demands.

The military government's stance towards the TTB was not much different from its position on trade unions. The TTB had already transcended the boundaries of a classical professional body and had begun to voice a socialist perspective towards healthcare in the 1970s. The military junta closed down the General Council of the TTB and jailed the head of the organisation. Once the TTB was reopened, the military government attempted to ensure that medical doctors working for public facilities were not required to be members of the TTB, with the objective of undermining their representative power and funding base. With the coup, the General Council of the TTB was moved to Ankara, and the MoH was authorised to monitor the finances and administration of provincial medical chambers. All these changes were directed towards the consolidation of state control over the TTB and thus the medical profession.

3.8.2 *The Motherland Party Period: Attempts to Liberalise Healthcare*

In the aftermath of the transfer of power from the military to a civilian government following the 1980 coup, ANAP came to power with an agenda of furthering economic liberalisation policies. By collaborating with the International Monetary Fund (IMF) and the WB to initiate the Structural Adjustment Programme (SAP), ANAP took steps to increase the role of private entrepreneurs in sectors that had previously been secured for the public sector, including healthcare delivery. Private hospitals, according to the approach adopted by ANAP, would help reduce the pressure on the SSK hospitals and the MoH hospitals. In other words, while ANAP did not call for the direct privatisation of public healthcare delivery – which would have hampered its re-election prospects – it aimed at introducing a private option that would operate alongside the public provision. ANAP's agenda for reform, however, was not limited to policy layering in healthcare provision; it also included NPM policies, which manifested themselves in the introduction of the Basic Law of Health Services, which injected private sector tools to healthcare services in the public sector (The Republic of Turkey 1987).

The main objectives of the Basic Law of Health Services were to transform public hospitals into individual health enterprises, to end the lifelong employment guarantee that had been granted to medical doctors in the public sector, to introduce flexible employment contracts and a performance-based payment model for health professionals, and to establish a compulsory contribution-based general health insurance system by integrating all schemes under one institution (The Republic of Turkey 1987). In response, the main centre-left political party of the time, the SHP, appealed to the Constitutional Court requesting the annulment of particular articles of the law. The Constitutional Court annulled some articles of the law, rendering its full implementation impossible (The Constitutional Court of Turkey 1988).

The success of the SHP in stopping the pro-market reform, using its power to file an appeal to the Constitutional Court, did not signal a consensus between the SHP and the Constitutional Court on the role of the state in healthcare financing and delivery. The SHP argued that the Law would introduce monetary exchange between patients and doctors in public hospitals. The SHP found this unacceptable in a country where access to healthcare services was defined as a citizenship right. The SHP stated, 'Healthcare, as a right of citizens and duty of the state, cannot become an issue of commercial undertake' (The Constitutional Court of Turkey 1988, p. 4). The Constitutional Court did not rule that the proposed transformation of public hospitals into individual health enterprises was unconstitutional, however. The Court annulled articles on the transfer of power to the government in unification of social security institutions as well as the introduction of performance-based payment for health workers (The Constitutional Court of Turkey 1988).

The detailed ruling demonstrates that the majority of the Constitutional Court members saw no contradiction between charging for access to services in public hospitals and people's right to healthcare.

The Constitutional Court decided that the SHP claim that the social state has to provide healthcare services free of charge at the point of service was invalid. Instead, it argued that public bodies could demand direct payments from citizens according to their income levels (The Constitutional Court of Turkey 1988).

Despite the fact that the ANAP government was unable implement the Basic Law of Health Services in its full version, the ANAP legacy left its footprint on healthcare with the introduction of revolving funds into public hospitals in 1987 (Buğra 2008, p. 213). The introduction of revolving funds into public hospitals symbolised the first step of the marketisation of public healthcare services in two ways and represented a form of policy layering. First, rather than extending benefit packages of public insurees and incorporating those who had been excluded from social security coverage, it enabled people to receive treatment by directly paying for services in public hospitals. Secondly, rather than increasing the salaries of doctors in public hospitals, it started to top up their salaries using revolving fund revenues collected from patients.

In the meantime, due to a gradual decrease in secure formal employment opportunities with the adoption of the export-led growth model, the privatisation of public sector institutions, the continuing migration from rural to urban areas and the outbreak of armed conflict between the Kurdistan Workers' Party militias (*Partiya Karkerên Kurdistan, or PKK*) and the Turkish army leading to internal displacement of people, the number of uninsured citizens began to increase substantially. In that context, while social risks associated with facing healthcare problems and incurring catastrophic health expenditures increased, no changes were made to the healthcare system to mitigate these risks, allowing this situation to be broadly categorised as policy drift.

The second footprint that ANAP left on healthcare was the promotion of private sector in healthcare delivery. Keyder reports that private healthcare provision started to gain visibility in the early 1990s due to the introduction of state incentives in the late 1980s (2007a, p. 18). Consequently, the inpatient bed capacity of private hospitals reached one-tenth of the total inpatient bed capacity in the middle of the 2000s (Keyder 2007a, p. 19). In addition, Günal notes that the number of beds in private hospitals almost doubled in the 1980s and the 1990s (2008, pp. 407–8).

The majority of these private hospitals were based in the major cities. Their services were focused mainly on specialties such as ophthalmology, dental health, obstetrics, gynaecology, microsurgery and transplantation.

The first seeds of the commodification of healthcare services occurred in specialties whose services were not covered by social health insurance schemes (e.g. dental health) or in specialty services which coexist with cultural ceremonial components attached to these services (e.g. giving birth, male circumcision).

The public sector continued to dominate in most healthcare services during this period, however. In 1990, it was reported that 78 per cent of all hospitals in Turkey were under the administration of the MoH, the SSK and public universities (Pricewaterhouse 1990, p. 66).

3.8.3 *The Introduction of the Green Card Scheme*

The Green Card scheme was a tax-funded social assistance program that granted the poor without social security coverage access to inpatient healthcare services. The introduction of the Green Card scheme was the only reform that aimed at facilitating access to healthcare services for the uninsured poor. It symbolised a counter-movement to the ANAP government's pro-market direction in healthcare policy.

The Green Card scheme was a collaborative policy initiative of the centre-left SHP and the centre-right DYP. In the 1987 general elections, SHP came in second, with almost one-fourth of the national vote. SHP was followed by the DYP, a centre-right party that represented a significant portion of the farmers, and the main competitor of ANAP in centre-right with roughly 20 per cent of all votes. After the significant fall in ANAP's votes in the 1991 general elections, the DYP and SHP formed a coalition government.

The SHP was against privatisation in healthcare services, as evidenced by its opposition to the ANAP government's pro-market reform attempt, while the DYP generally assumed a populist position on social policy issues. A major healthcare policy development in the DYP-SHP coalition government period was the introduction of the Green Card scheme in 1992 (The Republic of Turkey 1992). The scheme was essentially a social assistance scheme that gave the uninsured poor access to inpatient services in public hospitals. Buğra suggests that the introduction of the Green Card scheme represented a step toward the realisation of the right to healthcare services for all citizens (2008, pp. 214–15). She argues that the Green Card model symbolises a procedural formalisation to grant the poor access to healthcare services, especially in comparison to the former model, which required the poor to convince the local authorities or the physician who was chief of staff at the hospital that they were indeed indigent; otherwise, they would have to pay for services (Buğra 2008, pp. 214–15).

3.8.4 The Global Healthcare Reform Agenda Arrives in Turkey

In line with international trends, and as evidenced by the ANAP government's reform attempts, in the early 1990s the various Turkish governments were engaged in drafting healthcare reforms and attempting to legislate them. Four critical developments during this period contributed to the elevation of healthcare reform to the political agenda.

The first of these developments was the commencement of a partnership between the Turkish government and the WB on healthcare issues. The continuity of these partnerships throughout the 1990s was of critical importance in explaining how the WB changed the way healthcare bureaucrats perceive, talk about and act upon healthcare policies. Throughout the 1990s, the Turkish governments collaborated with the WB on healthcare policy issues, and the WB has continued to be one of the key players in Turkey's healthcare policy. The first WB project on healthcare started in 1990, and a second was launched in 1996.

The impact of the WB's pro-market discourse on draft reforms was visible in their problem definitions, as well as in the solutions they put forward. For instance, in a national health policy document, parallel to the WB's perspective, the Ministry questioned the centralised structure of healthcare delivery – which it aimed at strengthening in the previous period – the lack of managerial staff in public hospitals, the absence of awareness about costs among the staff and low motivation among medical doctors due to the nonexistence of performance-based payment mechanisms (The Ministry of Health 1993, p. 51). In the same year, the draft Law on Health projected the introduction of a basic benefit package for public health insurance plans and the formalisation of out-of-pocket contributions for the insured (The Republic of Turkey 1993). In 1997, a Ministry report entitled *Health Sector Reforms in Turkey* stated that purchaser and provider roles in Turkey's healthcare system should separate, competition should be established among different service providers and social insurance should cover the whole population (The Ministry of Health 1997, p. 29).

The second critical development was the publication of a report entitled the *Health Sector Master Plan*. PriceWaterhouse had been commissioned by the State Planning Organisation (*Devlet Planlama*

Teşkilatı, or DPT) to prepare this report, which declared that the state was incapable of planning Turkey's diverse healthcare system (Pricewaterhouse 1990, pp. 4–5). It also stated that the healthcare system had failed to provide equitable access to healthcare services and to integrate preventive and curative healthcare services (Pricewaterhouse 1990, p. 34). The report raised awareness among the various actors about the chronic problems of Turkey's healthcare system. It also popularised the discourse of health economics in terms of defining these problems and proposing solutions, thus contributing to the emergence of a new healthcare policy paradigm.

The third critical development was the revitalisation of the medical doctors' movement under the umbrella of the TTB at the end of the 1980s. Between 1988 and 1992, thousands of medical doctors marched in 'white protests' to call for the improvement of their working conditions and the realisation of a universal right to healthcare (Soyer 2005, pp. 189–90). With these protests, the TTB called for the establishment of a 'real' public healthcare system and once again emerged as a significant political actor in the politics of healthcare.

The fourth critical development that increased the politicians' and bureaucrats' attention to healthcare policy was the emerging income-expenses imbalance of the social security institutions. In the late 1980s and early 1990s, governments started to make transfers from the public budget to these institutions in order to strike a balance between their income and their expenses. The ES was the first institution to face a budget deficit in 1986, followed by the BAĞ-KUR in 1989 and finally by the SSK in 1991 (Yılmaz and Yentürk 2016a). The share of budget transfers to social security institutions reached 1 per cent of GDP in 1994 and this share continued to increase until 2000 (Yılmaz and Yentürk 2016a).

While these deficits emerged partly as a result of the various governments' using social security funds for external debt payments and borrowing from these funds interest-free, both the government and the mainstream media started conceptualising these deficits as a 'black hole' in the public budget. In fact, the share of social expenditures in Turkey's GDP was already comparatively low. Unlike other corporatist welfare regimes, the state did not contribute to social security funds for workers, farmers or the self-employed. Therefore, the budget deficits of the SSK and the BAĞ-KUR might well be interpreted as a need for the formalisation of regular state contributions to these funds per each public insuree, which would legitimately increase the share of social expenditures in Turkey. Nevertheless, in line with the neoliberal political hegemony, the fiscal deficit of social security institutions was interpreted as an intrinsic shortcoming of the public social insurance system that combined healthcare financing and provision. The popular portrayal of the fiscal deficit of social security institutions in Turkey in the 1990s as a black hole and a burden on public budget can be conceptualised as part of a process of 'the social construction of the need to reform' (Cox 2001, pp. 475–7).

A report by the Health Insurance Commission of Australia on the Turkish healthcare system concluded that Turkey was a low-spender on healthcare compared to other countries with similar levels of economic development (Health Insurance Commission of Australia 1995, p. 3). It went on to point out that a private insurance option would not be a viable solution to either the fiscal problems or the lack of coverage in Turkey's healthcare system (Health Insurance Commission of Australia 1995, p. 7). However, the deficits of the social security institutions were hardly handled within a conceptual framework that the Health Insurance Commission of Australia used at the time, which demonstrates the power imbalance between competing ideas in healthcare politics.

Despite differences in problem definitions and the solutions proposed, these four critical developments made it clear that there was a growing consensus that healthcare reform was needed in Turkey. However, the introduction of a reform did not follow automatically. A major reason for the failure of healthcare reform at the time was the fact that the country was run by a series of short-lived coalition governments and the presence of competing reform ideas among different political actors.

The policy drift in healthcare financing and in welfare policies in general, combined with the devastating impact that the coup had on left-wing politics, opened up a new platform for the rising Islamist populism to organise. In this context, the political Islamist Welfare Party (*Refah Partisi, or RP*) emerged as the new centre of attraction, especially among the urban poor and in the economically deprived regions of Eastern and Southeastern Anatolia. Their roots originated from the National Outlook (*Milli Görüş*) movement that combined a modest Islamic critique of capitalism with third-world nationalism. In contrast to the mainstream centre-right and centre-left parties at the time, the RP appeared as a religio-ideological movement and was able to mobilise significant numbers of committed activists who voluntarily worked for the party's success.

The first significant victory of the RP came in the 1994 municipal elections, when the RP received almost 20 per cent of the votes. In addition, Mr Recep Tayyip Erdoğan (now the President of Turkey) was elected mayor of the Istanbul Metropolitan Municipality. The RP's rise to power in district and provincial municipalities brought free healthcare services (mostly primary healthcare services and screening campaigns for diseases such as breast cancer) to the uninsured, which in turn popularised the RP among the urban poor.

The RP's wave of success continued in the 1995 general elections, when the RP won first place, marking the most significant victory of a political Islamist party in the history of the Republic. However, the Turkish army, based on its self-proclaimed role to protect secularism that it believed it was under threat at the time, forced the RP-DYP coalition government to resign. This event is known as the 28 February 1997 post-modern coup d'état.

Following the military coup, the centre-left Democratic Left Party (*Demokratik Sol Parti, or DSP*) led by Ecevit came first in the 1999 general elections and formed a broad coalition government with the Nationalist Action Party (*Milliyetçi Hareket Partisi, or MHP*) and ANAP. Despite the progress it had made with the European Union (EU) accession process, the coalition government proved to be unsuccessful in dealing with the ramifications of two serious earthquakes, and its economic policies paved the way for the largest economic crisis in the history of the Republic in 2001. Unsurprisingly, these political parties lost votes in the 2002 general elections and failed to win any seats in the Parliament because they were unable to meet the 10 per cent national threshold.

While the coalition government was in power, a group of politicians separated from the National Outlook movement and its newly founded Virtue Party (*Fazilet Partisi, or FP*) found the AK Party in 2001, which then gained a victory in the 2002 general election. It was in this context that the AK Party came to power as a single-party government in the 2002 general elections.

Before the AK Party came to power, the problems in Turkey's healthcare system had already been quite visible to the public and to different political actors. Throughout the 1990s, policy drift with respect to healthcare financing posed a significant obstacle to access to healthcare services. In a representative survey conducted in six cities, roughly 42 per cent of respondents stated that they had not been able to apply for healthcare services in the last 6 months due to financial difficulties (The Ministry of

Health 1999). Parallel to this, the first comprehensive study on health expenditures found that Turkey was among the OECD countries where citizens were making significant out-of-pocket expenditures for healthcare services. The share of out-of-pocket health expenditures in 2000 constituted roughly 29 per cent of total health expenditures (The Ministry of Health 2004, p. 36). In response, the AK Party promised a reform in healthcare system.

3.9 Turkey's Healthcare System Before the Reform from a Comparative Perspective

A healthcare system can be broadly defined as the whole set of regulations in a given country with respect to the financing, provision and regulation of healthcare services (Wendt et al. 2009, p. 77). Healthcare system typologies enable scholars to compare and contrast different national healthcare systems and to evaluate whether the direction of changes in different national healthcare systems diverge or converge (Blank and Burau 2010; Wendt et al. 2009; Hassenteufel and Palier 2007; Bambra 2005a; Wall 1996; Moran 1992).

While the healthcare systems approach is useful in explaining the major characteristics of national healthcare policies, it needs to be used with caution due to its tendency to treat national healthcare systems as coherent systems and to underestimate the internal contradictions of national healthcare policies. Freeman argues that healthcare policies generally do not constitute a conflict-free system, as each country's healthcare policies are based upon institutions that are superimposed on one another. These coexisting institutions can be complementary or conflicting (Freeman 1999, p. 89). In response, scholars call for an approach that pays attention to conflicts as well as tensions within the healthcare policy domain (Blank and Burau 2010, p. 224; Kasza 2002). The history of healthcare system development in the Turkish case exemplifies the validity of Freeman's position.

Bearing in mind these words of caution about using the healthcare systems approach, it is useful to first situate Turkey's healthcare system within a healthcare systems typology. Among various healthcare systems typologies (e.g. Wendt 2014; Blank and Burau 2010; Wendt et al. 2009; Hassenteufel and Palier 2007; Bambra 2005a; Rothgang et al. 2005; Wall 1996), I use Wendt et al.'s (2009) typology. As one of the most comprehensive and up-to-date typologies, it has the power to explain the diversity of contemporary healthcare systems due its multi-dimensional categorisation of healthcare systems.

For Wendt et al., there are three main ideal-types of healthcare systems: state healthcare systems, societal healthcare systems and private healthcare systems (2009, p. 81). The defining characteristic of the state healthcare systems is that the state undertakes financing, provision and regulation activities. In societal healthcare systems, societal actors, mostly in the form of independent autonomous social organisations (e.g. trade unions) are in charge of all three main pillars of the healthcare system. Lastly, in private healthcare systems, private actors control all the pillars of healthcare systems. On the basis of these three main ideal-types, they devised 27 combinations of healthcare system with different forms of control over different pillars of the healthcare system. According to Wendt et al.'s typology, Turkey's healthcare system before the introduction of the HTP most resembled state healthcare systems, as the state had been the dominant power in the financing, provision and regulation of healthcare services. Nevertheless, the reliance of a country on a state healthcare system, as the Turkish case shows, does not guarantee universal health coverage.

3.10 Healthcare Financing

The financing of healthcare services is a fundamental subsector of healthcare systems. By financing, scholars refer to the mechanisms through which the total amount of financial resources allocated to healthcare services are collected and how the conditions of access to healthcare services are determined (Blank and Burau 2010, p. 220).

The four main sources of healthcare service funding identified in the literature are general taxation, social insurance, private insurance and direct payments by the user (Blank and Burau 2010, p. 13; Normand 1997, p. 205). The healthcare systems of most countries rely on a combination of these sources. For instance, the healthcare system in the United States is financed primarily by private insurance schemes, but involves public funding to ensure the access of special groups, such as children, the disabled, the elderly and the indigent (via Medicaid) to healthcare services.

Despite the use of multiple sources of healthcare financing in most countries, one funding source is still usually dominant in each healthcare system (Normand 1997, p. 205). The dominant funding source gives the system its general characteristic and has equity implications in terms of access to healthcare. The financing of healthcare services is considered to be 'a pointer to power' (Blank and Burau 2010, p. 63) in a given healthcare system. The main institutional funder of the system tends to have more power over the system as a whole. Therefore, in terms of direct implications for access, reforms in healthcare financing are among the most critical reforms in healthcare systems.

Similar to most developing countries (Barrientos and Lloyd-Sherlock 2000, p. 417), Turkey's healthcare system relied upon a social health insurance model of financing. Turkey's welfare system resembled Rudra's protective welfare system (2007), social insurances in Turkey were founded to provide protection for state officials and urban formal sector workers after the Second World War, which then extended to farmers and the self-employed. Turkey's healthcare system before the reform had three public insurance schemes which combined retirement pensions with health insurance and constituted the main source of healthcare financing. These insurance entities were the SSK, ES and BAĞ-KUR.

The state in Turkey did not make financial contributions to these social insurance funds, with the exception of ES (for civil servants), to which it contributed. In other words, these insurance funds were financed mainly through employer and employee's contributions. Despite the fact that employees and employers financed these insurance funds, neither group was in charge of the administration of the funds. Instead, the majority of the members of these funds' executive boards were government employees. In this setting, governments could even use these funds arbitrarily for purposes other than paying retirement pensions and health expenditures (paying the government's debts to the IMF, for example).

The size of the formal sector determines the scope for the development of social health insurance (Normand 1997, p. 216). As in other developing countries (Lloyd-Sherlock 2006, p. 355; Barrientos and Lloyd-Sherlock 2000, p. 417,), the limited scope of the formal sector in Turkey decreased the ability of the social health insurance model to provide universal health coverage. In line with the developmentalist aspirations of the period between the end of WWII and the beginning of the 1980s, the uninsured population was expected to disappear as industrial development gained pace and created more formal jobs (Buğra and Keyder 2006, p. 17; Lloyd-Sherlock 2006, p. 365). These expectations of incorporation through economic development disappeared with Turkey's adoption of the neoliberal economic order after the military coup in 1980. In response, a separate non-contributory scheme – the

Green Card scheme – for the uninsured poor, financed out of the public budget, was introduced (Buğra 2008, p. 215). Such a move was in line with trends in other developing countries (Barrientos and Lloyd-Sherlock 2000, p. 417).

The number of citizens with private health insurance remained quite low in Turkey's healthcare system before the reform. In 2000, approximately 0.4 per cent of the population had private health insurance coverage (TÜSİAD 2005). Therefore, the private sector had no significant power in healthcare financing.

Before the introduction of the HTP, a significant share in healthcare financing came from out-of-pocket payments, which created an obstacle to citizens' accessing healthcare services, and this imposed an informal condition on public insurees' use of the healthcare services to which they were entitled. In 2000, out-of-pocket payments constituted 27.7 per cent of total health expenditures in Turkey (The Ministry of Health 2004, p. 33). Out-of-pocket payments included both formal and informal payments. To exemplify, formal payments were made to purchase medications and to pay for compulsory 'donations' to SSK hospitals (*Yeni Şafak Yeni Şafak* 2000). Another example of out-of-pocket payments was the informal payments made during a patient's visit to the private clinic of a medical doctor (one who holds a full-time post in a public hospital at the same time), with the expectation of getting timely and quality healthcare services in public hospitals in return. Due to the coexistence of formal social security system alongside high levels of informality, scholars identified Turkey's previous social security system as an 'eclectic system' (Buğra and Candaş 2011, p. 516).

3.11 Healthcare Delivery

The provision of healthcare services is another significant subsector of healthcare systems. Healthcare provision refers to rules and regulations with respect to the institutional means through which healthcare services are delivered in a given country. Healthcare systems rely on different forms of service delivery. With the exception of data on the number of beds in public and private hospitals, the lack of comparative data sources on the role of the state and the private sector in healthcare provision (Rothgang et al. 2005, p. 196) prevents international comparison.

There are three different forms of ownership of healthcare facilities.[3] Healthcare services may be delivered through public facilities, private facilities and/or non-profit facilities. There is a relationship between the dominant type of healthcare financing and the ownership of healthcare facilities. For instance, healthcare systems funded by tax revenues rely heavily on public hospitals as the main providers of healthcare services, while social health insurance-based systems depend both on public and private hospitals (Blank and Burau 2010, pp. 82–3). In healthcare systems that are funded primarily by private health insurance, the private sector is generally the largest healthcare provider. In line with contemporary health reforms, midway solutions, which combine non-profit ownership with a level of state guarantee, such as the hospital trusts in the United Kingdom and health maintenance organisations in the United States, have developed.

Turkey's healthcare system before the introduction of the HTP relied upon public provision of healthcare services. The public sector was divided into different institution types, most of which were owned by the MoH, the SSK and public universities, respectively. The number of private sector hospitals, including hospitals funded by foreign or minority foundations, constituted only a negligible portion of healthcare provision in the country (The Ministry of Health 2004, pp. 7–8). This picture started to change with the launch of state incentives for private sector involvement in healthcare delivery since the 1990s. More importantly, medical doctors in the public sector had the right to open and operate private clinics with outpatient services without giving up their positions in the public sector, which made private clinics an important component of Turkey's healthcare system before the HTP.

3.12 The Regulation of Healthcare Financing and Delivery

The last important component of the healthcare system is the regulation of services. The regulation of healthcare services refers to the course of the governance of healthcare delivery and healthcare financing (Wendt et al. 2009, p. 77). Wendt et al. argue that this dimension can only be analysed in qualitative terms, as it requires the examination of different actors' engagement in regulatory practices with respect to diverse subsectors of healthcare systems (2009).

As the state was the dominant party in the financing and provision of healthcare services in Turkey, the regulation took place mainly within the public administration. Indeed, neither professional organisations nor trade unions had any institutionalised regulatory power over healthcare services in Turkey's healthcare system.

Despite the fact that Turkey's healthcare system closely resembled state healthcare systems as defined in Wendt et al.'s healthcare system typology, it also relied upon a significant amount of out-of-pocket payments in healthcare financing and private provision of healthcare services in the form of the private practice of medical doctors. Given the importance of these components, it can be argued that the state's regulatory capacity was limited, as it failed to control the informality enmeshed into the formal healthcare system.

3.13 Conclusion

This chapter offered an analysis of the history of the healthcare system development in Turkey with reference to three periods of the politics of healthcare in Turkey and Turkish politics. In the first period, starting from the late nineteenth century, Turkey's healthcare system was consolidated as a result of a collection of policy efforts especially in the domain of preventive healthcare services. Relying upon the late Ottoman state-making legacy, the Republic incorporated members of the medical community as state officials with elite status into its nation-making endeavour. Healthcare policy developments concentrated mainly on the introduction and expansion of preventive healthcare services and initiatives for securing workers' health, especially in the mining sector.

In the second period, similar to welfare state developments in other parts of the world after the end of WWII, Turkey's programmes to consolidate its healthcare system included both preventive and curative healthcare services with a sound financing mechanism. In the domain of healthcare delivery, the geographical extension of primary healthcare services had been one of the major concerns of Turkish governments, which was addressed by the Socialisation Programme. In the domain of healthcare financing, governments initiated the establishment of occupation status-based social health insurance plans that facilitated access to curative healthcare services, although in a stratified manner. In this period, Turkey succeeded in establishing institutionalised models of solidarity in healthcare financing and provision, which made access to healthcare part of the social contract between the state and citizens. In this regard, Turkey is similar to countries with a state or societal healthcare system including Western European and Latin American countries; it does not resemble countries such as Lebanon, where public capacity is low and is compensated with fragmented non-state actors (Chen and Cammett 2012, p. 2).

A political analysis of the development of healthcare system shows that the process can hardly be explained with the power resources approach, as the role of trade unions and social democratic parties in establishing state healthcare system was not sufficiently strong. Partly reflecting the pluralist approach, the major dynamic behind the birth of Turkey's healthcare system in the 1950s was the transition to electoral democracy after the ruling bloc was divided between two political parties: the CHP and the DP. Aiming to secure their re-election chances, a series of governments made advances in the domain of healthcare policy and cumulatively paved the way for the emergence of Turkey's healthcare system. For the most part, the political system severely restricted class politics. Electoral politics, the political limits of which were set under the anti-communist political projects in the Cold War era, remained the only opportunity for citizens to influence welfare policy-making.

Despite the fact that the main parameters of Turkey's healthcare system resembled the corporatist welfare regimes in Western Europe, this corporatist character did not find an echo in the governance of social security institutions. In other words, the political system of Turkey did not permit trade unions and professional organisations to enjoy a veto power in the administration of social security funds or healthcare delivery, which limited the impact of both DİSK and TTB, among other actors, on healthcare policy outcomes.

In spite of the restrictions imposed on class politics and the lack of veto power that trade unions might have used in the governance of social security, the relatively liberal constitution of 1961 provided a restricted window of opportunity for the above-mentioned actors to emerge as autonomous. Parallel to the rise of social movements worldwide around 1968 and using the window of opportunity after the 1961 constitution, the DİSK and TTB emerged as powerful actors defending the social rights of citizens, including the right to healthcare. Therefore, these actors might have had an influence on the development of social policies in general and healthcare system in particular, as a cluster of actors that performed key functions in popularising a pro-public approach to healthcare policies (in influencing the CHP position, for example) and created a moral discursive foundation for public discussions on social welfare issues.

In the third period, with 1980 coup, neoliberalisation became ascendant in Turkey. The engagement of the WB with Turkey's healthcare system during the 1990s appears to have had an immense impact on the framing of the problems of the system and on ideas to solve these problems. However, the healthcare system in Turkey did not undergo large-scale reform in this period. The concept of policy drift can best describe the general tendency in the domain of healthcare policy in Turkey throughout the 1990s. The failure of Turkey's healthcare system to provide universal coverage and the organisational problems of the system were visible to all actors in the 1990s, but this did not lead to any significant policy response with the exception of incremental changes towards passive privatisation in healthcare delivery and introduction of the Green Card scheme for the uninsured poor. Meanwhile, the Political Islamist National Outlook movement benefited from the policy drift and recruited outsiders into its ranks. The AK Party, as a successor of the National Outlook movement, inherited the popularity among the urban poor that it acquired thanks to the RP legacy. While the general atmosphere in the realm of healthcare policies is characterised by the notion of policy drift, limited yet important policy revisions were introduced during this period. Among these, one can list the introduction of revolving funds in public hospitals, the granting of incentives to the private sector in healthcare delivery and the introduction of the Green Card scheme that granted the uninsured poor access to inpatient services. These policy revisions in particular symbolised a trend towards policy layering, which introduced private sector delivery as an alternative to the public sector, incorporated the reception of out-of-pocket payments in public hospitals, injected additional income for medical doctors that stemmed from out-of-pocket payments by uninsured patients again in public hospitals and expanded public health insurance coverage to the uninsured poor.

Notes

1. As Buğra suggests, the Turkish state adopted a similar policy in housing. As the migration from rural to urban areas gained pace, the state started to let migrants from the rural areas settle in public lands and construct houses on public land rather than developing social housing projects.
2. Later scholars considered around one-third of all voters in Turkey to be traditionally left leaning, and the remaining two-thirds traditionally right leaning (Ayata 1993a, p. 32).
3. Different rules and regulations may apply to the provision of primary and secondary healthcare services in a particular country. To exemplify, the NHS

treats general practitioners as individual entrepreneurs and works with them on a contractual basis. GPs in the United Kingdom are involved in the delivery of primary care services and are permitted to establish private practices while remaining as employees of a health authority or hospital trust. See: Rothgang, H., Cacace, M., Grimmeisen, S., Wendt, C. 2005. The Changing Role of the State in Healthcare Systems. *European Review*, 13, 187–212.

References

Ayata, A. (1993a). Ideology, social bases, and organizational structure of the post-1980 political parties. In A. Eralp, M. Tünay, and B. Yeşilada (eds.), *The political and socioeconomic transformation of Turkey* (pp. 31–51). Westport, Connecticut and London: Praeger.

Aydın, E. (2002). *Türkiye'de sağlık teşkilatlanması tarihi (The history of health organisation in Turkey)*. Ankara: Naturel Yayınları.

Bambra, C. (2005a). Health status and the worlds of welfare. *Social Policy & Society*, 5(1), 53–62.

Barrientos, A., and Lloyd-Sherlock, P. (2000). Reforming health insurance in Argentina and Chile. *Health Policy and Planning*, 15(4), 417–423.

Blank, R. H., and Burau, V. (2010). *Comparative health policy*. Hampshire: Palgrave Macmillan.

Boratav, K. (2010). *Türkiye iktisat tarihi 1908–2007 (Economic history of Turkey 1908–2007)*. Ankara: İmge Kitabevi.

Brenner, N., and Theodore, N. (2002). Cities and the geographies of actually existing neoliberalism. *Antipode*, 34(3), 349–379.

Buğra, A. (1997). *Devlet ve işadamları (State and businessmen)*. Istanbul: İletişim.

Buğra, A. (2008). *Kapitalizm, yoksulluk ve Türkiye'de sosyal politika (Capitalism, poverty and social policy in Turkey)*. Istanbul: İletisim Yayınları.

Buğra, A., and Candaş, A. (2011). Change and continuity under an eclectic social security regime: The case of Turkey. *Middle Eastern Studies*, 47(3), 515–528.

Buğra, A., and Keyder, Ç. (2006). The Turkish welfare regime in transformation. *Journal of European Social Policy*, 16(3), 211–228.

Chen, B., and Cammett, M. (2012). Informal politics and inequity in access to health care in Lebanon. *International Journal for Equity in Health*, 11(1), 1–8.

CHP. (1973). *Ak günlere: CHP 1973 seçim bildirgesi (To bright future: Election declaration of the CHP in 1973)*. Ankara: CHP.

Cox, R. H. (2001). The social construction of an imperative: Why welfare reform happened in Denmark and the Netherlands but not in Germany. *World Politics*, 53(3), 463–498.

Ellison, N. (2006). *The transformation of welfare states?*. London and New York: Routledge.

Emre, Y. (2015). Why has social democracy not developed in Turkey? Analysis of an atypical case. *Journal of Balkan and Near Eastern Studies*, 17(4), 392–407.

Ersoy, T. (1998). *Türkiye tıp tarihi için materyalist notlar (Materialist notes for Turkey's medical history)*. Istanbul: Sorun Yayınları.

Freeman, R. (1999). Institutions, states and cultures: Health policy and politics in Europe. In J. Clasen (ed.), *Comparative social policy: Concepts, theories and methods* (pp. 80–94). Oxford and Massachusetts: Wiley-Blackwell.

Giaimo, S. (2005). *Markets and medicine: The politics of healthcare reform in Britain, Germany, and the United States*. Ann Arbor: The University of Michigan University Press.

Giaimo, S., and Manow, P. (1999). Adapting the welfare state: The case of healthcare reform in Britain, Germany, and the United States. *Comparative Political Studies*, 32(8), 967–1000.

Günal, A. (2008). *Health and citizenship in Republican Turkey: An analysis of the socialization of health services in Republican historical context*. Ph.D. Istanbul: Boğaziçi University.

Günal, İ. (2014, March 13). 12 Mart darbesi ve bilim (12th March coup d'état and science). *Sol*.

Hacker, S. J. (2004). Privatizing risk without privatizing the welfare state: The hidden politics of social policy retrenchment in the United States. *American Political Science Review*, 98(2), 243–260.

Harrison, S., and McDonald, R. (2008). *The politics of healthcare in Britain*. London: SAGE Publications.

Hassenteufel, P., and Palier, B. (2007). Towards neo-Bismarckian healthcare states? Comparing health insurance reforms in Bismarckian welfare systems. *Social Policy & Administration*, 41(6), 574–596.

Health Insurance Commission of Australia. (1995). *Final health financing report: Policy options study for Turkiye*. The Ministry of Health: Ankara.

Heper, M. (1991). The state and interest groups with special reference to Turkey. In M. Heper (ed.), *Strong state and economic interest groups: The post-1980 Turkish experience* (pp. 3–23). Berlin and New York: Walter de Gruyter.

Immergut, E. M. (1992). *Health politics: Interests and institutions in Western Europe*. Cambridge, New York and Melbourne: Cambridge University Press.

Jacobs, L. R., and Skocpol, T. (2010). *Healthcare reform and American politics: What everyone needs to know*. Oxford and New York: Oxford University Press.

Kasza, G. J. (2002). The illusion of welfare 'regimes'. *Journal of Social Policy*, 31(2), 271–287.

Keyder, Ç. (2007a). Giriş (Introduction). In Ç. Keyder, N. Üstündağ, T. Ağartan, and Ç. Yoltar (eds.), *Avrupa'da ve Türkiye'de sağlık politikaları (Health Policies in Europe and in Turkey)*. Istanbul: İletişim.

Keyder, Ç. (2007b). *Türkiye'de devlet ve sınıflar (State and Class in Turkey)*. Istanbul: İletişim.

Lloyd-Sherlock, P. (2006). When social health insurance goes wrong: Lessons from Argentina and Mexico. *Social Policy & Administration*, 40 (4), 353–368.

Marshall, T. H. (2008). Citizenship and social class. In S. Leibfried and S. Mau (eds.), *Welfare states: Construction, deconstruction, reconstruction* Volume *I* (pp. 89–137). Cheltenham and Northampton: Edward Elgar.

Moran, M. (1992). The health-care state in Europe: Convergence or divergence?. *Environment and Planning C: Government and Policy*, 10(1), 77–90.

Moran, M. (2000). Understanding the welfare state: The case of healthcare. *British Journal of Politics and International Relations*, 2(2), 135–160.

Navarro, V. (1994). *The politics of health policy: The US reforms, 1980–1984*. Oxford & Cambridge: Blackwell.

Normand, C. (1997). Health insurance: A solution to the financing gap?. In C. Colclough (ed.), *Marketizing education and health in developing countries: Miracle or mirage?* (pp. 205–221). Oxford: Clarendon Press.

Özbek, N. (2006). *Cumhuriyet Türkiyesi'nde sosyal güvenlik ve sosyal politikalar (Social Security and Social Policies in Republican Turkey)*. Istanbul: Tarih Vakfi.

Pricewaterhouse. (1990). *Health sector masterplan study*. Ankara: State Planning Organisation, Republic of Turkey.

Rothgang, H., Cacace, M., Grimmeisen, S., and Wendt, C. (2005). The changing role of the state in healthcare systems. *European Review*, 13(Suppl. 1)), 187–212.

Rudra, N. (2007). Welfare states in developing countries: Unique or universal?. *The Journal of Politics*, 69(2), 378–396.

Schmitter, P. (1974). Still the century of corporatism?. *The Review of Politics*, 36(1), 85–131.

Şenses, F. (1993). Turkey's labor market policies in the 1980s against the background of its stabilization program. In A. Eralp, M. Tünay, and B. Yeşilada (eds.), *The political and socioeconomic transformation of Turkey* (pp. 97–109). Westport, Connecticut and London: Praeger.

Soyer, A. (2005). *Bir muhalefet odağı olarak tabip eylemleri, bir eylem biçimi olarak beyaz eylemler (Protests of medical doctors as a node of opposition, white protests as a form of opposition)*. Istanbul: Sorun Yayınları.

Talas, C. (1992). *Türkiye'nin açıklamalı sosyal politika tarihi (History of social policy in Turkey)*. Ankara: Bilgi Yayınevi.

The Constitutional Court of Turkey. (1988). *Temel Sağlık Hizmetleri Kanunu'nun bazı maddelerinin iptaline ilişkin (Request for cancellation of some of the clauses of the Basic Health Services Law). 1988/8*.

The Ministry of Health. (1993). *Ulusal sağlık politikası (National health policy)*. Ankara: The Ministry of Health, Health Project General Coordination Unit.

The Ministry of Health. (1997). *Health sector reforms in Turkey*. Ankara: The Ministry of Health, Health Project General Coordination Unit.

The Ministry of Health. (1999). *Sağlık hizmet kullanıcıları memnuniyet araştırması (Satisfaction with health services survey)*. Istanbul: MAKRO Araştırma.

The Ministry of Health. (2004). *Turkey national health accounts 1999–2000*. Ankara: The Ministry of Health of Turkey, Refik Saydam School of Public Health.

The Ministry of Health and Social Assistance. (1966). *Sağlık ve Sosyal Yardım Bakanlığında 10–12 Ekim 1966 günlerinde tedavi edici sağlık hizmetlerinin bir elden idaresi konusunda yapılan seminer çalışmaları (Seminar on the administrative unification of curative healthcare services in the Ministry of Health and Social Assistance on 10–12 October 1966)*. Ankara: The Ministry of Health.

The Republic of Turkey. (1921). *Ereğli Havzai Fahmiye Maden Amelesinin Hukukuna Müteallik Kanun (Law on the Rights of Coal Mine Workers in Ereğli Basin). 151.*

The Republic of Turkey. (1928). *Tababet ve Şuabatı Sanatlarının Tarzı İcrasına dair Kanun (Law on the Practice of Medicine). 1219.*

The Republic of Turkey. (1930). *Umumi hıfzısıhha kanunu (Public health law). 1593.*

The Republic of Turkey. (1947). *Sendikalar Kanunu (Law on Trade Unions). 5018.*

The Republic of Turkey. (1949). *Türkiye Cumhuriyeti Emekli Sandığı Kanunu (Law on the Republic of Turkey Retirement Fund). 5434.*

The Republic of Turkey. (1950). *Hastalık ve Analık Sigortası Kanunu (Law on Sickness and Maternity Insurance). 5502.*

The Republic of Turkey. (1955). *Hastaneler Talimatnamesi (Hospitals Ordinance).*

The Republic of Turkey. (1961). *Sağlık Hizmetlerinin Sosyalleştirilmesi Hakkında Kanun (Law on the Socialization of Health Services). 224.*

The Republic of Turkey. (1963a). *Sendikalar Yasası (Law on Trade Unions). 274.*

The Republic of Turkey. (1963b). *Toplu İş Sözleşmesi, Grev ve Lokavt Yasası (Law on Collective Bargaining, Industrial Action and Lock-out). 275.*

The Republic of Turkey. (1964). *Sosyal Sigortalar Kanunu (Social Insurances Law). 506.*

The Republic of Turkey. (1971). *Esnaf ve Sanatkarlar ve Diğer Bağımsız Çalışanlar Sosyal Sigortalar Kurumu Kanunu (Law on Shopkeepers, Artisans and Other Self-Employed Social Insurances Institution). 1479.*

The Republic of Turkey. (1978). *Sağlık Personelinin Tam Süre Çalışma Esaslarına Dair Kanun (Law on Full-time Working Principles for Health Personnel). 2162.*

The Republic of Turkey. (1983a). *Sendikalar Kanunu (Law on Trade Unions). 2821.*

The Republic of Turkey. (1983b). *Toplu İş Sözleşmesi, Grev ve Lokavt Yasası (Law on Collective Bargaining, Industrial Action and Lock-out). 2822.*

The Republic of Turkey. (1987). *Sağlık Hizmetleri Temel Kanunu (The Basic Health Law). 3359.*

The Republic of Turkey. (1992). *Ödeme Gücü Olmayan Vatandaşların Tedavi Giderlerinin Yeşil Kart Verilerek Devlet Tarafından Karşılanması Hakkında Kanun (Law on the Provision of Green Card that would Cover The Treatment Costs of Citizens Who do not Have the Ability to Pay). 3816.*

The Republic of Turkey. (1993). *Sağlık Kanunu Tasarısı Taslağı (Draft Proposal of Health Law).*

Thelen, K. (2004). *How institutions evolve: The political economy of skills in Germany, Britain, the United States, and Japan*. Cambridge: Cambridge University Press.

TİP. (1964). *Türkiye İşçi Partisi programı (The program of the Labour Party of Turkey)*. Ankara: TİP.

Toprak, Z. (1982). *Türkiye'de 'Milli İktisat' 1908–1918 ('National Economy' in Turkey 1908–1918)*. Ankara: Yurt Yayınları.

TÜSİAD. (2005). *Charting the way forward: Healthcare reform in Turkey*. Istanbul: TÜSİAD Publications.

Wall, A. (1996). *Healthcare systems in liberal democracies*. London and New York: Routledge.

Wendt, C. (2014). Changing healthcare system types. *Social Policy & Administration*, 48(7), 864–882.

Wendt, C., Frisina, L., and Rothgang, H. (2009). Healthcare system types: A conceptual framework for comparison. *Social Policy & Administration*, 43(1), 70–90.

Yeldan, E. (2001). *Küreselleşme sürecinde Türkiye ekonomisi (Turkish economy in the process of globalisation)*. Istanbul: İletişim.

Yeni, Şafak. (2000). SSK'daki bağış soygununa son (Giving end to the 'donation' robbery in the Social Insurance Institution). *Yeni Şafak*, 2 October 2000.

Yılmaz, V., and Yentürk, N. (2016a). *Yeniden ayarlama ve özelleştirme ikiliğinde Türkiye'de sosyal güvenlik reform: sosyal güvenlik harcamalarının uzun dönemli analizi (Social security reform in Turkey in between recalibration and privatisation: Long-term analysis of social security expenditures)*. Istanbul: Istanbul Bilgi Üniversitesi Sivil Toplum Kuruluşları Eğitim ve Araştırma Birimi.

CHAPTER 4

The Health Transformation Programme in Turkey Within the Context of Healthcare Reforms in Other Emerging Market Economies

4.1 Introduction

Turkey was not an exception to global wave of healthcare reforms. Due to rising healthcare costs and ageing populations, along with changes in the power dynamics that favoured pro-market political actors, many Western European countries introduced incremental pro-market healthcare reforms. In the case of emerging market economies, the intensity and the direction of healthcare reforms took more radical pathways, exemplified in the case of radical pro-market reform in Chile under Pinochet.

Replacing the previously central role of the WHO in global health policy, the WB had been at the forefront of the promotion of pro-market healthcare reforms in the emerging market economies of Latin America and the transition countries of Eastern Europe and Central Asia since the late 1980s. In addition to the WB, the IMF was also active in imposing conditionalities on developing country governments, including spending less on public healthcare services as part of stabilisation programmes or structural adjustment programs.

Despite the fact that most post-1980s' healthcare reforms, particularly those in emerging market economies, generally shared a strong marketisation dynamic, it would be erroneous to portray these reforms as carbon copies of one another. While a marketisation tendency was evident in most reforms, healthcare reforms took unique shapes in different national

V. Yılmaz, *The Politics of Healthcare Reform in Turkey*,
DOI 10.1007/978-3-319-53667-5_4

settings owing to diverse political dynamics. The major objective of this chapter is to describe the main tenets of the HTP in Turkey and to situate it within the context of post-1980s' healthcare reforms in emerging market economies.

4.2 The Main Parameters of the Health Transformation Programme in Turkey

The AK Party government came to power in the 2002 general elections and launched the HTP in 2003. Ağartan argues that the election results that led to a single-party government opened a 'rare window of opportunity' (Ağartan 2015a) for a fundamental reform in the healthcare system. The reform paved the way for the restructuring of healthcare financing, healthcare provision and the regulation of healthcare services, which led scholars to view the HTP as a large-scale reform (Ağartan 2015a; Sparkes et al. 2015; Akıncı et al. 2012).

The HTP had eight goals: (1) to transform the MoH into a planning and a monitoring body, (2) to unify the existing public health insurance schemes under the umbrella of compulsory general health insurance, (3) to facilitate access to healthcare services, (4) to increase the motivation of human resources in healthcare, (5) to establish educational institutions to support the new model, (6) to introduce quality measures for the healthcare sector, (7) to support the rational use of medications and (8) to establish a health information system (The Ministry of Health 2003, pp. 26–36). My discussion of these HTP components will focus on the changes they effected in the domains of healthcare financing and delivery, leaving aside any discussion on changes to the provision of primary healthcare and to pharmaceutical policy.

4.2.1 Changes in Healthcare Financing

The HTP aimed to establish a compulsory general health insurance model that would cover all citizens of Turkey. Compulsory general health insurance was put into practice in 2008 (The Republic of Turkey 2006). With this change, three public health insurance schemes and the Green Card scheme were united. The SGK replaced the previous stratified system for different occupational groups, namely, the ES, BAĞ-KUR and SSK. The reform also equalised the benefit packages of all three social insurance schemes and the Green Card scheme.

The general health insurance model kept the existing social insurance-based financing model of Turkey's healthcare system intact. It did not change the residual tax-financed component that had financed the non-contributory Green Card scheme for the indigent. In contrast to the previous model, all citizens are now obliged to contribute to the public health insurance fund regardless their employment status. The only exceptions to this rule are those whose income (or lack of it) make them eligible for an exemption or a state subsidy.[1] Unlike in the previous healthcare financing model, the state contributes to the public health insurance fund an amount equal to 25 per cent of all premiums collected monthly, which, in fact, incorporated the former public budget transfers to cover deficits in social security funds into the formal financing mechanism. Continuity in the social insurance-based financing model for healthcare, coupled with formalised regular support from the public budget, strengthened the financial sustainability of the healthcare system in Turkey and can be viewed as a recalibration of the former system rather than as a radical departure from it.

The new financing model, however, not only consolidated the social insurance-based financing model of Turkey's healthcare system, but also introduced additional sources of healthcare financing. These sources included patient contributory payments for all hospital visits and medications, additional payments for private hospital visits (most of which began to accept public health insurance after the reform) and optional supplementary private health insurance.

Patients are now obliged to make flat rate contributory payments when receiving outpatient healthcare services in public hospitals and medications as part of public health insurance coverage.[2] The amount is calculated on the basis of the number of hospital visits and the number of prescribed medications. The contributory payment rate varies according to the hospital type – a public university hospital, or a public education and research hospital, for example. Patients are not required to make contributory payments when they visit primary healthcare services. In addition, patients with defined health conditions (e.g. an emergency patient or patient with a metastatic cancer) and those living under the official poverty threshold are exempt from making contributory payments.

In the early days of the reform, the government argued that contributory payments were introduced in order to promote rational use of healthcare services and medications. Contributory payments were presented, therefore, as part of economisation. Nevertheless, a study on changes to the contributory payment rate points to an increase throughout the reform process (TTB 2011a). Indeed, these increases resulted in the tripling of the total revenue collected from contributory payments from 2009 to 2010 (Medimagazin 2011a). In 2014, the total revenue collected from contributory payments, having increased each year since its inception, approximated 3 million TL, which is equal to approximately more than 800,000 Euros (Takvim 2015). I have argued elsewhere that the increasing trend in the rate of contributory payments over time suggests that these payments might become an important source of healthcare financing and might go beyond the objectives of economisation, eventually leading to the marketisation of healthcare services (Yılmaz 2013).

The second new component of healthcare financing was the introduction of additional payments for private hospital visits. The HTP led to the establishment of a sizeable private healthcare delivery sector that it integrated into the system as service providers for the publicly insured. Citizens can only get access to private hospital services if they are able and willing to make additional payments to top up their public health insurance plan. The Council of Ministers determines the maximum amount of additional payment that a private hospital can charge. The introduction of additional payments implied marketisation of healthcare services, and started to undermine the function of public health insurance for the upper-middle income group.

Similar to the level of contributory payments, the maximum rate of additional payments demonstrates an increasing trend that signifies an increasing marketisation of healthcare services over time. The SGK specified the maximum amount of additional payment in 2012 as 90 per cent of the full price for private hospital services (Habertürk 2012), which then rose to 200 per cent over a single year (*NTVMSNBC* 2013). In addition, the rate of additional payments varies according to where a private hospital stands in the MoH service quality rankings, which consolidates an income-based stratification among citizens in their access to healthcare services (Yılmaz 2013).

Lastly, the HTP introduced a basic benefit package for public health insurance. After the reform, the SGK became responsible for defining the basic benefit package of public health insurance. Every year the SGK issues the type, amount and duration of diagnostic services, medications and treatment services that are financed by the public health insurance fund.

While the basic benefit package is still comprehensive, some changes such as the introduction of the base price principle for subsidising medications might have increased patients' out-of-pocket payments.

These developments in the domain of healthcare financing seem to encourage the purchase of private health insurance plans. Indeed, the number of citizens with private health insurance increased from roughly 850,000 in 2004 (TSB 2012) to approximately 2,800,000 in 2013 (TSB 2014). Despite the fact that the total share of citizens with private health insurance has still not exceeded 2 per cent of the total population, the increase in private health insurance uptake is nevertheless noteworthy.

In addition, the HTP also introduced an optional supplementary private health insurance. The main aim of this insurance component is to top up the public health insurance by offering financial protection for additional payments in private hospitals that offer services to the publicly insured (Mapfre Genel Sigorta 2012). The number of citizens with supplementary private health insurance reached only around 300,000 at the end of 2016 (TSB 2016), which demonstrates that the uptake of this component has not yet met expectations of the insurance industry.

4.2.2 Changes in Healthcare Delivery

Prior to the reform, different types of public hospitals (MoH hospitals, SSK hospitals, public university hospitals) and private clinics of medical doctors dominated healthcare delivery in Turkey's healthcare system. Two major components of the HTP sought to restructure healthcare delivery and create a quasi-market in healthcare provision. While the first of these components was the transformation of the MoH into a planning and monitoring body, the second aimed to establish health enterprises that would operate from public hospitals and increase the role of the private sector in healthcare delivery.

The first step that the government took in altering the structure of healthcare delivery was to transfer the SSK hospitals to the MoH (The Republic of Turkey 2005a). It then restructured the MoH to fit into its new overseer and monitoring role and granted administrative and partial financial autonomy to public hospitals (The Republic of Turkey 2011a). In line with these legislative changes, Public Hospital Unions (*Kamu Hastane Birlikleri*) were established to bring together geographically close public hospitals and to grant them financial and administrative autonomy. The government also began to establish new public hospitals with a new financing mechanism that resembled the Private Finance Initiatives (PFI) in the United Kingdom (The Republic of Turkey 2013). Reminiscent of the build-transfer-operate model, private sector actors built new large public hospitals on public land, received rent from the state and got permission to provide commercial services in these hospitals.

Another major step the government took was to provide incentives for private investors to open new private hospitals and allow the SGK to purchase services from private hospitals for its insurees. These changes implied the launch of the quasi-market model in healthcare delivery. On the one hand, purchasing services from private sector providers was not new to the healthcare system in Turkey. Prior to the reform, public hospitals were free to purchase diagnostic and maintenance services from private providers. In addition, it was not uncommon for the ES to purchase services from private hospitals, though this was limited in scope. On the other hand, with the implementation of the HTP, the state began to purchase healthcare services from the private sector on a much larger scale than it had in earlier periods. As a result, both the share of private sector investments in the healthcare sector and the share of expenditures from the SGK to private hospitals increased drastically during the reform (Sönmez 2011, pp. 60–71), which resulted in a clear privatisation trend in healthcare delivery.

Private clinics of medical doctors used to function as an important component of the healthcare delivery structure before the reform. With the launch of the HTP, the government's insistence on introducing a full-time work requirement for medical doctors and to exclude private clinics from the public health insurance plan led to a decline in the number of private clinics (Kaban 2010). This decrease was a direct result of the government's policy decision that favoured larger actors in healthcare delivery market.

Another significant development occurred in the provision of medications. Before the HTP, SSK beneficiaries did not have easy access to medications. SSK beneficiaries were obliged to use pharmacies owned by the SSK, whose service capacity was limited. As a result, getting necessary medications on time had been a challenge to SSK insurees. Green Card beneficiaries did not have the right to free medications at all. The only mechanism through which Green Card beneficiaries were able to access medications was to apply for a social assistance scheme, a laborious and lengthy application process that did not guarantee access in the end. With the launch of the HTP, beneficiaries of the SSK began to access medications through privately owned pharmacies, which essentially solved the problems of that group. The reform granted equal benefit packages for Green Card users, including access to medications through privately owned pharmacies, which implied a clear improvement in Green Card beneficiaries' access to healthcare.

4.2.3 *The Results of the Health Transformation Programme So Far*

One of the results of the HTP was an increase in the share of public health expenditures in the GDP. Figure 4.1 indicates this increase.

The figure also illustrates that, despite the policy drift between 1988 and 2002, the share of public health expenditures in the GDP rose from 0.9 per cent in 1988 to 3.6 per cent in 2002. After the introduction of the HTP in 2003, the increase in the share of public health expenditures in the GDP continued. The share of public health expenditures in the GDP rose from 3.7 per cent in 2003 to 4.6 per cent in 2013.[3] This increase can be explained by the various components of the reform as the equalisation of benefit packages for all public insurees, including the beneficiaries of the Green Card scheme, an increase in the number of Green Card beneficiaries – from under 7 million in the early 2000s (SGK 2010c) to

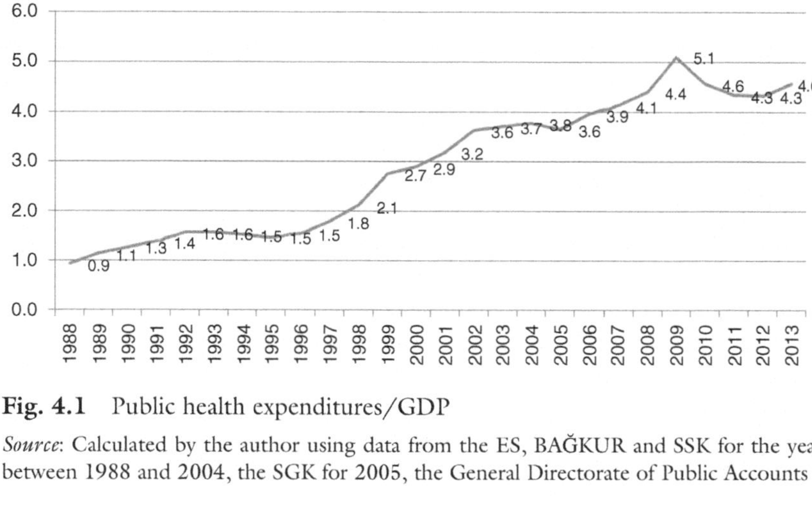

Fig. 4.1 Public health expenditures/GDP

Source: Calculated by the author using data from the ES, BAĞKUR and SSK for the years between 1988 and 2004, the SGK for 2005, the General Directorate of Public Accounts

nearly 12.5 million by April 2014 (SGK 2014) – and the introduction of public transfers for services of private hospitals to public insurees. In another study, we found that the increase in the share of public healthcare expenditures in the GDP originated mainly from expenditures for treatments (Yılmaz and Yentürk 2016b).

Despite increased demand and increased ease of access, Ökem and Çakar rightly point out that the government has been largely successful in controlling public healthcare expenditures (2015, p. 1154). Parallel to this finding, based on the Court of Accounts report (2013), public health insurance fund was self-sustaining as of 2013 (Yılmaz and Yentürk 2016a).

The HTP, in fact, increased the state's responsibility to finance universal public health insurance coverage by keeping means-tested public support for the very poor, incorporating public contribution to an insurance fund for each worker and equalising benefit packages for all. The latter is evidenced in a study that concluded public expenditures for healthcare were more fairly distributed among different occupational status groups since the introduction of the HTP (Teksöz et al. 2009).

However, because the HTP kept the insurance-based financing model and income means-testing for the very poor intact, the new system still does not automatically provide the very poor with insurance coverage. Based on survey data collected in 2011, scholars found that more than two-fifths of those eligible for exemption from paying premiums due to poverty did not have public health insurance coverage (Erus et al. 2015). Given that younger people and those without urgent need to access healthcare services are less like to register, scholars also calculated the non-take-up rate for people with chronic illnesses. They found that more than one-third of those with chronic illnesses did not have public health insurance coverage (Erus et al. 2015, p. 102). Those without public health insurance coverage are more likely to avoid seeing a doctor, either for fear they will not be able to afford it or the possibility of having to make higher of out-of-pocket payments (Erus et al. 2015, p. 105). This study evidences the obstacle posed by the use of income means-testing in providing public health insurance coverage for people living below the official poverty threshold. An ethnographic study also provided evidence that there are inherent uncertainties in the application and status determination process for poor people's access to public health insurance, which leads to poor people employing tactical manoeuvres to get public health insurance, while at the same time disempowering others who do not employ or are not capable of employing those strategies (Yoltar 2009).

Elsewhere I have argued that the introduction of contributory payments for public healthcare services and medications as well as additional payments for private healthcare services would lead to a regressive healthcare financing model (Yılmaz 2013). A review of the literature on healthcare reform in Turkey also reveals that the reform failed to reverse the regressive feature of out-of-pocket payments in the healthcare system (Ökem and Çakar 2015, p. 1159). While the HTP made public expenditures for healthcare more fairly distributed, out-of-pocket payments it formalised might have been hampering its egalitarian impacts.

The prevalence of informal payments in healthcare delivery was one of the factors that the government used to legitimise the reform and introduce the full-time work requirement for medical doctors working in public hospitals. A survey study conducted in Ankara, however, shows that the HTP did not put a stop to informal payments in healthcare provision in the public sector. It found that almost one-third of the participants declared that they had made informal payments, three-fourths of whom belonged to low-income groups (Tengilimoğlu et al. 2015).

Despite the obstacles poor people had to overcome to get public health insurance coverage and the regressive character of out-of-pocket payments – including informal payments that did not disappear with the reform – a survey revealed that the general public perceived the short-term impacts of the contemporary health reform as largely positive. The rate of highly and very highly satisfied citizens increased from 40 per cent in 2003 to roughly 75 per cent in 2013 (TÜİK 2014, p. 78). A study on changes in service satisfaction after the HTP indicates that satisfaction in the lowest 30 per cent income group increased more than that in the highest 70 per cent income group (Hazama 2015, p. 48). Parallel to this evidence, Alkan interpreted the AK Party's consecutive victories in general elections as a result of the government's success in reforming healthcare (2011).

This drastic increase in citizens' satisfaction – especially the satisfaction of low-income individuals – can be partly attributed to the increased ease of access: it was reported that per capita hospital visits rose from 2 in 2002 to 5.1 in 2012 (The Ministry of Health 2013, p. 91). Doctor consultations per capita increased from 2.8 in 2000 to 8.3 in 2014 (OECD).

Ease of access without a corresponding increase in the healthcare workforce comes with a human cost and at the expense of service quality. A study on the healthcare workforce rightly suggests that this drastic rise in doctor consultations during the HTP significantly increased the workload of healthcare professionals (Ağartan 2015b, p. 1624).

Studies evaluating the HTP's impact on efficiency in healthcare provision, which was one of the main objectives of the reform, point in conflicting directions. Scholars suggest that NPM reforms in public hospitals, such as the introduction of the pay for performance system for medical doctors, increased the efficiency of public hospitals (Gok and Altındağ 2015). Another study, however, demonstrates that the establishment of an internal market in healthcare delivery, and thus the introduction of competition, did not affect hospital efficiency (Narcı et al. 2015). More research on healthcare delivery after the HTP is needed to uncover the HTP's impact on efficiency in healthcare provision.

In the literature, scholars disagree on the overall impact of the reform on three fronts: access to healthcare, the working conditions of health workers and the sustainability of the healthcare system. Some scholars argue that the reform had a positive impact on citizens' access to healthcare services by simply easing their access to healthcare services and abolishing the former occupational status-based inequalities in access to healthcare (i.e. Dorlach 2015; Atun et al. 2013; Baris et al. 2011; Karadeniz 2009; Teksöz et al. 2009; Ağartan 2008, 2007; Keyder 2007a). In response, others suggest that the reform's pro-market components pose significant obstacles to the consolidation of a universal healthcare system (i.e. Yılmaz 2013; Ağartan 2012; Civaner 2011; Etiler and Urhan 2011; Sönmez 2011; TTB 2011b; Yaşar 2011; Yaşar and Uğurluoğlu 2011; Ucku and Elçi 2010; Üstündağ and Yoltar 2007; Pala 2007).

Studies also examined the impact of the HTP on women's access to healthcare services under three headings. First, the reliance on a social insurance-based model of financing healthcare services perpetuated gender inequality in getting public health insurance coverage in a country where female labour force participation rate is lower than all EU and OECD countries (Kılıç 2008). In this social insurance-based model, women outside the formal labour market get public health insurance either as dependents of their husband or through income means-testing (Ağartan 2012a). Secondly, the introduction of the HTP coincided with a significant shift in the population policy in Turkey from ante-natalism to pro-natalism, which led to the undermining of a previously strong family planning component in healthcare provision (Him and Hoşgör 2015). Thirdly, related to the second impact, scholars suggested that women's health has been placed at the intersection of neoliberalism and neoconservatism during the HTP, which undermines women's agency in determining if they need healthcare services and, if so, which type (Acar and Altunok 2013).

4.3 The Post-1980s' Healthcare Reforms in Latin America, Southern Europe and East Asia

In this section, I provide a brief review of the post-1980s' healthcare reforms in emerging market economies without claiming they are comprehensive or up-to-date. In doing so, I situate the HTP within a comparative healthcare policy reform framework.

4.3.1 Background

Before the consolidation of the Washington Consensus, healthcare reforms in developing countries aimed to extend the scope of and to facilitate access to healthcare services. A combination of anti-colonialist sentiment, positive international political atmosphere crowned by the Alma Ata Declaration of 1978 and the ideals of socialism and social democracy, made 'health for all' the common reference point for most if not all developing country governments in their healthcare policies.

Unlike most advanced capitalist countries, developing countries were not able to achieve universal coverage for all citizens before the early 1980s. The majority of healthcare systems in high- and middle-income developing countries traditionally rely on a social insurance system for civil servants and other formal sector employees (Barrientos and Lloyd-Sherlock 2000, p. 417). In line with the developmentalist objectives of the post-WWII period, it was expected that public health insurance schemes for the formally employed would gradually cover all citizens, either as workers or as dependents of these workers.

Since the late 1970s and early 1980s, healthcare reforms have become part of the political agenda in both emerging market economies and advanced capitalist countries. In advanced capitalist countries, several factors account for the rise of healthcare reforms in the political agenda: ageing populations and chronic diseases, which led to a rise in healthcare expenditures; an increase in demand for healthcare services; intensive use of health technologies such as computerised axial tomography (CAT) scanners, magnetic resonance imaging (MRI) and positron emission tomography (PET) (Wessen 1999, p. 386; Abel-Smith and Mossialos 1994, p. 90); and the need to contain increasing healthcare expenditures accordingly (Blank and Burau 2010, pp. 96–7). Indeed, scholars note that the increasing rate of healthcare costs has exceeded the rate of economic growth in advanced capitalist countries (Blank and Burau 2010, p. 19). With regard to the factors that led to significant increases in healthcare expenditures, Moran suggests that Western European governments made a conscious political choice to prioritise protecting the global competitiveness of their health industries over the sustainability of the provision of free health service for all (1998, p. 26).

Do pro-market healthcare reforms decrease healthcare spending? The evidence indicates the answer is not affirmative. State healthcare systems seem better able to accommodate healthcare costs (Abel-Smith and Mossialos 1994, p. 125). Societal healthcare systems tend to be less effective than state healthcare systems in containing costs, yet they fare better than private healthcare systems (Blank and Burau 2010, p. 76). As the case of the United States demonstrates, greater private actor involvement in healthcare services tends to result in reduced government ability to control health costs (Blank and Burau 2010, p. 107).

How has the US private healthcare system emerged as the model for healthcare reforms in Western Europe and elsewhere? While the US healthcare system has failed in terms of providing universal coverage and containing healthcare expenditures, it is nevertheless a leader in the global healthcare market. The strength of the US position within the global healthcare market makes it a reference point for healthcare reforms, while the United Kingdom has one of the best-performing healthcare systems in terms of cost containment and universal coverage (Moran 1999, p. 18).

If pro-market healthcare reforms do not support cost-containment, what makes them suitable for democratic societies? Some sectors of Western European societies find pro-market healthcare reforms appealing for a variety of reasons. Scholars suggest that upper and upper-middle classes in particular have been dissatisfied with state healthcare systems. This discontent was not unfounded, as rationing mechanisms led to problems such as long waiting times and delays, especially in access to specialty healthcare services (Leys 2010, p. 19; Moran 2000, p. 150; Ranade 1994, p. 43). Moran emphasises that even though state healthcare systems perform well in controlling the system and providing access to all, free of charge at the point of service, they are more likely to be insensitive to consumer demand and inefficiencies (1998, p. 19). As a result, the neoliberal discourse of healthcare reforms has become a voice for high-income groups' demands for better and faster healthcare services in these countries (Moran 1998,

p. 30). Finally, the fact that pro-market healthcare reforms lack evidence does not weaken their popularity. The power of neoliberalism manifested itself in the recognition of the basic premises of a pro-market approach to healthcare among policymakers in particular and the public in general.

In the aftermath of the fall of Keynesianism and the consolidation of first the Washington Consensus and then the Post-Washington Consensus, the political atmosphere that favoured the establishment and proliferation of state and societal healthcare systems in the developing world started to disappear. The WB emerged as the key institution in global health policy. The first WB report on financing health services in emerging market economies was published in 1987 (World Bank 1987). The report promoted pro-market healthcare reforms and contributed substantially to the increasing political urgency attached to healthcare reforms in emerging market economies. The WB approach was clearly pro-market in healthcare delivery, but it pushed for the state to take on a financier role to remain intact (World Bank 1993, p. 65). In this period, managers and economists became part of healthcare policy debates, challenging the power of the medical profession in healthcare politics (Walt and Gilson 1994, p. 357).

Therefore, the post-1980s' healthcare reforms in emerging market economies emerged as part of neoliberalisation. Emerging market economies differed from advanced capitalist countries in terms of the financial resources available to them and the unmet needs they had to serve. Schieber and Maeda examined the WB statistics on healthcare to show that developing countries – home to 84 per cent of the world's population – account for only 11 per cent of the world's healthcare spending (1999, p. 194). In this context, Structural Adjustment Programmes (SAPs) and Stabilisation Programmes that laid the basic tenets of the neoliberalisation of emerging market economies, and public sector transformation in these countries became part of the political context within which healthcare reforms gained primacy. Pro-market healthcare reforms were sometimes introduced as part of the conditionalities attached to loans provided by international donor organisations in times of economic crises (Hall 2003, p. 87).

Nevertheless, it would be erroneous to conclude that healthcare systems are simply converging to private healthcare systems. For OECD countries, Rothgang et al. suggest that there is a relative retreat of the state from healthcare financing, while the differences between healthcare system types remain relatively stable over time (2005, pp. 194–6). Research on specific country cases points to a reverse dynamic in private healthcare systems. For instance, the Obama government in the United States managed to introduce a healthcare reform to increase the regulatory power of the state over the health insurance market, aiming to ensure access to healthcare services, especially for seniors, the sick and middle-class Americans (Jacobs and Skocpol 2010, p. 122). After the recent election of Trump to the presidency, the future of Obamacare is bleak and a new pro-market intervention to the US healthcare system is highly likely. Therefore, evidence supports the claim that healthcare reforms all around the world are ongoing political processes, the pace and scope of which vary according to the political and economic dynamics in different domestic contexts. Studies of individual healthcare reforms especially in emerging market economies are needed to see if there is a common trend in their health system transformations after the 1980s.

Against this background, the selected country cases discussed below indicate that the political trajectories of post-1980 healthcare reforms in emerging market economies have been diverse with respect to the content of these reforms as well as the changes they produced.

4.3.2 Healthcare Reforms in Latin America

Most post-1980 healthcare reforms in Latin America were introduced as part of SAPs during economic crises. In line with the policy direction of roll-back neoliberalism, the majority of Latin American healthcare reforms had strong pro-market components throughout the 1980s and 1990s. In the 2000s, most Latin American countries revitalised their promises to provide healthcare for all and reversed the marketisation trend (for the Venezuelan healthcare reform, see Muntaner et al. 2006; and for the Plan AUGE in Chile, see Pribble 2013; Ewig and Kay 2011).

Most Latin American countries and Turkey had social insurance-based healthcare systems that failed to provide coverage for those outside the formal labour market. While Turkey's healthcare reform did not start during an economic crisis or as a result of SAP, as was the case in most Latin American reforms, it still shares some features of a pro-market approach with the Latin American reforms. Therefore, an analysis of three Latin American experiences of post-1980 healthcare reforms may shed light on discussions about the Turkish healthcare reform. Latin American cases also provide important reference points for analysing what might be the lock-in effects of increased private sector involvement on healthcare reform towards universalism during the early 2000s. With this objective, reform experiences in three countries are examined here: El Salvador, Chile and Argentina.

4.3.2.1 Healthcare Reform in El Salvador

El Salvador witnessed healthcare reform during its public sector restructuring after the 1980 economic crisis and the 1992 peace agreement with Farabundo Martí National Liberation Front. The WB was seen as the most critical international partner of the El Salvadorian government during the reform process (Homedes et al. 2000, pp. 66–7). The government established the Health Reform Group, which led the reform process without consultation with trade unions, peasant organisations, professional organisations or the MoH (Homedes et al. 2000, p. 75). The reform resulted in decentralised healthcare services, a limited role for the public sector in healthcare, new user fees for healthcare services and a basic benefit package that included only primary healthcare services (Homedes et al. 2000, pp. 71–3).

4.3.2.2 Healthcare Reform in Chile

Chilean healthcare system traditionally relied on a centralised public healthcare delivery system funded by a set of social health insurance schemes (Barrientos 2000, pp. 95–6). As in the El Salvadorian experience, the first set of post-1980 healthcare reforms in Chile came into place as part of the SAP. In addition, the country was under the rule of the US-backed military dictatorship of Pinochet that had overthrown democratically elected Salvador Allende's government. The dictatorship separated healthcare financing from healthcare provision, introduced private health insurance and extended coverage to blue-collar workers in the late 1970s and early 1980s (Pribble 2013; Barrientos 2000). However, until the end of the 1990s, private health insurance covered just over a quarter of the citizenry, which included mostly low-risk individuals and high-income earners (Barrientos 2000, p. 94).

Chile's transition to an electoral democracy after 1989 brought the centre-left party to power, which led to the strengthening of the public component of its healthcare system. A second set of Chilean healthcare reforms, the Plan AUGE, attempted to reverse the marketisation process initiated by the Pinochet dictatorship and established universal health insurance for all, one which would eliminate differences in benefit packages among different sectors of society (Ewig and Kay 2011). However, for the majority of women, this reform did not ensure equal access to healthcare. The reform also failed to eradicate income-based inequalities that blocked access to healthcare services (Dannreuther and Gideon 2008). With the reform, the strengthened public component of the Chilean healthcare system functioned as a 'provider of last resort' (Barrientos 2000, p. 94). The resulting healthcare system rendered a strong stratification in citizens' access to healthcare services (Barrientos 2000, p. 111).

4.3.2.3 Healthcare Reform in Argentina

During the 1990s, the Argentinean government carried out a comprehensive healthcare reform in collaboration with the WB. Before the reform, the Argentinian healthcare system had been built upon a tripartite structure: the publicly funded sector, social insurance funds and private healthcare (Lloyd-Sherlock 2005, p. 1895). The publicly funded sector suffered from underfunding, and, due to the lack of state regulation, small-sized social insurance funds were meagre compared to healthcare providers (Lloyd-Sherlock 2005, p. 1895). Throughout the 1990s, the private sector component grew (Lloyd-Sherlock 2005, p. 1895).

Similar to the experience of most other Latin American countries, the Argentinean healthcare reform was initiated at a time when the economy was under the influence of the SAP in the 1990s. One of the key components of the Argentinean healthcare reform was the introduction of a competitive market in health insurance, which gave citizens the option to exit the social health insurance scheme and switch to private health insurance (Lloyd-Sherlock 2005, p. 1897). Secondly, the reform transformed public hospitals into health enterprises with their own management authorities, with the exception that the provincial administration still had authority over the hospital staff (Lloyd-Sherlock 2005, p. 1898).

4.3.3 Healthcare Reforms in Southern Europe

Southern European countries, specifically, Greece, Italy, Spain and Portugal, are historically similar to Turkey in terms of their political-economic structures and their reliance on social insurance-based healthcare financing (e.g. Buğra and Keyder 2006, p. 212). Günal points out, however, that Greece and Italy took a different route in terms of their healthcare systems after the end of the 1970s. While Turkey chose to consolidate its social insurance-based financing model with the HTP, Greece and Italy switched to a national health services model (Günal 2008, pp. 13–14). Although these three countries took different paths towards healthcare reform, it is still useful to examine the reforms in Greece and Italy to see whether it was the different political dynamics in these countries that resulted in a switch to a national health services model.

Before discussing individual cases, I would like to note the political-economic contexts within which national healthcare systems are embedded in Southern European countries as opposed to those which are at play in other countries with state healthcare systems such as the UK and the Scandinavian countries. First of all, Southern European countries had societal healthcare systems before the reforms, and these systems were transformed into state healthcare systems. By contrast, Britain and the Scandinavian countries established their healthcare systems as state healthcare systems from the very start (Petmesidou and Guillén 2008, p. 107). Secondly, Britain and the Scandinavian countries set up their state healthcare systems in times of steady economic growth and prosperity, while Southern European countries moved to this model during periods of economic austerity (Petmesidou and Guillén 2008, p. 107) and the permanent austerity that the Maastricht criteria imposes upon EU member states. Not unlike Latin American countries that were obliged to undertake SAPs under the influence of the WB and the IMF, Southern European countries were required to meet the Maastricht criteria in order to join the European Monetary Union (EMU) (Petmesidou and Guillén 2008, p. 107).

In line with historical institutionalist predictions, Moran suggests that national healthcare services in Southern European countries did not function in the same way as the systems of Northern European countries (2000, p. 154). Co-payments increasingly became the biggest source of healthcare financing, while universal coverage remained more an ideal than a reality (Moran 2000, p. 154). According to Moran, the partial failure of the national healthcare service model in Southern Europe was due to the fact that Southern European healthcare reforms were undertaken at a time of fiscal austerity that hampered the prospects of public investment in healthcare infrastructure and human resources. Lastly, Moran draws attention to the role of the political culture in these countries, which resulted in corruption and what became the common practice of medical doctors setting up their own private clinics (Moran 2000, p. 155).

4.3.3.1 Healthcare Reform in Greece

After the fall of the military junta in the middle of the 1970s, the New Democracy Party of Karamanlis won the general elections in Greece. However, it was not until 1981 that the Pan Hellenic Socialist Movement (PASOK) initiated healthcare reform and established a national health service (Kondilis et al. 2011, pp. 32–3). As part of the reform, the establishment of new private healthcare facilities was banned. This reform led to an increase in the capacity of public healthcare facilities (Kondilis et al. 2011, p. 33).

However, reformers failed to unite social security funds due to strong opposition by trade unions (Kondilis et al. 2011, p. 33). As a result, while almost two-thirds of total health expenditures were funded through general taxation in Spain and Italy, only around 20 per cent were financed through general taxation in Greece in 2004 (Petmesidou and Guillén 2008, p. 111). Petmesidou and Guillen suggest that the main reason for Greece's failure to unite separate social security funds was the 'statist-clientelistic' political culture and the consequent polarised political structure (2008, p. 110).

After the fall of the social democrats, the conservative government lifted the ban on the establishment of private healthcare facilities, introduced co-payment and user charges, subsidised private health insurance, abolished employment security for medical doctors (Kondilis et al. 2011, p. 34) and permitted medical doctors working for public hospitals to engage in private practice (Petmesidou and Guillén 2008, p. 110).

As mentioned earlier, the European Union's (EU) Maastricht criteria, coupled with preparations for the transition to a monetary union in Europe, undermined the Greek government's control of the public budget during the reform process (Kondilis et al. 2011, p. 34). As a result, the consolidation of the national healthcare services model could not be pursued properly. Instead, the government concerned itself with cost-containment in healthcare services, which then resulted in the further marketisation of healthcare services (Kondilis et al. 2011, pp. 34–5). Therefore, Tountas et al. point out that despite the introduction of the NHS model, the role of the private sector increased over time (2005, p. 168). They argue that the main reason for the increased private sector presence in healthcare was the public sector's failure to provide quality services while citizens' disposable income increased, thereby fostering 'passive privatisation' (Tountas et al. 2005, p. 169).

The private hospitals sector witnessed mergers and acquisitions during the late 1990s and early 2000s. This process led to the establishment of an oligopolistic market in private healthcare provision dominated by three multinationals (Kondilis et al. 2011, p. 37). In his study of the concentration of the private hospitals sector, Boutsioli too reports that the private hospitals sector had become an oligopolistic market, as it became increasingly concentrated over time and only a few companies controlled the market (2007, p. 223). The current Greek healthcare system, which has low satisfaction rates among the public, is a mixed healthcare system that is composed of different forms of financing and delivery structures (Kondilis et al. 2011, pp. 40–1).

4.3.3.2 Healthcare Reform in Italy

The Italian government introduced healthcare reform to transform the country's healthcare system into a national health service in 1978. The major aim of this reform was to establish tax-based financing, free access for all to services and public provision of services (Donatini et al. 2001, p. 91). However, the reform could not be fully implemented, and private healthcare providers flourished due to limited public capacity for delivering healthcare services. In addition, costly co-payments created an obstacle for patients wishing to access healthcare services during the 1980s and early 1990s (Donatini et al. 2001, p. 92).

In response, the Italian government initiated a new reform project in the early 1990s. In line with changes in the British NHS, the main objectives of this reform were to create an internal market for healthcare delivery and to decentralise healthcare services (Donatini et al. 2001, p. 92). Nevertheless, these changes did not work in tandem due to the lack of regulatory capacity of the regional governments.

In 1999, the Italian healthcare system once again witnessed a reform. This time, the reform strengthened the regulatory role of the state but left the administration of healthcare delivery to the autonomous regions (Donatini et al. 2001, p. 93). The reform authorised autonomous regions to permit the establishment of new healthcare facilities, which increased state power over the private providers (Donatini et al. 2001, p. 99).

In the Italian case, the reform ended the dual practice of medical doctors (Donatini et al. 2001, p. 100). Instead, public hospitals reserved 6–12 per cent of their bed capacity for doctors' private patients, provided that these doctors paid a specific percentage of their privately earned income to the hospital (Donatini et al. 2001, p. 100).

4.3.4 *Healthcare Reforms in East Asia and Southeast Asia*

The social policies of East Asian and Southeast Asian countries have traditionally been enmeshed with outward-oriented developmentalist aspirations, which are categorised as 'productive welfare systems' (Rudra 2007). East Asian and Southeast Asian countries also witnessed welfare system transformations after the 1980s. Since the literature on political economy has compared Turkey with Malaysia and South Korea (e.g. Eder 1993), healthcare reforms of those countries are discussed briefly below.

4.3.4.1 Healthcare Reform in Malaysia

The Malaysian healthcare system was traditionally a state healthcare system (Ramesh 2009, p. 73). While the Malaysian government included healthcare in its privatisation plan in 1983 (Ramesh 2009, p. 75), the government did not implement this practice for fear that it might hamper its re-election chances (Ramesh 2009, p. 75).

The Malaysian government, on the other hand, pursued a policy-layering strategy that encouraged the private healthcare sector to develop as an alternative to the public sector without undertaking direct privatisation (Leng and Barraclough 2007, p. 21). As the national income of Malaysia rose dramatically in the 1990s and 2000s, private hospitals flourished, validating the success of the government's 'passive privatisation' strategy (Leng and Barraclough 2007, p. 24). For example, the share of private hospital beds in the total number of hospital beds increased from 5 per cent in 1980 to 25 per cent in 2002 (Leng and Barraclough 2007, p. 9). In this new setting, roughly less than half of the medical doctors worked in the private sector, while more than half were employed in the public sector (Ramesh 2009, p. 75).

Malaysia relied upon various forms of healthcare finance tools, including government transfers, user charges, out-of-pocket payments and a tiny proportion of social security funds and private health insurance funds (Ramesh 2009, p. 76). Government transfers to healthcare services accounted for a little more than half of total healthcare expenditures in 1998 and in 2002 (Ramesh 2009, p. 77).

Ramesh reports that the Malaysian government had been concerned about the containment of healthcare costs since the mid-1980s (2009, p. 79). The government plans to transform the country's healthcare finance model from a tax-based model to a social insurance-based one. However, Ramesh suggested in 2009 that the government had not yet been successful in reaching these objectives due to a fear of possible electoral backlash (2009, p. 79).

4.3.4.2 Healthcare Reform in South Korea

South Korea, similar to Turkey, has one of the lowest levels of social expenditures in the OECD. In his book on the South Korean social policy, Woo argues that the main reason for low social expenditures resulted from the state's primary political objectives: commitment to economic development and national competitiveness in the international economy. These objectives subjected social policy development to economic development. In order to strengthen its developmentalist strategy, Woo explains that the South Korean state worked with the owners of large companies to create a cooperative labour force using company-level trade unions (Woo 2004, p. 135). In fact, the Korean Tripartite Commission, which is composed of government, business and labour representatives, functioned as a corporatist governance body in South Korea. In this setting, the company-level welfare provision increased in scope, yet the development of a universal welfare state remained limited (Woo 2004, p. 135).

Woo explains that the South Korean healthcare system began to develop during the economic boom of the 1960s and 1970s under an authoritarian regime. This system provided healthcare coverage mainly for those working in the largest companies. However, the Medical Aid Programme, similar to the Green Card scheme in Turkey, was introduced in 1977 as a tax-financed welfare programme to provide free healthcare services for those living below the officially determined poverty threshold (Chun et al. 2009, p. 26).

According to Woo, health insurance for the general population and other social programs began to appear only after the relative democratisation of the country in the late 1980s, similar to the history of healthcare system development in Turkey (2004, p. 130). For instance, in the late

1980s, health insurance schemes for the self-employed became available (Chun et al. 2009, p. 141). Woo states that the largest increase in health insurance coverage came about after the financial crises of 1997 and 1998 in order to reinstate the legitimacy of the state (2004, p. 130). Kwon also suggests that the democratisation of Korean politics and the financial crises of 1997 and 1998 made the developmentalist Korean state a more socially inclusive one in the domain of healthcare policies (2005, p. 494).

In 1998, the South Korean government, a single-party government of the then centre-left Democratic United Party, launched its plan to unite health insurances. As trade unionism was confined to the company level, the largest trade union of the country, the Federation of Korean Trade Unions, opposed any proposal to unify social insurances and establish a national health service (Woo 2004, p. 134). The largest business organisation also opposed the unification proposal and suggested instead the extensive use of private health insurance (Woo 2004, p. 109).

Despite strong opposition to the proposed reform, the Democratic United Party's centre-left government legislated the reform, and the constitutional court ruled the unification of health insurance funds constitutional (Woo 2004, p. 109). As a result, the National Medical Insurance Corporation was established in 1998 to merge 227 social insurance funds under the umbrella of a single public body (Chun et al. 2009, p. 142).

Despite the legislative victory and the ruling, the Grand National Party, the major conservative party of South Korea, and the Federation of Korean Trade Unions continued to work against the actual unification of social insurance funds. Indeed, Woo suggests that the fate of the financial unification of health insurance funds was still unclear as of 2002. The anti-unification camp managed to persuade the government to delay the financial merger until after the 2002 general elections (Chun et al. 2009, p. 144). Woo argues that the political division between the Federation of Korean Trade Unions, who were against the unification, and the Korean Confederation of Trade Unions, who were in favour of the unification, decreased the chance of full-fledged unification of health insurances being realised (2004, p. 120). Finally, after the electoral victory of the centre-left Democratic United Party in the 2002 presidential elections, the financial merger was implemented in 2003 (Chun et al. 2009, pp. 144–5).

After the mid-2000s, the Medical Aid Programme began to be perceived as a significant burden on the public budget (Kwon 2007). As a result, the South Korean government introduced cost sharing for outpatient care services with a ceiling on user charges and limited access to certain healthcare providers (Kwon 2007). Kwon reports that progressive civic groups opposed these changes to the Medical Aid Programme, yet failed to stop the reform (2007).

4.4 Conclusion

This concluding section, after summarising the main tenets of the HTP, explores the similarities and differences between the HTP in Turkey and reforms in Latin American, Southern European and East Asian countries. In doing so, it offers insight into the unique features of Turkey's HTP from a comparative perspective. Last but not least, this section shows that it is important to take into account the significance of the actors that played key roles in healthcare reforms in other emerging market economies when examining the politics of healthcare in Turkey.

The HTP, as a large-scale healthcare reform, strengthened the social insurance-based financing model in healthcare finance in Turkey. As a result, the share of public healthcare expenditures increased in the GDP – which was the case even before the HTP – and most of this increase was due to an increase in expenditures for curative healthcare services rather than medications. Despite the unification of all social insurance schemes under the compulsory general health insurance with a broadly defined basic benefit package, healthcare expenditures in Turkey did not increase drastically.

Health insurance coverage and access to healthcare services increased, but there still is a considerable rate of non-take-up in those who are in need of healthcare services. The HTP also introduced new financing mechanisms, including user fees for public healthcare services and medications, as well as contributory payments for private healthcare services. These new financing mechanisms introduced an income-based stratification among citizens' access to healthcare services. The HTP failed to eliminate the regressive character of out-of-pocket and informal payments, which might have, in fact, perpetuated these inequalities.

A drastic increase in the number of doctor consultations came at the expense of a heavier workload for medical doctors and possibly reduced service quality due to shortened consultation times in public hospitals.

The marketisation dynamic is most visible in the changes made in healthcare delivery. The HTP provided incentives for increased private sector involvement in healthcare provision primarily in the form of hospitals and opened these facilities for public insurees who were able and willing to make additional payments. While abolishing the occupational status-based inequalities in access, the HTP replaced them with income-based inequalities in access.

The first conclusion is that there is a general trend towards marketisation in the different components of healthcare systems in emerging market economies. The dominant global 'policy paradigm' of pro-market healthcare reforms for the governments of emerging market economies has been by and large the same. International organisations, especially the WB, have been at the forefront of promoting this discourse through various means.

This global policy paradigm, however, did not secure a teleological route for emerging market economies to restructure their healthcare systems along with marketisation. Even if two countries seem to take a similar reform path (e.g. providing more room for private health insurance schemes), whether and how this path is implemented on the ground depends on numerous and varied domestic and global political factors.

The HTP has similarities and differences with healthcare reforms in the selected countries of Latin America, Southern Europe and East Asia. On the one hand, the main tenets of the reform in Turkey are common in most of the healthcare reforms discussed above, including the purchaser-provider split, the social insurance funds merger, user chargers to outpatient services, and a greater role for the private sector in healthcare delivery. On the other hand, the HTP is a product of a rather different political and economic context than most healthcare reforms in Latin American countries in the 1980s and 1990s that were under military dictatorships and were implementing SAPs. The Turkish healthcare reform was introduced by a single-party government aiming at generating public legitimacy in its first-term rule and during an economic boom period that lasted until the mid-2010s.

As far as the outcomes of the reforms are concerned, passive privatisation is a general trend in electoral democracies, rather than the selling of public healthcare institutions to the private sector and direct privatisation of social health insurances. Turkey is no exception to this passive privatisation trend especially in healthcare delivery. As is the case of Greece, changes in the healthcare delivery market in Turkey have led to an oligopolistic market in the healthcare delivery. Similar to the Malaysian experience, a rise in national income has strengthened the use of private healthcare facilities in the Turkish case. During the post-1980 healthcare reforms, hardly any of the emerging market economies examined were investing significantly in public healthcare facilities. In line with the trend in Greece, Turkey also began to employ public-private partnership models (similar to the UK's PFI) in the construction of public hospitals. Therefore, it can be argued that the rise of private actors in healthcare delivery and passive privatisation emerged as a common trend in the aftermath of post-1980 healthcare reforms in emerging market economies.

A major difference between the HTP and reforms in other selected emerging market economies is the continued dominant role of the Turkish state in healthcare financing. For instance, unlike the reform in Argentina, the Turkish healthcare reform did not allow for opting out of general health insurance. This can be partially explained on the basis of the contextual differences within which the reforms were introduced in these two countries. While the healthcare reform in Argentina was introduced in times of austerity, the Turkish healthcare reform came into place during a period of steady economic growth, which provided the government with the financial means to implement a reform that increased public healthcare expenditures (Atun et al. 2013). The second difference is the limited power of political actors in other countries examined when compared to the successive AK Party governments in Turkey. South Korean consultative bodies such as the Tripartite Commission did not exist in Turkey's political system. And while the power of trade unions and other actors delayed the implementation of healthcare reform in South Korea and blocked reform in Greece, no political actors succeeded in delaying or blocking the reform of the single-party government in Turkey that transferred SSK hospitals to the MoH.

The selected case studies suggest that there are important political actors that have to be taken into account when examining the politics of healthcare reform processes. These actors include the role of international organisations, governments and their power within the country's political system, and the role of trade unions and business organisations.

There are also general lessons to be learnt from these case studies. For instance, if a country has a working electoral democracy, those governments seem to care about their electoral prospects in carrying out healthcare reforms, which inevitably hampers government attempts to pursue direct privatisation. In other words, when governing parties have competitors in the political system, they may choose not to pursue direct privatisation but undertake passive privatisation instead. In addition, depending on the nature of industrial relations, trade unions in emerging market economies can act to protect their members' relatively privileged positions within healthcare systems or to establish broader alliances to push for the establishment of universal healthcare system. Their position on universalisation in healthcare varies on the basis of their political vision as well as the industrial relations systems within which they operate. Finally, neoliberalism limits public investment in healthcare systems by decreasing the ability of emerging market economies to tax the rich in a tight fiscal environment.

Last but not least, these cases suggest that significant political clashes are likely to occur once a reform is enacted. These clashes can even block the implementation of a reform, give it a new shape, or make a significant amendment to it. Therefore, the tendency in the literature to examine the political processes that result in the enactment of reforms but neglect the political processes after the primary legislative victory of the proponents of the reform might not be well grounded. Political negotiations and conflicts over a reform do not come to an end once the primary decision is made.

Notes

1. For example, for the period between 1 June and 31 December 2012, income ranges and premium levels apply to these ranges of monthly incomes per person in a family: (1) No premium to be paid for people living under less than one-third of minimum wage (313.50 TL = approx. €135), (2) 37.62 TL (approx. €16) premium to be paid for people living on monthly incomes between one-third of minimum wage (313.50 TL = approx. 135 €) and minimum wage (940.50 TL = approx. €405), (3) 112.86 TL (approx. €49) premium to be paid for people living on monthly incomes between minimum wage (940.50 TL = approx. €405) and two minimum wages (1881 TL = approx. €810 and (4) 225.72 TL (approx. €97) premium to be paid for people living on monthly incomes above two minimum wages (1881 TL = approx. €810).
2. Up-to-date rates of contributory payments at the time this article was drafted were as follows: (1) 5 TL (=approx. €2.15) for each outpatient visit to a public hospital, (2) 12 TL (= approx. €5.17) for each outpatient visit to a private hospital that offers services to the publicly insured, (3) 3 TL (= approx. €1.29) for each prescription including up to three items of medication and (4) an additional 1 TL (= approx. €0.43) for each item of medication over three.
3. The highest share of public health expenditures in GDP in 2008 was due to the shrinkage of the GDP by 4.8 per cent during the economic crisis.

References

Abel-Smith, B., and Mossialos, E. (1994). Cost containment and healthcare reform: A study of the European Union. *Health Policy*, 28(2), 89–132.

Acar, F., and Altunok, G. (2013). The 'politics of intimate' at the intersection of neoliberalism and neoconservatism in contemporary Turkey. *Women's Studies International Forum*, 41(1), 14–23.

Adıyok, M. (2012). Turkey's healthcare: A bad prognosis. *Turkish Review*, 2(4), 26–31.

Ağartan, T. İ. (2007). Turkish health policy in a globalizing world: The case of 'Transformation of Health' program. *ISA Research Committee 19 Annual Academic Conference*. Florence: ISA.

Ağartan, T. İ. (2008). *Turkish health system in transition: Historical background and reform experience*. Ph.D., State University of New York.

Ağartan, T. İ (2012a). Gender and health sector reform: Policies, actions and effects. In A. Y. Elveren and S. Dedeoğlu (eds.), *Gender and society in Turkey: The impact of neo-liberal policies, political Islam and EU accession* (pp. 155–173). London and New York: IB Tauris.

Ağartan, T. I. (2015a). Explaining large-scale policy change in the Turkish healthcare system: Ideas, institutions, and political actors. *Journal of Health Politics, Policy and Law*, 40(5), 971–999.

Ağartan, T. I. (2015b). Health workforce policy and Turkey's healthcare reform. *Health Policy*, 119(12), 1621–1626.

Akıncı, F., Mollahaliloğlu, S., Gürsöz, H., and Öğücü, F. (2012). Assessment of the Turkish healthcare system reforms: A stakeholder analysis. *Health Policy*, 107(1), 21–30.

Alkan, H. (2011, June 1). AKP'nin sağlık kozu (AKP's healthcare trump). *BBC Türkçe*.

Atun, R., Aydın, S., Chakraborty, S., Sümer, S., Aran, M., Gürol, İ, Nazlıoğlu, S., Özgülcü, Ş., Aydoğan, Ü., Ayar, B., Dilmen, U., and Akdağ, R. (2013). Universal health coverage in Turkey: Enhancement of equity. *The Lancet*, 382(9886), 65–99.

Bank, World (1987). *Financing health services in developing countries: An agenda for reform*. Washington, DC: The World Bank.

Baris, E., Mollahaliloğlu, S., and Aydın, S. (2011). Healthcare in Turkey: From laggard to leader. *British Medical Journal*, 342, 579–582.

Barrientos, A. (2000). Getting better after neoliberalism: Shifts and challenges of health policy in Chile. In P Lloyd-Sherlock (ed.), *Healthcare reform & poverty* (pp. 94–111). London: Institute of Latin American Studies.

Barrientos, A., and Lloyd-Sherlock, P. (2000). Reforming health insurance in Argentina and Chile. *Health Policy and Planning*, 15(4), 417–423.

Blank, R. H., and Burau, V. (2010). *Comparative health policy*. Hampshire: Palgrave Macmillan.

Boutsioli, Z. (2007). Concentration in the Greek private hospital sector: A descriptive analysis. *Health Policy*, 82(2), 212–225.
Buğra, A., and Keyder, Ç. (2006). The Turkish welfare regime in transformation. *Journal of European Social Policy*, 16(3), 211–228.
Chun, C. B., Kim, S. Y., Lee, J. Y., and Lee, S. Y. (2009). Republic of Korea: health system review. *Health Systems in Transition*, 11(7), 1–184.
Civaner, M. (2011). 'Transforming' our health by privatisation-Response to Baris et al. *British Medical Journal*, 342.
Dannreuther, C., and Gideon, J. (2008). Entitled to health? Social protection in Chile's Plan AUGE. *Development and Change*, 39(5), 845–864.
Donatini, A., D'ambrosio, A. R. M. G., Scalzo, A. L., Orzella, L., Cicchetti, A., and Profili, S. (2001). Healthcare systems in transition: Italy. *Healthcare Systems in Transition*, 3(4), 1–131.
Dorlach, T. (2015). The prospects of egalitarian capitalism in the global South: Turkish social neoliberalism in comparative perspective. *Economy and Society*, 44(4), 519–544.
Eder, M. (1993). *Crises of late industrialization: A comparative study of the automotive industry in Brazil, South Korea and Turkey*. Ph.D. Virginia: University of Virginia.
Erus, B., Yakut Çakar, B., Cali, S., and Adaman, F. (2015). Health policy for the poor: An exploration on the take-up of means-tested health benefits in Turkey. *Social Science & Medicine*, 130(C), 99–106.
Etiler, N., and Urhan, B. (2011). Working conditions of physicians employed in public institutions in Turkey. In J. Lister (ed.), *Europe's health for sale: The heavy cost of privatisation* (pp. 83–93). Oxfordshire: Libri Publishing.
Ewig, C., and Kay, S. J. (2011). Postretrenchment politics: Policy feedback in Chile's health and pension reforms. *Latin American Politics and Society*, 53(4), 67–99.
Gok, M. S., and Altındağ, E. (2015). Analysis of the cost and efficiency relationship: Experience in the Turkish pay for performance system. *The European Journal of Health Economics*, 16(5), 459–469.
Günal, A. (2008). *Health and citizenship in Republican Turkey: An analysis of the socialization of health services in Republican historical context*. Ph.D. Istanbul: Boğaziçi University.
Habertürk. (2012, March 18). Özel hastanede farka dikkat! (Pay attention to the additional payments in private hospitals). *Habertürk Ekonomi*.
Hall, D. (2003). Multinational corporations and the pattern of privatisation in healthcare. In K. Sen (ed.), *Restructuring health services: Changing contexts & comparative perspectives* (pp. 77–92). London and New York: Zed Books.
Hazama, Y. (2015). Health reform and service satisfaction in the poor: Turkey 2003–11. *Turkish Studies*, 16(1), 36–53.
Him, M.S., and Hoşgör, A.G. (2015). An implication of health sector reform for disadvantaged women's struggle for birth control: A case of Kurdish rural-

urban migrant women in Van, Turkey. *Health Care for Women International*, 36(9), 969–987.

Homedes, N., Paz-Narvaez, A. C., Selva-Sutter, E., Solas, O., and Ugalde, A. (2000). Health reform: Theory and practice in El Salvador. In P Lloyd-Sherlock (ed.), *Healthcare reform & poverty* (pp. 57–77). London: Institute of Latin American Studies.

Jacobs, L. R., and Skocpol, T. (2010). *Healthcare reform and American politics: What everyone needs to know*. Oxford and New York: Oxford University Press.

Kaban, Ş. (2010, March 9). Sağlık Bakanı Recep Akdağ: 20 bin olan özel muayenehane sayısı 4 bine düştü (Minister of Health Recep Akdağ: Number of private clinics fell from 20 thousand to 4 thousand). *Türkiye.*

Karadeniz, O. (2009). *Annual national report 2009-Pensions, health and long-term care.* Brussels: European Commission DG Employment, Social Affairs and Equal Opportunities.

Keyder, Ç. (2007a). Giriş (Introduction). In Ç. Keyder, N. Üstündağ, T. Ağartan, and Ç. Yoltar (eds.), *Avrupa'da ve Türkiye'de sağlık politikaları (Health Policies in Europe and in Turkey).* Istanbul: İletişim.

Kılıç, A. (2008). The gender dimension of social policy reform in Turkey: Towards equal citizenship?. *Social Policy & Administration*, 42(5), 487–503.

Kondilis, E., Smyrnakis, E., Giannakopoulos, S., Zdoukos, T., and Benos, A. (2011). Privatising the Greek healthcare system - a story of corporate profits and rising health inequalities. In J. Lister (ed.), *Europe's health for sale: The heavy cost of privatisation* (pp. 29–43). Oxfordshire: Libri Publishing.

Kwon, H. (2005). Transforming the developmental welfare state in East Asia. *Development and Change*, 36(3), 477–497.

Kwon, S. (2007). Reform of the medical aid program. *Health Policy Monitor.*

Leng, C. H., and Barraclough, S. (2007). Introduction: The transformation of healthcare in Malaysia. In C. H. Leng and S. Barraclough (eds.), *Healthcare in Malaysia: The dynamics of provision, financing and* access (pp. 1–16). Oxon and New York: Routledge.

Leys, C. (2010). Health, healthcare and capitalism. *Socialist Register*, 46(46), 1–28.

Lloyd-Sherlock, P. (2005). Health sector reform in Argentina: A cautionary tale. *Social Science & Medicine*, 60(8), 1893–1903.

Medimagazin. (2011a, March 27). Tedavi giderleri arttı, ilaç giderleri sabit kaldı (Expenditures for treatment increased, while expenditures for medications stayed the same). *Medimagazin.*

Moran, M. (1998). Explaining the rise of the market in healthcare. In W. Ranade (ed.), *Markets and healthcare: A comparative analysis* (pp. 17–33). London and New York: Longman.

Moran, M. (1999). *Governing the healthcare state: A comparative study of the United Kingdom, the United States and Germany.* Manchester and New York: Manchester University Press.

Moran, M. (2000). Understanding the welfare state: The case of healthcare. *British Journal of Politics and International Relations*, 2(2), 135–160.

Muntaner, C., Salazar, R. M. G., Benach, J., and Armada, F. (2006). Venezuela's Barrio Adentro: An alternative to neoliberalism in healthcare. *International Journal of Health Services*, 36(4), 803–811.

Narcı, H. Ö., Ozcan, Y. A., Şahin, İ, Tarcan, M, and Narcı, M. (2015). An examination of competition and efficiency for hospital industry in Turkey. *Healthcare Management Science*, 18(4), 407–418.

NTVMSNBC. (2013, October 14). Özel hastanelerin fark ücreti 2 kat arttı (Additional payments of private hospitals doubled). *NTVMSNBC*.

Ökem, Z. G., and Çakar, M. (2015). What have health care reforms achieved in Turkey? An appraisal of the 'Health Transformation Programme'. *Health Policy*, 119(9), 1153–1163.

Pala, K. (2007). Türkiye sağlık sistemi nereye gidiyor? (Where is Turkey's health system heading?). *Toplum ve Hekim*, 22(1–2), 62–69.

Petmesidou, M., and Guillén, A. M. (2008). 'Southern-style' National Health Services? Recent reforms and trends in Spain and Greece. *Social Policy & Administration*, 42(2), 106–124.

Pribble, J. (2013). *Welfare and party politics in Latin America*. New York: Cambridge University Press.

Ramesh, M. (2009). Malaysian health policy in a comparative perspective. In C. H. Leng and S. Barraclough (eds.), *Healthcare in Malaysia: The dynamics of provision, financing and access* (pp. 72–84). Oxon and New York: Routledge.

Ranade, W. (1994). *A future for the NHS? Healthcare in the 1990s*. London and New York: Longman.

Rothgang, H., Cacace, M., Grimmeisen, S., and Wendt, C. (2005). The changing role of the state in healthcare systems. *European Review*, 13(Suppl. 1), 187–212.

Rudra, N. (2007). Welfare states in developing countries: Unique or universal?. *The Journal of Politics*, 69(2), 378–396.

Schieber, G., and Maeda, A. (1999). Healthcare financing and delivery in developing countries. *Health Affairs*, 18(3), 193–205.

SGK. (2010c). *Primsiz Ödemeler Genel Müdürlüğü Aralık ayı istatistik bülteni (Directorate General of Non-contributory Payments December statistics bulletin)*. http://www.sgk.gov.tr/wps/wcm/connect/896ed4e3-9bf2-4aa7-add2-be5d97e65d1c/2010_12_bulten.pdf?MOD=AJPERES. Accessed 25 December 2010.

SGK. (2014). *Monthly basic indicators-April*. Ankara: SGK.

Sigorta, Mapfre Genel. (2012). *Tamamlayıcı sağlık sigortası (Supplementary health insurance)*.

Sönmez, M. (2011). *Paran kadar sağlık: Türkiye'de sağlığın ticarileşmesi (Healthcare as much as you have money: The commercialisation of health in Turkey)*. Istanbul: Yordam Kitap.

Sparkes, S. P., Bump, J. B., and Reich, M. R. (2015). Political strategies for health reform in Turkey: Extending veto point theory. *Health Systems & Reform*, 1(4), 263–275.

Takvim. (2015, July 3). Özel hastanelerde ek ücret vurgunu (Additional payment sack in private hospitals). *Takvim*.

Teksöz, T., Kaya, Y., and Helvacıoğlu, K. (2009). *Sağlık reformunun sonuçları itibariyle değerlendirmesi (Analysis of health reform by examining its results)*. Istanbul: Türkiye Ekonomi Politikaları Araştırma Vakfi (Economic Policy Research Foundation of Turkey.

Tengilimoğlu, D., Güzel, A., Toygar, A., Akıncı, F., and Dziegielewski, S. F. (2015). Informal payments in health systems: Purpose and occurrences in Turkey. *Journal of Social Service Research*, 41(5), 684–696.

The Ministry of Health. (2003). *Transformation in health*. Ankara: The Ministry of Health.

The Ministry of Health. (2013). *Sağlık istatistikleri yıllığı 2012 (Health statistics yearbook 2012)*. Ankara: Ministry of Health.

The Republic of Turkey. (2005a). *Bazı Kamu Kurum ve Kuruluşlarına Ait Sağlık Birimlerinin Sağlık Bakanlığına Devredilmesine Dair Kanun (Law on the Transfer of Health Institutions of Other Public Institutions to the Ministry of Health). 5283.*

The Republic of Turkey. (2006). *Sosyal Sigortalar ve Genel Sağlık Sigortası Kanunu (Social Insurances and General Health Insurance Law). 5510.*

The Republic of Turkey. (2011a). *Sağlık Bakanlığı ve Bağlı Kuruluşlarının Teşkilat ve Görevleri Hakkında Kanun Hükmünde Kararname (Statutory Decree on the Organisation and Duties of the Ministry of Health and its Subsidiary Institutions). KHK/663.*

The Republic of Turkey. (2013). *Sağlık Bakanlığınca Kamu Özel İş Birliği Modeli İle Tesis Yaptırılması, Yenilenmesi ve Hizmet Alınması ile Bazı Kanun ve Kanun Hükmünde Kararnamelerde Değişiklik Yapılmasına Hakkında Kanun (Law on the Permittance of the Establishment and Renovation of Healthcare Facilities with the Public-Private Partnership Model and Purchasing of Services for the Ministry of Health and on the Changes* in Some Legislations *and Decrees). 6428.*

Tountas, Y., Karnaki, P., Pavi, E., and Souliotis, K. (2005). The 'unexpected' growth of the private health sector in Greece. *Health Policy*, 74(2), 167–180.

TSB. (2012). *İstatistikler (Statistics)*. Istanbul: TSB.

TSB. (2014). *Sağlık istatistikleri (Health Statistics)*. Istanbul: TSB.

TSB. (2016). *İstatistikler (Statistics)*. Istanbul: TSB.

TTB. (2011a, May 24). Sağlıklı seçim, seçimlerde sağlık (Healthy election, health in elections). *Ttb.org.tr*.

TTB. (2011b, May 25). AKP sağlık politikası: Yalanlar ve gerçekler (Health policy of the AKP: Lies and truths). *Bağımsız İletişim Ağı*.

TÜİK. (2014). *Yaşam memnuniyeti araştırması 2013 (Life satisfaction survey 2013)*. Ankara: Turkish Statistical Institute.

Ucku, R., and Elçi, O. C. (2010). Turkey. In J. A. Johnson and C. H. Stoskopf (eds.), *Comparative health systems: Global perspectives* (pp. 273–286). Boston, Toronto, London and Singapore: Johns and Bartlett Publishers.

Üstündağ, N., and Yoltar, Ç. (2007). Türkiye'de sağlık sisteminin dönüşümü: bir devlet etnografisi (Transformation of Turkey's healthcare system: A state ethnography). In Ç. Keyder, N. Üstündağ, T. Ağartan, and Ç. Yoltar (eds.), *Avrupa'da ve Türkiye'de sağlık politikaları* (pp. 55–95). Istanbul: İletişim.

Walt, G., and Gilson, L. (1994). Reforming the health sector in developing countries: The central role of policy analysis. *Health Policy and Planning*, 9(4), 353–370.

Wessen, A. F. (1999). Structural differences and healthcare reform. In F. D. S. Powell and A. F. Wessen (eds.), *Healthcare systems in transition: An international perspective* (pp. 369–392). Thousand Oaks, London and New Delhi: Sage Publications.

Woo, M. (2004). *The politics of social welfare policy in South Korea: Growth and citizenship*. Maryland: University Press of America.

World Bank. (1993). *World Development Report: Investing in health*. New York: World Bank.

Yaşar, G. Y. (2011). Review: 'Health transformation programme' in Turkey: An assessment. *International Journal of Health Planning and Management*, 26(2), 110–133.

Yaşar, G. Y., and Uğurluoğlu, E. (2011). Can Turkey's general health insurance system achieve universal coverage?. *International Journal of Health Planning and Management*, 26(3), 282–295.

Yılmaz, V. (2013). Changing origins of inequalities in access to healthcare in Turkey: From occupational status to income?. *New Perspectives on Turkey*, 48, 53–75.

Yılmaz, V., and Yentürk, N. (2016a). *Yeniden ayarlama ve özelleştirme ikiliğinde Türkiye'de sosyal güvenlik reform: sosyal güvenlik harcamalarının uzun dönemli analizi (Social security reform in Turkey in between recalibration and privatisation: Long-term analysis of social security expenditures)*. Istanbul: Istanbul Bilgi Üniversitesi Sivil Toplum Kuruluşları Eğitim ve Araştırma Birimi.

Yılmaz, V., and Yentürk, N. (2016b). *Türkiye'de kamusal sağlık harcamalarının tarihsel seyri: betimleyici bir değerlendirme (Historical trajectory of public healthcare expenditures in Turkey: A descriptive analysis)*. Istanbul: Istanbul Bilgi Üniversitesi Sivil Toplum Kuruluşları Eğitim ve Araştırma Birimi.

Yoltar, Ç. (2009). When the poor need healthcare: Ethnography of state and citizenship in Turkey. *Middle Eastern Studies*, 45(5), 769–782.

CHAPTER 5

The Impact of the World Bank on Healthcare Reform in Turkey

5.1 Introduction

Domestic political dynamics (within the limits of global economic dynamics) are often used to account for the emergence of healthcare reforms in Western European and North American advanced capitalist countries (Giaimo 2016; Jacobs and Skocpol 2010; Klein 2010; Ewert 2009; Ham 2009; Harrison and McDonald 2008; Giaimo 2005; Lister 2005; Salter 2004; Freeman 1999; Moran 1999; Freeman 1998; Moran 1998; Abel-Smith and Mossialos 1994; Navarro 1994; Ranade 1994; Walt 1994; Moran 1992; Immergut 1992). By contrast, in emerging market economies the role of international organisations is particularly emphasised when explaining factors leading to healthcare reforms (Ağartan 2008, 2007; Lloyd-Sherlock 2006; Homedes and Ugalde 2005; Armada et al. 2001; Berman and Bossert 2000; Sen and Koivusalo 1998). In exploring the influence of international organisations on policies at the national level, the global social policy approach has been useful. Scholars characterise all international organisations, including the WB, as public actors, albeit with a shaky legitimacy (Kaasch and Martens 2015, pp. 9–10).

Mandates of international organisations vary in their response to changing political and economic contexts (Kaasch and Martens 2015, p. 234). WB's involvement in healthcare policy is a relatively new phenomenon. Before the establishment of the Washington Consensus, in fact, it was the WHO that was the most important international actor driving the global

V. Yılmaz, *The Politics of Healthcare Reform in Turkey*,
DOI 10.1007/978-3-319-53667-5_5

healthcare policy agenda. In the late 1970s, the WB replaced the WHO as the new key global development actor and began directing considerable amounts of financial resources to the reform of healthcare systems in developing countries.

The World Bank Group (WBG) institutions, which were primarily established during the Bretton Woods Conference in 1944 to assist the reconstruction of Europe after WWII, changed shape as the neoliberal political agenda took off, first in the United States and the United Kingdom and then it spread to other countries. As the voting structure of the WB allowed advanced capitalist states to dominate its policy choices (Armada et al. 2001, p. 732), political changes, especially in the United States and the United Kingdom, proved to be influential in reshaping the policy priorities of the WB, alongside the Washington Consensus. In this process, the WB emerged as one of the largest global development actors and pioneers of pro-market healthcare reforms in emerging market economies.

Starting in the late 1970s, the WB increased the scope of its funds for healthcare services, which by the 1990s had exceeded the total budget of all health-related UN organisations. In addition to its financial resources, the WB also established an international 'epistemic community', which, as Freeman indicates (Freeman 1998, p. 398), began to claim expertise in reforming healthcare systems, especially those in emerging market economies. With these changes, the WB started to engage in the domestic policies of its aid recipient countries, including in the restructuring of public administration, and in the domains of social policy and healthcare policy (Laurell and Arellano 1996, p. 2). The WB began to act as a reference point for healthcare reforms in emerging market economies (Homedes and Ugalde 2005, p. 94; Buse and Gwin 1998; Walt 1998, p. 434, 1994, p. 127).

The WB, a member of the WBG, is comprised of two institutions: the International Bank for Reconstruction and Development (IBRD) and the International Development Association (IDA). In addition to the WB, the International Finance Corporation (IFC), also a member organisation of the WBG alongside the Multilateral Investment Guarantee Agency (MIGA) and International Centre for Settlement of Investment Disputes (ICSID), has also been influential in the healthcare domain in emerging market economies. The IFC is 'the world's largest multilateral investor in the private health sector in emerging markets' (IFC 2012b) that works to support the growth of the private sector in healthcare.

After the release of two WB reports entitled *Financing Health Services in Developing Countries: An Agenda for Reform* (World Bank 1987) and *Investing in Health* (World Bank 1993), the mandate of the WB over the global healthcare policy agenda and the discourse of healthcare reform was consolidated. In this period, Turkey became one of the WB's target countries. The Turkish government started to collaborate with the WB in order to determine the shortcomings of its healthcare system and to formulate possible solutions to overcome them.

Against this background, this chapter addresses the question of how and to what extent the WB has been influential in the healthcare reform process in Turkey. This question is critical in exploring the drivers of 'policy diffusion', in Weyland's terms (2005), in the case of healthcare reform in Turkey. While the existing scholarship explains the role of the WB in the HTP on the basis of conditionality and funding (Ağartan 2016, p. 61), I suggest that these factors fail to describe the WB's role in the HTP fully. With the objective of exploring the role of the WB and its impact on the reform, this chapter examines the interaction between the WB and the AK Party government and the MoH bureaucracy in the domain of healthcare policy, and both the historical and ongoing institutional ties established between the WB and the Turkish government that feed into the contemporary partnership between these two actors. In doing so, this chapter draws on a qualitative content analysis of WB documents, as well as interviews with WB experts who worked in partnership with the Turkish government in the HTP and the members of the government's reform team.

5.2 The World Bank's Approach to Healthcare Reform in Emerging Market Economies

This section explores the following questions: Does the WB have a blueprint for healthcare reforms? If it does, what are the main parameters of the blueprint? One way of exploring these questions is to examine official WB documents on healthcare reforms. The World Development Report entitled *Investing in Health* is considered the foundation of the WB approach to healthcare reform in emerging market economies. In this report, as Laurell and Arellano succinctly state, the WB presented healthcare both 'as an end in itself and as a means to foster development' (1996, p. 2). This dual portrayal of healthcare can be argued to echo the contemporary nature of the healthcare domain, both as a matter of human rights and as a global commodity.

Despite the fact that the WB describes healthcare both as a public good and as a profitable sector, scholars argue that WB healthcare reform proposals in practice aim to foster healthcare as a profitable sector, only to disregard its public good feature. Laurell and López Arellano argue that the WB gives priority to healthcare as a means to foster development (1996, p. 2) rather than as a human right to be instituted. As WB proposals are centred on the idea of healthcare as a means to development (implying economic development only), scholars associate the WB approach to healthcare with neoliberalism (Armada et al. 2001, p. 735; Laurell and Arellano 1996, p. 11), which in this context implies a political project that aims to increase the commodification of goods and services formerly out of the market relations.

The WB backs up its contemporary healthcare reform blueprint with three arguments. These are (1) that the state does not have enough money for universal healthcare, (2) that public financing and provision of healthcare services are bound to be inefficient and (3) that instituting equity in access to healthcare services is not possible.

The WB comes up with a set of policy tools that it promotes as a panacea to the ills of healthcare systems in emerging market economies. This set of policy tools includes the consolidation of individual-based forms of healthcare financing (specifically, user charges and private health insurance) at the expense of tax-based and social insurance-based financing models. The approach of the WB also includes the introduction of a purchaser-provider split and the promotion of private sector involvement in healthcare financing and delivery (Collins et al. 1999, pp. 69–70).

Nevertheless, insiders do not always see their tendency to be blueprint in the WB. One of my informants, holding an important position at WB headquarters, argued:

> We do not have a reform blueprint for countries.... It is better to think of it as a loose jacket. It is shaped according to the political economy of each country. (Interview no. 25)

As the informant stated, the WB offers 'loose jacket' guidelines to developing country governments rather than a reform blueprint. In his understanding, the WB does not impose the specifics of healthcare reform but rather provides governments with a general perspective on healthcare policy issues and equips them with up-to-date evidence.

However, not all WB experts agree with this view. Another informant working in the WB office in Ankara took a step forward to criticise the WB's tendency to use a blueprint in its healthcare reform proposals for emerging market economies:

> We tend to give a blueprint. We go to every country and say the same things. Hospital autonomy, purchaser-provider split... The reality is that every country has to contextualize these reforms. (Interview no. 22)

As the interviewee suggests, the 'loose jacket' of the WB has a specific colour. The WB, according to this informant, needs to be more responsive to varied political and economic factors at play in different countries. However, she does not question the WB healthcare reform blueprint. For her, the problem is not about the jacket itself, but the way the WB expects emerging market economies to wear it.

Where does this 'loose jacket' of healthcare reform come from? When I put this question to informants affiliated with the WB, they all unequivocally referred to scientific evidence. For instance, one suggested:

> There are some principles that science proves to us, such as the provider-purchaser split. Science teaches us that. We use an evidence-based policy approach. (Interview no. 25)

Another informant from the WB office in Turkey argued:

> Co-payments – everybody recognises that even in health insurance systems and basic economics tells you that if you don't ask people to pay something, there is a moral hazard issue. (Interview no. 21)

For WB experts, it therefore seems that the main parameters of the 'loose jacket' approach to healthcare reform originate from scientific evidence. By scientific evidence, they refer mainly to the discipline of health economics. Having expertise on different healthcare reforms, therefore, may bestow a sense of authority on WB experts in such a way that they are confident in presenting their knowledge as universal truth. In this sense, the WB policy proposals appear as a manifestation of this universal truth. Alternatives are deemed political or ideologically driven and therefore lack face validity.

The validity of the WB's general claims, however, is contested in the literature. With respect to the first claim about the lack of public resources for universal healthcare, scholars argue that the WB fails to analyse the distribution of public expenditures, including health expenditures in government budgets, and does not consider alternative solutions that may increase public social and health expenditures (Laurell and Arellano 1996, p. 9). With regard to the second claim, that is, on the inefficiency of public healthcare service provision, scholars argue that the WB disregards the negative impacts of the SAPs on the efficiency and effectiveness of public financing and delivery of healthcare services (Laurell and Arellano 1996, p. 10). With respect to the WB's last claim – about the inequitable nature of public financing and delivery of healthcare – scholars emphasise that this problem might well be eliminated by introducing universal public health insurance to replace the formerly inequitable access requirements, rather than allowing more private sector involvement in financing and provision (Laurell and Arellano 1996, p. 10). Nevertheless, the WB disregards the aforementioned alternatives. Therefore, scholars argue that the all-encompassing discourse of the WB on healthcare actually excludes all alternative solutions without a valid scientific base (Laurell 2001; Laurell and Arellano 1996).

While the pro-market character of the WB healthcare reform blueprint has not changed, its approach to the role of the state in the healthcare sector has not remained constant over time. In the early days of the Washington Consensus, the WB called for a 'minimal' state. Later, with the rise of the Post-Washington Consensus, the WB replaced the 'minimal' state idea with the idea of the 'effective' state (Archer 1994, p. 13). This discursive change, consolidated in the 1990s, became known as 'the governance agenda'.

Some scholars viewed this change in the approach of the WB as a sign of a move to give a larger role to the state in public policies (Archer 1994, p. 13). Nevertheless, not all scholars have attributed a similar significance to this change. In response to Archer, Crawford argued that the WB approach in its revised form continues to subordinate the role of the state to the market (Crawford 2006, p. 115). In the WB's approach, good governance is nothing but pro-market governance (Crawford 2006, p. 120). On the one hand, Crawford rightly emphasises the continuity in the WB's approach in favouring the private sector over the public sector in the provision of public services. On the other hand, it can be argued that Archer's emphasis on the difference between the two discourses of the WB signifies a noteworthy alteration of the WB's policy tools. Therefore, this change in the WB paradigm might imply that the WB may continue to favour the marketisation of healthcare services, while ensuring that the state monitors and regulates the marketisation process.

Why did the WB feel the need to give the state a larger role in existing healthcare markets? Laurell and López Arellano provide us with an elaborate explanation of why the WB has made this discursive change. For them, the approach of the WB to healthcare reform faces a dilemma. This dilemma resembles the foundational contradiction of the modern capitalist state: promoting capital accumulation while regulating class conflict (Laurell and Arellano 1996, p. 3). While the analogy is insightful, it needs further elaboration. In fact, the WB differs from the modern capitalist state in its institutional setup, accountability structures and ideological makeup.

One of the most striking differences between the WB and democratic capitalist states is that the WB's activities have no popular democratic control, thus their legitimacy rest on shaky ground (Kaasch and Martens 2015, pp. 9–10). Therefore, unlike in democratic capitalist welfare states, it can be argued that the WB solution to the dilemma between the promotion of capital accumulation and the regulation of class conflict (or soothing the masses through the provision of social policies) tends to favour the former objective over the latter. Nevertheless, the lack of popular democratic control in the WB does not necessarily imply that it is totally exempt from the need to establish legitimacy for its pro-market reform proposals; it has to work with democratically elected governments in most emerging market economies in order to introduce pro-market healthcare reforms.

Another difference between the WB and a modern capitalist state is the level of responsiveness to different business interest groups. While the former is expected to think primarily in terms of global markets and serve global business interests (e.g. multinational companies), the latter is expected to consider the needs of the domestic market and at least take into account the interests of domestic business interests.

The WB healthcare reform proposals in emerging market economies generally support the above-mentioned analysis. The WB encourages governments of emerging market economies to promote a larger role for the private sector in the financing and delivery of healthcare services. The WB also promotes the targeting of public expenditures to provide low-cost services to the bottom income quintiles (Laurell and Arellano 1996, p. 3). While the former proposal might be regarded as the WB's primary objective to foster more private sector participation in the provision of public services, the second proposal can be considered the WB's quest for public legitimacy in its pro-market healthcare reforms.

It is argued here that the approach of the WB to healthcare reforms in emerging market economies forms a coherent paradigm that might well be considered a blueprint. In fact, this blueprint sits very well with the WB's general pro-market approach to reforms in other public policy domains.

As the WB informants suggested, the WB tries to be responsive to the political economic differences between countries. However, this responsiveness is limited, as it only implies 'contextualising' the WB blueprint in different institutional environments in order to establish legitimacy, rather than considering other alternatives. The WB's approach to healthcare reforms has been fine-tuned over time. In its current form, the WB calls for a strong presence of the state with a stewardship role in the healthcare market. It has adopted a more responsive and flexible approach to domestic political economic differences in working with emerging market economies and recommends a public guarantee for access to basic healthcare services for the very poor. However, its approach is still not sufficiently flexible to accommodate a universal option as a legitimate policy option.

5.3 The History of the Partnership Between the World Bank and Turkey in Healthcare and Its Impact on the Health Transformation Programme

This section presents a brief history of the partnership between the WB, Turkish governments and the MoH bureaucracy in the realm of healthcare policies. The relationship of the WB with the Turkish government tightened in the aftermath of the coup d'état in 1980. The coup was significant not only because it suspended democratic rule in the country, but it also paved the way for the neoliberalisation of the Turkish economy and the alteration of the country's main development strategy from import substitution industrialisation to export-oriented growth. As Turkey's economy transformed, the WB and the IMF began to get directly involved in economic policy-making processes (Yalman 2009; p. 251).

The WB has been involved in various policy domains in Turkey. For instance, in 2012 the WB had 27 ongoing projects in Turkey. The sectoral distribution of these projects ranged from secondary education to renewable energy and energy efficiency (World Bank, 2012). The WB's multi-sector engagement with Turkey may have provided it with higher leverage vis-à-vis the Turkish government, equipping it with the necessary know-how about the modus operandi of Turkey's public administration.

As of the late 2000s, WB loans to Turkey constituted an important portion of all WB loans. According to 2008 WB data (World Bank 2008, p. 20), Turkey was the largest borrower country in Europe and the Central Asia region and ranked third among all borrower countries in terms of the loan size in the three years leading up to the report. Turkey has also been a member of another important member institution of the WBG, the ICF, since 1956. In 2010, Turkey ranked fifth among all countries benefiting from ICF operations (IFC 2012a).

The partnership between the WB, the Turkish government and the MoH bureaucracy on healthcare policy dates back to the late 1980s. The WB's primary engagement started with the launch of the First Health Project in 1990, which provided the Turkish government with $75 million in funds. As part of this project, the government was expected to extend the geographical access to healthcare services in eight particularly underserved provinces, to enhance the efficiency of healthcare delivery, to improve the financial sustainability of the healthcare system and to support the management capacity in the MoH (World Bank 2004, p. 27). The Second Health Project came in 1994, with a $130 million loan released in 1995. Similar to the objectives of the first project, the second project aimed to extend access to essential healthcare services, this time in 23 underserved eastern provinces, and to strengthen the management capacity of the MoH (World Bank 2004, p. 27).

Following the second project, the WB and the Turkish government initiated the Primary Healthcare Services Project in 1997. This project included a $14 million loan to the government with the aim of developing a family physician model for Turkey, applying this model nationwide, establishing an effective referral system and developing the economic analysis capacity of the MoH (World Bank 2004, p. 27). This project, however, was not implemented due to the inability of a succession of unstable coalition governments to pass necessary legislative amendments in the Turkish parliament.

The fourth and last collaboration between the WB and the Turkish government came in the early 2000s. Although none of the previous three partnerships between the WB and Turkish governments had produced satisfactory outcomes, they provided the WB with strong know-how in working with Turkish governments and healthcare bureaucracy. Furthermore, these partnerships helped the WB to promote its approach to healthcare policy within the MoH. For instance, Ministry officials who attended WB training sessions on healthcare policy learned how to approach these issues from a health economics perspective and became part of the WB epistemic community on healthcare policy issues. Moreover, the WB succeeded in institutionalising its discourse within the Ministry in the form of a directorate, namely, the Health Project General Directorate (*Sağlık Projesi Genel Koordinatörlüğü, or SPGK*). In fact, some Directorate officials served in key posts during the introduction of the HTP.

I argue that the partnerships between the WB and the successive Turkish governments throughout the 1990s laid the foundation for the introduction of a pro-market healthcare reform in Turkey. This argument is elaborated in Section 5.6, where I demonstrate how the WB 'policy paradigm' on healthcare policies was later adopted in policy documents of Turkish public administration. In fact, scholars demonstrate how the HTP was a product of the healthcare bureaucracy, but not of the social security bureaucracy, and in fact, it was at the expense of the latter (Sparkes et al. 2015, p. 271). The preference of the healthcare bureaucracy, which shares the WB's approach to healthcare reform over the social security bureaucracy, can be taken as an indicator of the AK Party government's political preference for a pro-market direction.

5.4 The Partnership of the World Bank and the AK Party Government on Healthcare Reform

The AK Party period signified a closer partnership between Turkey and the WB. In 2003, a year after the AK Party came to government, the WB released a policy note identifying the main public policy areas that needed to be reformed in Turkey. The note clearly prioritised healthcare policy. It called for 'fundamental and systemic changes' in Turkey's healthcare system that would include separating the financing and provision of healthcare, improving resource mobilisation and allocation, enhancing access to healthcare services, increasing the utilisation of healthcare services in accordance with the needs of the population, improving efficiency in production and delivery of healthcare services and enhancing the clinical effectiveness of the healthcare services (World Bank 2003a, pp. 31–2). In the same policy note, the WB also declared its enthusiasm for and readiness to support a new healthcare reform project in Turkey and expressed its willingness to provide both policy advice and loans to the government and bureaucracy (World Bank 2003a, p. 33).

Following its electoral victory in 2002, the AK Party government launched its Urgent Action Plan to initiate a comprehensive healthcare reform. This Plan declared that the government would take policy actions, including the restructuring of the MoH, granting administrative and financial autonomy to public hospitals, unifying all hospitals under the umbrella of the MoH, splitting purchaser and provider functions in healthcare, introducing universal compulsory social health insurance and providing incentives to private sector initiatives in healthcare (The Republic of Turkey 2003, pp. 99–101). Given the similarities between the components of the government's reform plan and the WB's proposals, it can be argued that the AK Party and the WB had a shared vision for a large-scale healthcare reform, even before the establishment of the actual partnership.

The actual collaboration between the AK Party government and the WB started with the launch of the Health Transition Project in 2004. The government and the WB designed this project that would facilitate the implementation of the HTP. The Health Transition Project had two phases. In the first phase, initiated in 2004, the WB's objective was the following:

> ... to assist the government to strengthen the institutional environment for the implementation of the Health Transformation Programme that will improve system stewardship, streamline financing and service delivery, and build the institutional capacity to extend health insurance coverage to the whole population in a fiscally sustainable manner. (World Bank 2004, pp. ii)

Completed by 2007, the Health Transition Project included the release of a roughly $61 million loan (World Bank 2003b, p. 11). While previous WB healthcare projects in Turkey had invested the majority of the loan funds into building infrastructure and purchasing equipment (World Bank 2004, p. 6), most of this project's budget was allocated to training and consultancy services (World Bank 2003b, pp. 10–11).

The second project, called the Health Transformation and Social Security Reform Project, came into effect in 2009 and was completed by 2013. The main objectives of this project were to improve the effectiveness of the SGK and the MoH in developing and implementing reforms on provider payments and healthcare systems performance, and piloting output-based financing for non-communicable diseases prevention and control (World Bank 2009, p. iv). With this project, the WB supplied approximately $75 million (World Bank 2009, p. iv). Most of the project's budget was dedicated to capacity-building in the MoH, aiming for them to claim a stewardship role and retreat from their dominant role in the healthcare delivery (World Bank 2009, p. v).

In addition to the Health Transition Project and the Health Transformation and Social Security Reform Project, the WB financially supported the government through two loans for the Programmatic Public Sector Development Policy and two more loans for the Restoring Equitable Growth and Development Policy. Implemented between 2004 and 2011, these four projects did not address healthcare policies exclusively, but each had strong healthcare policy components. One of the four programme development objectives specifically addressed healthcare reform. This objective was expressed as follows:

> ... reforming substantially the country's social protection system, which covers social security, universal health insurance and social assistance to address growing deficits in the social security system, to make structural and administrative improvements in the provision of social security benefits and social assistance, and to support universal access to health services while increasing the efficiency of their provision. (World Bank 2012, p. viii)

The WB loans for these four consecutive projects ranged from \$400 million to \$1.3 billion (World Bank 2012, p. i). The share of loans directed to healthcare reforms ranged from 11 per cent to 25 per cent (world Bank 2012, pp. v–vi).

In between the two phases of the Health Transition Project, the WB published a three-year (2008 and 2011) country partnership strategy document for Turkey, which set the WB priorities for the partnership. The WB presented its main domains of interest in Turkey as (1) improved competitiveness and employment, (2) equitable human and social development and (3) efficient provision of high-quality public services (World Bank 2008, p. i). Under the pillar of equitable human and social development, the WB once again affirmed that making the healthcare system more effective was its priority (World Bank 2008, p. ii).

In the three-year country partnership strategy document, the main objectives of the WB in healthcare policies were presented as improving the cost-effectiveness of healthcare services and increasing the responsiveness of these services to the needs of the population (World Bank 2008, p. 32). In order to achieve these general objectives, the WB declared it would continue providing financial support in the form of lending, technical assistance, just-in-time policy notes, monitoring and evaluation of the impacts of the ongoing healthcare reform and training in the form of healthcare reform flagship programmes for policymakers and practitioners (World Bank 2008, p. 32).

In addition to the WB's engagement through partnerships with the government, the ICF was also active in the healthcare sector in Turkey. Unlike the WB, which primarily collaborates with governments, the ICF works directly with the private sector. The WBG declared that the ICF was committed to support higher levels of private sector provision in healthcare services. As stated in the WB Country Partnership Strategy for Turkey, the IFC, in collaboration with domestic banks, would lend its support specifically to companies that aimed to become national healthcare service providers, expand their domestic or foreign operations, establish specialised centres of excellence and/or have smaller hospitals and clinics (World Bank 2008, p. 32). Following the launch of the HTP in 2003, the IFC identified Turkey as a 'high priority country in the health sector' (Albawaba Business 2003).

In line with the prioritisation of Turkey in the health sector investments, the IFC released a $11 million loan for the Mesa group with the objective of supporting the construction of a private hospital in the capital city of Ankara (Albawaba Business 2003). Another notable project of the IFC was its support for the Acıbadem Healthcare Group with a $20 million loan (IFC 2007) that was then followed by another corporate loan of up to $40 million in 2006 (Joseph 2006). The total amount of ICF loans to private sector institutions in healthcare exceeded the total amount of the WB loans to the government in the Health Transition Project.

5.5 The Importance of World Bank Loans for Healthcare Reform in Turkey: Is It Overrated?

The WB uses different instruments to initiate, support and influence reforms in emerging market economies, including Turkey. Loan agreements are one of the most commonly used instruments of the WB. For some scholars, continuous WB loans directed to the restructuring of healthcare services in Turkey provide sufficient empirical data to argue that the HTP has been a top-down WB project (Savaş 2012, pp. 18–37). Indeed, similar arguments were made about healthcare reforms supported by the WB in other emerging market economies (e.g. Armada et al. 2001, p. 731).

Nevertheless, both the reform team and the WB team members argue against the claim that the WB has been influential throughout the reform process as a result of its financier role. For instance, one informant who worked as a member of the healthcare reform team in Turkey pointed out the limitations of the WB's power. He said:

> If you look at the World Bank loan agreements in social sectors in particular, these are not huge amounts of money. Indeed, these are quite symbolic amounts within the overall budgets of countries. This is valid for Turkey, at least. It may not be so in Uganda, however. From this angle, the World Bank's impositions on social sectors cannot be effective in countries like Turkey. (Interview no. 22)

Members of the reform explained their financial and intellectual autonomy from the WB on the basis of the economic strength of the country as well as the government's commitment to the reform. The WB report on the politics of the healthcare reform in Turkey also supports this informant's claim, suggesting that the WB loan for healthcare reform did not provide the Bank with significant leverage, since its amount was small compared to other loans that the government was managing at the time (Rosetti, 2004, p. 24).

Similarly, an informant who worked as a team leader on one of the WB health projects argued:

> The AK Party did not come to the World Bank for money. Indeed, the total amount of the loan was around 0.5 per cent of the total health budget. The AK Party wanted to benefit from World Bank know-how. It wanted to use the World Bank for legitimacy. If the reform went well, it would be the AK Party's reform. If it did not, it would be the World Bank's. In addition, it was useful to have a small, flexible budget. Therefore, we can list three reasons: technical advice, legitimacy and flexible money. (Interview no. 25)

As the informant suggested, acquiring loans was not the main motive of the AK Party government in approaching the WB to collaborate on healthcare reform. Neither the WB experts nor the members of the reform team suggested that the WB loans provided the WB with a strong decision-making capacity with respect to the content of the reform.

In fact, the low level of importance attributed to the loan components of the WB partnership throughout the reform process might be due to contextual economic factors. Scholars suggested that governments of developing countries had the lowest capacity to negotiate with the WB in adverse macroeconomic contexts and therefore complied with WB policy proposals in order to access loans and international aid (Batley 2004, pp. 54–5; Laurell and Arellano 1996, p. 13). In contrast to the Latin American reform experiences, the WB and Turkish government healthcare reform partnership on HTP was established at a time of steady economic growth of the Turkish economy. According to the WB data, Turkey's economy experienced a boom, especially between 2003 and 2007, with economic growth rate over 5 per cent, a factor which might have increased the control of the Turkish government vis-à-vis the WB over the specifics of the reform project.

I argue, therefore, the WB loans for healthcare reform in Turkey are not sufficient to explain the WB's influence on the HTP. This evidences that the drivers of policy diffusion may not be constant over time (see Weyland 2005), may instead change according to the political economic context within which diffusion occurs.

5.6 The Influence of the World Bank's Know-How and Policy Advice on the Reform

Despite the emphasis given in the literature to WB loans when explaining the WB impact on healthcare reform in Turkey, the effectiveness of other WB tools in shaping the reform agenda, such as know-how support and policy advice, has been generally overlooked. In fact, in the case of Turkey, the WB has long been active in researching the healthcare sector, promoting healthcare reform ideas and providing strategic political advice to the government in order to make a pro-market healthcare reform politically feasible in Turkey.

The WB was the pioneering institution in producing knowledge about the problems of the healthcare system of Turkey before the reform. An informant who had previously worked for the SPGK and then became part of the reform team during the preparation and implementation of the HTP argued that there was a consensus on the general parameters of the healthcare reform, even before the AK Party came to power, among different sections of the bureaucracy. He said:

> In the early 2000s, a programme called the Health Transformation Programme came onto the agenda. In fact, this was a new version of [previous] healthcare reforms.... In that period [before 2003], technical preparations by related ministries had already been made. The undersecretaries of the Ministry of Finance, the Ministry of Labour and Social Security, the State Planning Organisation, the Treasury and the Ministry of Health had already prepared

> letters of agreement. As of 2003, the general philosophy of these agreements was kept intact and took the name of Health Transformation Programme. (Interview no. 32)

The informant might have been implying that the AK Party's input, along with the contestations between the AK Party and the WB throughout the preparation and implementation of the HTP, did not lead to a significant change in the content of the reform draft. It was the earlier partnership between the WB and successive governments that shaped the major parameters of the reform.

In addition to the input that earlier partnership between the WB and successive governments into the HTP, one of the moments when the World Bank contributed to 'the social construction of the need to reform', in Cox's terms (2001, pp. 475–7), was the release of its report on Turkey's healthcare system in 2003 (World Bank 2003b). This study was influential in setting the main parameters of the political debates on Turkey's healthcare system and it then constituted a point of reference for the AK Party government's HTP (World Bank 2010, p. ix).

In that report, the WB called for 'fundamental and systemic changes' in Turkey's healthcare system (World Bank 2003b, p. iii) and listed the fundamental systemic changes that needed to be made, which included the introduction of compulsory universal social health insurance with optional supplementary private health insurance, the development of an essential healthcare services package, better targeted public spending, the reorganisation of public hospitals by granting them financial and administrative autonomy, the transformation of the role of the MoH from a healthcare service provider to a stewardship body that would oversee and guide the provision of healthcare services and the transformation of the role of the SSK from acting both as financier and provider of healthcare services to a purely social insurance body (World Bank 2003b, pp. iv–vi). In fact, the HTP covers almost all of the above-mentioned WB proposals that were made in the 2003 WB study.

Some political actors interpreted the similarity between the WB proposals and the government's healthcare reform as evidence that the reform was a replication of a WB blueprint. One of the informants, the former head of the TTB, suggested:

> Before I compared the two documents, I thought this claim [that the reform is a replication of a World Bank blueprint] was inspired by our standard

> leftist perspective.... Although this might sound like a slogan, I think the discourse that suggests this reform was a World Bank project is nothing but the manifestation of reality. (Interview no. 14)

Another informant, who was head of a leading trade union in the healthcare sector, made a similar comment on the reform. She argued, 'This programme in healthcare is totally a World Bank programme. In fact, it is a word-for-word translation. The AKP is the direct subcontractor of the World Bank' (Interview no. 31).

Both the TTB and this healthcare sector trade union opposed the HTP. Proving that the reform was a replication of the WB blueprint was important to them, as they thought it would undermine the legitimacy of the reform in the eyes of the general public. For these actors, the WB symbolised the interests of the transnational capitalist class and of advanced capitalist countries, especially the United States. They argued that this blueprint reform, implemented by the AK Party, furthered the interests of these actors rather than the interests of the citizens of Turkey.

In response, one member of the reform team contested the perception that HTP was merely a replication of the WB blueprint. He stated:

> I would really want that. If only somebody could bring in an already-implemented healthcare reform experience that we could be inspired by and then come up with an adaptation for Turkey, I would really want that, as a person involved in this process. But we did not have that chance.... In the final analysis, we know the sector, we know the country, and we know the world. We started with needs, the needs of the citizens and the needs of the sector.... I can safely argue that this model is specific to Turkey. (Interview no. 8)

In contrast to the anti-reform camp's critique of the blueprint reform, this informant stressed that the government's reform team had been decisive in preparing Turkey's healthcare reform and that the resulting reform was unique to Turkey. He emphasised both the competency of the reform team and their responsiveness to both citizenry and sector interests. Another informant, also a member of the government's reform team, also argued against the claim that the HTP was a carbon copy of a WB blueprint:

> This is a perception that I always contest, a perception that the WB and the IMF imposed this. Indeed, advances in healthcare financing from all over the

> world are reflected in Turkey. But instead of perceiving this as an imposition of the World Bank and the IMF – because it is not true – I think it is possible to view it as the accumulation of experience and institutional memory in Turkey that was enriched by the WB's consultancy support. (Interview no. 32)

This informant agreed with the previous one that the reform was not a top-down WB imposition on Turkey. However, unlike the previous informant, he acknowledged that the history of WB partnerships throughout the 1990s provided significant input into the HTP. Unlike the informant who presented the reform as a completely original one, this informant acknowledged the importance of WB input. He suggested, for instance, that international policy trends in healthcare financing, which he conceptualised as 'scientific advances', also resonated in this reform. Similar to the way WB experts presented policy trends as up-to-date scientific evidence, this informant portrayed international policy trends in healthcare as scientific, and thus beyond politics.

The WB experts also claimed that, while the main parameters of the HTP included WB proposals for healthcare reform in Turkey, this did not necessarily imply that the reform was a WB-imposed one. Indeed, one informant who worked in the WB as a policy expert stated in his public speech:

> The starting point of all partnerships [between the World Bank and governments] is, as I said, the development program of the countries. The World Bank does not come and tell the governments to do something. It does not work like this. Here the public sector is the decision-maker. (Public Speech no. 4)

Indeed, five-year development plans prepared mainly by bureaucrats with the input of a selected group of academics long before the introduction of HTP included the following policy priorities:

- A five-year development plan for 1985–89: Establishing universal health insurance (DPT 1984, p. 2), increasing service efficiency in health facilities, supporting the establishment of new private health facilities, allowing private health facilities to freely determine prices for their services, preventing of the Social Insurance Institution from establishing new health facilities (DPT 1984, p. 152).

- A five-year development plan for 1990–95: Provision of incentives to integrate private health providers into the public healthcare delivery system (DPT 1989, p. 291), diversification of sources of healthcare financing, the introduction of universal health insurance (DPT 1989, p. 357).
- A five-year development plan for 1996–2000: Establishing a purchaser-provider split in healthcare, transforming the MoH into a stewardship body and limiting its role in healthcare provision, granting administrative and financial autonomy to public hospitals, (DPT 1995, p. 46) and providing incentives to the private sector to increase its presence in healthcare domain (DPT 1995, p. 48).
- A five-year development plan for 2001–05: Providing incentives to private health insurance companies (DPT 2000, p. 225), establishing a purchaser-provider split in healthcare, increasing the efficiency of management of public hospitals (DPT 2000, p. 223).

One should not disregard the historical origins of these ideas in Turkish policy circles that gradually became dominant with the neoliberalisation process after the coup. The WB's role in promoting these ideas among bureaucrats was pivotal. In fact, the WB played a significant role in the restructuring of the Turkish economy after the 1980 coup d'état and in the implementation of policy trends, alongside with the policy trends of the Washington Consensus. Therefore, it can be argued that the WB historically contributed to the emergence of pro-market ideas in healthcare in line with domestic and global political changes and had made local allies since the 1980s.

As a result, during the preparation and implementation of the HTP, WB experts and the government's reform team were in general agreement on the main parameters of the reform and worked together as a large team. One of my informants, who worked as a project leader with the WB, commented on the uniqueness of the Turkish case, compared to healthcare reform experiences in other countries:

> Every single person in the MoH knows what the programme is about. In some other countries,... people only know when it happens.... The wealth of our discussions with the MoH here, the level of discussion is impressive. It is actually technical. You cannot underestimate the power of that. Everything is understood and thought through. (Interview no. 21)

While this quotation reveals that the WB carried out top-down reform projects in countries where even state officials were unaware of what the programme was about before it was implemented, it also demonstrates that the WB experts perceived the competence of state officials in Turkey. This perceived competency might well be attributed to the common language originating from earlier partnerships between the WB and the government that incorporated healthcare bureaucrats into the WB epistemic community.

One informant, a former member of the government's reform team, supported the WB team leader's suggestion that the government's reform team was confident in their competencies:

> We should not overestimate the WB. I attended the WB training session. But please do not misunderstand. We do listen. But why should we look down on our people? Why should we look down on our own politicians? We do listen. We can listen to anyone. Am I stupid? Can't I analyse what has been said there? Am I not aware of my country's reality? (Public Speech no. 5)

As the quotation suggests, the members of the reform team did not feel intimidated by the WB's role in the preparation and implementation of the reform. For this informant, the decision-making power in the reform lay in the hands of the government's reform team and the government rather than with the WB experts. They were in a position to attend WB training sessions and to assess for themselves the applicability of this information to the Turkish case. In other words, his perception is in line with those scholars who conceptualise the relationship between the WB and the reform team as a process of cross-national policy learning (Ağartan 2016). However, both he and the scholars seem to underestimate the power asymmetry in the learning process and the historical process that made healthcare bureaucrats in Turkey students of the World Bank.

In sum, the WB provided the institutional channel through which pro-market healthcare reform idea could be channelled to the healthcare bureaucracy in Turkey. In other words, the major impact of the WB in the HTP was its constitutive role in the emergence of the policy paradigm within which policymakers operated throughout the preparation and implementation of the HTP. During the introduction and implementation of the HTP, the role of the WB was one of policy consultancy. In the end, the government's confident reform team had a shared vision with the WB and contextualised the WB healthcare reform blueprint.

5.7 The Reform as a Closed Process

The preparation and the implementation of the HTP was largely a process that was closed to most domestic actors, which was in line with top-down policy-making tradition in Turkey (Ağartan 2016, pp. 60–1). An informant, who worked as the project leader of the WB, acknowledged this fact as follows: 'The way you do business here is very different. You would never go to a big public meeting and talk about such things. You would do that through your one-to-one relationships' (Interview no. 22).

As the informant above indicated, the modus operandi in policymaking in Turkey consists of closed-door person-to-person negotiations. Governments generally do not favour open discussions on policy issues. In response, the WB expert felt the need to follow local conventions and so kept his criticisms of official policy for private meetings with the Turkish politicians and high-level bureaucrats. Not only did he decide to work within these limits, he later appreciated this form of policy formation and strong leadership as main factors in the success of the HTP. He stated, 'the Health Transformation Project happened only because it had the support of the prime minister and a very strong minister of health' (Interview no. 22). As this quotation suggests, the informant, who had worked as a WB team leader in healthcare projects in Turkey, argued that strong leadership was one main reason for the success of the HTP. It might also serve as evidence that the WB prefers a strong executive to a democratically vibrant political atmosphere, the latter of which could slow down the reform process or cause the eventual reform to diverge from the WB blueprint.

A similar perspective can be seen in a collaborative report of the OECD and the WB that portrayed even the institutional checks and balances in the Turkish political system as obstacles to the introduction of a comprehensive healthcare reform before 2003. The report suggested:

> Governance arrangements in the health sector were fragmented and considerable power ultimately belonged with the Constitutional Court and Grand National Assembly. (OECD and World Bank 2008, p. 38)

OECD and the WB report presented the power of the Constitutional Court and Turkish Parliament as obstacles to the introduction of reform projects of the MoH before 2003. While Turkey already had a top-down policy-making tradition before the 2000s, the Constitutional Court and Grand National Assembly had not been easily ruled out as they were parts of a system of checks and balances. The WB's overemphasis on strong leadership, however, challenges the status quo and evidences the 'elective affinity' between the enactment of neoliberal reform ideas and de-democratisation.

Following the completion of the Health Transition Project, the WB confidently stated that the HTP was good practice (World Bank 2009, p. 26). Turkey's HTP was one of 12 projects to receive an award for having 'improved the lives of people in Europe and Central Asia' in 2010. The OECD and the WB report also presented the reform as a success story:

> The Health Transformation Programme in many ways reflects best practice in the development and implementation of a major health sector reform including UHI [universal health insurance] coverage in an OECD country. Strong government commitment and leadership, along with major financing reforms and aided by strong economic growth, have been complemented by sequential delivery system reforms. While it is too early to evaluate the impacts of the HTP on all aspects of health status, financial protection, and consumer satisfaction, the preliminary indications from the available data suggest that there has been important progress in all three areas. Turkey is closing the performance gap with other OECD countries and, on a number of measures including overall costs, performs well in relation to other comparable upper middle-income countries. There may be much that other countries can learn from the recent health reforms in Turkey. (OECD and World Bank 2008, pp. 128–9)

As the above quotation suggests, despite the lack of empirical evidence on the impact of the reform, the WB and the OECD began to present the HTP as a best practice that could be replicated in other emerging market economies (Chakraborty 2009). Even a commentary co-authored by the editor-in-chief of *The Lancet* about an article authored by members of the reform team suggested that 'Turkey's own story, independently reviewed and assessed, [is] about a remarkable revolution in health' (Horton and Lo 2013). They went on to claim that the HTP had been a product of democratisation and was in line with the extension of civil and political rights in Turkey (Horton and Lo 2013).

5.8 The Partnership of the World Bank and the Government: Any Disagreements?

Interviews with WB experts indicate that the partnership between the WB and the Turkish government and the reform team had been a close and relatively problem-free one. However, there had also been disagreements during its implementation.

According to the OECD and WB report, the government was not able to complete the restructuring of the MoH that would transform it into a stewardship body, nor had it been able to strengthen the capacity of the SGK to implement incentive-based payment systems in purchasing services from healthcare providers, or to transfer regulatory functions to quasi-public institutions until the end of Phase I of the HTP (OECD and World Bank 2008, p. 110).

In fact, an informant who was part of the reform team acknowledged the tension between the WB team and the government surrounding decisions on the public presence in healthcare provision:

> At times, we will take measures as part of this Programme that the WB might not accept. Indeed, we have already been doing it. Let me give you an example. In the WB tailor-made projects for developing countries, nationalisation of hospitals has no place. On the contrary, they [WB tailor-made projects for developing countries] include decentralisation of hospitals. They might even include the privatisation of hospitals. In the Health Transformation Programme, nowhere can you find any trace of the privatisation in public hospitals. In fact, Social Insurance Institution's hospitals were nationalised. (Interview no. 20)

In the quotation above, the informant claimed that the reform had been swimming against the current of WB-sponsored pro-market healthcare reforms, especially with regard to the role of the state in healthcare provision. While the WB encourages emerging market economies to decentralise and even privatise healthcare delivery, the informant argued that the Turkish reform had nationalised the social insurance fund's hospitals and had not put forth any privatisation agenda.

A former WB team leaders did not perceive this as a significant point of contestation between the Bank and the government. She argued:

> Some of the analytical advice [that appears in the WB report] was initially not taken on board by the government.... This is normal for us, by the way,

> because our objective is to advise the government based on available evidence.... In all countries, health reforms are guided by political economy decisions.... Even though you provide the best technical advice, there is no guarantee that any government will move on all directions. They have to evaluate the political situation. (Interview no. 22)

As seen in the above quotation, a former WB team leader suggested that their responsibility had been to support the government with the best policy advice in line with the WB perspective. However, whether or not the government took the advice was the decision of the government. A decision might go against WB advice if the government did not agree with the WB on a specific policy issue, or it might derive from the fact that the government thought the moment was not right to implement that particular policy advice for political reasons.

In fact, it could be argued that the steps that the government took in healthcare delivery discredits a former member of the reform team who argued that the government's healthcare reform would not lead to decentralisation and privatisation. While it could still be argued that the government did not put an end to the dominant role of the state in healthcare provision, the HTP clearly increased the role for private actors in healthcare provision and introduced private finance initiatives in public hospital constructions. It was pointed out earlier (Chapter 4) that the government restructured the Ministry so as to make it fit into its new role of overseer and monitor, granted administrative and partially financial autonomy to public hospitals and established a quasi-autonomous public body known as the Public Hospitals Institution of Turkey (*Türkiye Kamu Hastaneleri Kurumu, or TKHK*), all with the aim of coordinating healthcare delivery (The Republic of Turkey 2011a). In line with these legislative changes, public hospital unions were established to bring together public hospitals that were geographically close to each other and grant them financial and administrative autonomy. The TKHK was responsible for overseeing and monitoring the activities of the public hospital unions.

On the one hand, the government's further steps to decentralise the structure of healthcare delivery, transfer the Ministry's powers to a quasi-autonomous public body and establish public hospital unions as healthcare enterprises might be interpreted as evidence of the government's perfect agreement with the WB's policy advice. This interpretation would also render support for the former head of the WB team leader, who claimed that the government was willing to but could not take necessary steps to decentralise and privatise the public hospitals at the time due to the unfavourable political atmosphere. It can be argued that, once the government had the chance to go further, it did not hesitate to do so.

On the other hand, the alterations to the healthcare delivery structure and the governance of this structure did not fully comply with the WB blueprint. The TKHK is still affiliated with the MoH. In addition, the TKHK is legally responsible for implementing the Ministry's policies and targets. It can be argued that the dominant role of the state in the healthcare delivery structure was not challenged even after the 2011 changes. From the WB perspective, the dominant role of the state in healthcare delivery might distort market dynamics. However, the government might have an interest in retaining the public sector presence in healthcare provision: to secure public support for the reform, ensure their re-election and/or to suppress the prices of private hospitals services. Therefore, despite overall agreement between the WB and the government on the main tenets of the reform, the government's other political interests might have resulted in a reform that would diverge from the WB blueprint.

5.9 Conclusion

This chapter explored how and to what extent the WB was influential in the preparation and implementation of the HTP. Concurrent with the proliferation of the health economics discourse worldwide, the WB came up with pro-market healthcare reform suggestions for emerging market economies. While the core of this approach has been sustained, its components have changed over time. Earlier WB projects on healthcare reform in emerging market economies, especially in Latin American countries, had a sharp and sudden privatisation agenda. Later on, the WB adopted a more balanced approach to healthcare reforms that gave significant regulatory powers to the state in the establishment and operation of private healthcare systems.

The historical partnership between successive Turkish governments and the WB resulted in the institutionalisation of pro-market healthcare reform discourse within Turkey's MoH, which then manifested itself in the establishment of the Health Project General Directorate. In addition, this partnership helped Turkish state officials become part of the WB-sponsored international epistemic community on healthcare reforms. Throughout the 1990s, successive governments attempted to introduce pro-market healthcare reforms in collaboration with the WB. However, all these attempts failed. Despite the failure of these reform projects, the collaboration of the WB and the MoH resulted in the consolidation of a bureaucratic consensus on the need for a pro-market reform in Turkey's healthcare system. As of the 2000s, the pro-market approach towards healthcare reform appeared as a non-alien approach in healthcare policy circles in Turkey.

In fact, the AK Party's healthcare reform proposal bore a close resemblance to the WB suggestions for reform in Turkey's healthcare system and its reform blueprint. Nevertheless, it is argued here that this was not due to the WB's imposing the reform on the AK Party government by providing loans. In practice, the WB provided loans of relatively insignificant amounts (0.5 per cent of the total public expenditures spent on healthcare) to the government. Contextual factors, including steady economic growth and the favourable political conditions empowered the AK Party government vis-à-vis the WB during the partnership.

Members of the government reform team did not accept the criticism that the reform was a top-down WB blueprint for reform. They argued that they had the power and competency to design the reform in line with the needs of Turkish citizens and the healthcare sector in Turkey (disregarding any possible conflict between these two set of needs). However, I argue here that the policy paradigm that they shared with WB experts, coupled with the fact that there was no alternative to the pro-market reform from their perspective, made the WB and the government partnership a problem-free one.

The analysis presented in this chapter makes it clear that the AK Party government chose to work with the WB not because it was in need of WB loans, but because it shared a similar policy perspective and thus took advantage of WB know-how and expertise on healthcare reforms. The result was a success story not only for the Turkish government but also for the WB. The WB appreciated the Turkish reform experience and started to promote it as one of the best practices in healthcare.

The WB experts had a strong commitment to the government in implementing the reform as the recipe for success in the Turkish healthcare reform. They did not question the design of the reform process as a closed one that did not allow democratic participation of significant stakeholders. Therefore, as the case of Turkey's healthcare reform suggests, the WB not only disregards the need for democratic participation in reform processes; it instead presents checks and balances in democratic systems as obstacles to the success of reform projects. The WB's technocratic approach legitimised the government's exclusion of significant stakeholders from policy-making processes.

Despite the fact that the WB and the AK Party government were in agreement on the general parameters of the reform, it has become clear that their final destinations did not totally coincide. While the WB's final destination is a private healthcare system with a targeted health insurance component for the poor, the government has been hesitant to retreat from the financing and provision of healthcare services altogether. Even though the government took steps to increase the financial and administrative autonomy of public hospitals, to promote private sector involvement especially in healthcare delivery and introduced strong private-sector management methods into the operation of these hospitals, it did not put an end to the MoH dominating control of healthcare provision. This discrepancy between the intended final destination of the WB and that of the government may spring from their different primary political interests. Unlike the WB, the government has to secure its electoral success, and it might not want to lose its political mandate over healthcare provision.

The WB impacted the reform in two different ways. First, as it is argued here, the growing dominance of the WB over the global healthcare reform agenda since the late 1970s and the engagement of the WB with healthcare bureaucracy since the late 1980s popularised the pro-market healthcare reform paradigm among Turkish policy circles. This paved the way for the acceptance of a pro-market policy paradigm. Analysis of interviews shows that both WB officials and members of the government reform team see a pro-market approach to healthcare policy reform as scientifically sound and evidence-based instead of a purely political decision. An article co-authored by the Minister of Health in charge of the HTP presented the reform as a product of the government's 'comprehensive strategy informed by evidence' (Atun et al. 2013, p. 71). The common belief in an objective scientific basis for a pro-market healthcare reform led to the framing of all other policy options as 'ideological' and therefore non-scientific.

In conclusion, this chapter maintains that the WB influence on the healthcare reform in Turkey can be better understood if the WB is perceived both as a structure that predated the rise of the AK Party and as an actor that collaborated with the AK Party government. While the former role of the WB originates from its long-lasting ideological investment in the domain of healthcare, its latter role as an actor in healthcare reforms is subject to change due to contextual factors. The strength of the WB's ideological dominance in the domain of healthcare has a clear implication for the main tenets of healthcare reform. Nevertheless, given the considerable room for manoeuvring that the AK Party government had in times of economic growth and popular support, the government had the power to alter these tenets by introducing different policy formulations and by adjusting the timing of various parts of the reform.

Globally dominant ideas did matter in shaping the content of healthcare reform in Turkey. However, the Turkish case suggests that such ideas make inroads into a domestic policy setting, but not always through the direct imposition of the WB through loans and its conditionalities in times of austerity. They can also be effective through the establishment of an ideological consensus on how to approach healthcare policy, with the help of long-term WB investments in knowledge production and policy advice and the establishment of epistemic communities.

References

Abel-Smith, B., and Mossialos, E. (1994). Cost containment and healthcare reform: A study of the European Union. *Health Policy*, 28(2), 89–132.

Ağartan, T. İ. (2007). Turkish health policy in a globalizing world: The case of 'Transformation of Health' program. *ISA Research Committee 19 Annual Academic Conference*. Florence: ISA.

Ağartan, T. İ. (2008). *Turkish health system in transition: Historical background and reform experience*. Ph.D., State University of New York.

Ağartan, T. I. (2016). Learn, frame and deploy? Cross-national policy ideas and comparisons in Turkey's health reform. *Journal of Comparative Policy Analysis*, 18(1), 54–69.

Archer, R. (1994). Markets and good government. In A. Clayton (ed.), *Governance, democracy and conditionality: What role for NGOs?* (pp. 7–34). Oxford: Intrac.

Armada, F., Muntaner, C., and Navarro, V. (2001). Health and social security reforms in Latin America: The convergence of the World Health Organization, the World Bank, and transnational corporations. *International Journal of Health Services*, 31(4), 729–768.

Atun, R., Aydın, S., Chakraborty, S., Sümer, S., Aran, M., Gürol, İ, Nazlıoğlu, S., Özgülcü, Ş., Aydoğan, Ü., Ayar, B., Dilmen, U., and Akdağ, R. (2013). Universal health coverage in Turkey: Enhancement of equity. *The Lancet*, 382(9886), 65–99.

Batley, R. (2004). The politics of service delivery reform. *Development and Change*, 35(1), 31–56.

Berman, P. A., and Bossert, T. J. (2000). Decade of health sector reform in developing countries: What have we learned?. In *Data for decision making project-Appraising a decade of health sector reform in developing countries.* Washington DC: Harvard School of Public Health.

Buse, K., and Gwin, C. (1998). The World Bank and global cooperation in health: The case of Bangladesh. *The Lancet*, 351(9103), 665–669.

Business, Albawaba. (2003, July 22). IFC makes first investment in Turkey's health sector. *Albawaba Business.*

Chakraborty, S. (2009). Health systems strengthening: Lessons from the Turkish experience. *World Bank Europe and Central Asia Knowledge Brief*, 12. Washington D.C.: The World Bank.

Collins, C., Green, A., and Hunter, D. (1999). Health sector reform and the interpretation of policy context. *Health Policy*, 47(1), 69–83.

Cox, R. H. (2001). The social construction of an imperative: Why welfare reform happened in Denmark and the Netherlands but not in Germany. *World Politics*, 53(3), 463–498.

Crawford, G. (2006). The World Bank and good governance: Rethinking the state or consolidating neo-liberalism?. In A. Paloni and M. Zanardi (eds.), *The IMF, World Bank and policy reform* (pp. 115–141). Oxon and New York: Routledge.

DPT. (1984). *Five Year Development Plan for 1985–1989.* Ankara: DPT.

DPT. (1989). *Five Year Development Plan for 1990–1995.* Ankara: DPT.

DPT. (1995). *Five Year Development Plan for 1996–2000.* Ankara: DPT.

DPT. (2000). *Five Year Development Plan for 2001–2005.* Ankara: DPT.

Ewert, B. (2009). Economization and marketization in the German healthcare system: How do users respond?. *German Policy Studies*, 5(1), 21–44.

Freeman, R. (1998). Competition in context: The politics of healthcare reform in Europe. *International Journal of Quality in Healthcare*, 10(5), 395–401.

Freeman, R. (1999). Institutions, states and cultures: Health policy and politics in Europe. In J. Clasen (ed.), *Comparative social policy: Concepts, theories and methods* (pp. 80–94). Oxford and Massachusetts: Wiley-Blackwell.

Giaimo, S. (2005). *Markets and medicine: The politics of healthcare reform in Britain, Germany, and the United States.* Ann Arbor: The University of Michigan University Press.

Giaimo, S. (2016). *Reforming health care in the United States, Germany and South Africa: Comparative Perspectives on Health.* Hamsphire and New York: Palgrave Macmillan.

Ham, C. (2009). *Health policy in Britain.* Hampshire and New York: Palgrave MacMillan.

Harrison, S., and McDonald, R. (2008). *The politics of healthcare in Britain.* London: SAGE Publications

Homedes, N., and Ugalde, A. (2005). Why neoliberal health reforms have failed in Latin America. *Health Policy*, 71(1), 83–96.

Horton, R., and Lo, S. (2013). Turkey's democratic transition to universal health coverage. *The Lancet*, 382(9886), 3.

IFC. (2007). Financing private healthcare in Turkey: Acibadem Healthcare Group. Reducing poverty, improving lives. http://www.ifc.org/wps/wcm/connect/9522e0004970c18b9f3edf336b93d75f/Reduce%2BPoverty%2BAcibadem.pdf?MOD=AJPERES. Accessed 21 July 2012.

IFC. (2012a). Investing in private healthcare in emerging markets. *ICF in Turkey*. http://www1.ifc.org/wps/wcm/connect/region__ext_content/regions/europe+middle+east+and+north+africa/ifc+in+europe+and+central+asia/countries/turkey+country+landing+page. Accessed 10 February 2012.

IFC. (2012b). *IFC in health – Key facts*. http://www1.ifc.org/wps/wcm/connect/Industry_EXT_Content/IFC_External_Corporate_Site/Industries/Health+and+Education/Health+Sector/KeyFacts/. Accessed 10 February 2012.

Immergut, E. M. (1992). *Health politics: Interests and institutions in Western Europe*. Cambridge, New York and Melbourne: Cambridge University Press.

Jacobs, L. R., and Skocpol, T. (2010). *Healthcare reform and American politics: What everyone needs to know*. Oxford and New York: Oxford University Press.

Joseph, L. (2006, March 8). IFC invests in Turkish healthcare company. *International Finance Corporation*.

Kaasch, A., and Martens, K. (2015). *Actors and agency in global social governance*. New York: Oxford University Press.

Klein, R. (2010). *The new politics of the NHS: From creation to reinvention*. Oxon: Radcliffe Publishing.

Laurell, A. C. (2001). Health reform in Mexico: The promotion of inequality. *International Journal of Health Services*, 31(2), 291–321.

Laurell, A. C., and Arellano, O. L. (1996). Market commodities and poor relief: The World Bank proposal for health. *International Journal of Health Services*, 26(1), 1–18.

Lister, J. (2005). *Health policy reform: Driving the wrong way?*. Middlesex: Middlesex University Press.

Lloyd-Sherlock, P. (2006). When social health insurance goes wrong: Lessons from Argentina and Mexico. *Social Policy & Administration*, 40(4), 353–368.

Moran, M. (1992). The health-care state in Europe: Convergence or divergence?. *Environment and Planning C: Government and Policy*, 10(1), 77–90.

Moran, M. (1998). Explaining the rise of the market in healthcare. In W. Ranade (ed.), *Markets and healthcare: A comparative analysis* (pp. 17–33). London and New York: Longman.

Moran, M. (1999). *Governing the healthcare state: A comparative study of the United Kingdom, the United States and Germany*. Manchester and New York: Manchester University Press.

Navarro, V. (1994). *The politics of health policy: The US reforms, 1980–1984.* Oxford & Cambridge: Blackwell.

Ranade, W. (1994). *A future for the NHS? Healthcare in the 1990s.* London and New York: Longman.

Rosetti, A. G. (2004). *Strategic options for the implementation of the health sector transformation in Turkey.* Ankara: Ministry of Health and the World Bank.

Salter, B. (2004). *The new politics of medicine.* Hampshire and New York: Palgrave Macmillan.

Savaş, N. (2012). 'Sağlıkta dönüşüm sürecinde Dünya Bankası'nın ulusal sağlık mevzuatımıza etkisi' (The impact of the World Bank on our national health legislations). In *15. Ulusal Halk Sağlığı Kongresi: Sağlık Reformları.* Bursa.

Sen, K., and Koivusalo, M. (1998). Healthcare reforms and developing countries: A critical overview. *International Journal of Health Planning and Management*, 13(3), 199–215.

Sparkes, S. P., Bump, J. B., and Reich, M. R. (2015). Political strategies for health reform in Turkey: Extending veto point theory. *Health Systems & Reform*, 1(4), 263–275.

The Republic of Turkey. (2003). *T.C. 58. Hükümet Acil Eylem Planı (58th Government of Republic of Turkey Urgent Action Plan).* Ankara: The Republic of Turkey.

The Republic of Turkey. (2011a). *Sağlık Bakanlığı ve Bağlı Kuruluşlarının Teşkilat ve Görevleri Hakkında Kanun Hükmünde Kararname (Statutory Decree on the Organisation and Duties of the Ministry of Health and its Subsidiary Institutions). KHK/663.*

Walt, G. (1994). *Health policy: An introduction to process and power.* Johannesburg: Witwatersrand University Press, London and New Jersey: Zed Books.

Walt, G. (1998). Globalisation of international health. *Lancet*, 351(9100), 434–437.

Weyland, K. (2005). Theories of policy diffusion: Lessons from Latin American pension reform. *World Politics*, 57(2), 262–295.

World Bank (1987). *Financing health services in developing countries: An agenda for reform.* Washington DC: The World Bank.

World Bank. (1993). *World Development Report: Investing in health.* New York: World Bank.

World Bank (2003a). *Turkey: Greater prosperity with social justice. Policy notes.* Washington DC: The World Bank.

World Bank. (2003b). *Turkey reforming the health sector for improved access and efficiency.* Human Development Sector Unit, Europe and Central Asia Region: The World Bank.

World Bank. (2004). *Project appraisal document on a proposed load in the amount of 49.40 million Euro to the Republic of Turkey for a Health Transition Project in support of the first phase of the program for Transformation in Health*. Human Development Unit-Europe and Central Asia Region: The World Bank.

World Bank. (2008). *Country partnership strategy with the Republic of Turkey for the period 2008–2011*. Turkey Country Management Unit-Europe and Central Asia Region, International Finance Cooperation-Central and Eastern Europe Department, Multilateral Investment Guarantee Agency: The World Bank.

World Bank. (2009). *Project appraisal document on a proposed loan in the amount of Euro 56.10 million (US$75.12 million Equivalent) to the Republic of Turkey for a health transformation and social security reform project in support of the second phase of the health transformation program*. Human Development Sector Unit, Turkey Country Unit, Europe and Central Asia Region: The World Bank.

World Bank. (2010). *Implementation completion and results report on a loan in the amount of Euro 49.40 million to the Republic of Turkey for a Health Transition Project*. Human Development Unit, Turkey Country Unit, Europe and Central Asia Region: The World Bank.

World Bank. (2011). *Country partnership strategy with the Republic of Turkey for the period 2012–2015*. Turkey Country Management Unit-Europe and Central Asia Region, International Finance Cooperation-Central and Eastern Europe Department, Multilateral Investment Guarantee Agency: The World Bank.

World Bank. (2012). *World Bank*-Turkey. http://www.worldbank.org.tr. Accessed 10 February 2012.

Yalman, G. L. (2009). *Transition to neoliberalism: The case of Turkey in the 1980s*. Istanbul: Istanbul Bilgi University Press.

CHAPTER 6

The AK Party and the Politics of Healthcare in Turkey in the Last Decade

6.1 Introduction

This chapter focuses on the role of the AK Party throughout the healthcare reform process in Turkey between 2003 and 2013. The role of the AK Party might seem obvious to some. However, there are further important questions to explore in order to fully understand why the AK Party focused its energy on healthcare reform, how and to what extent the AK Party exerted its influence on the content of the reform, tackled political conflicts throughout the reform process, made the reform politically possible and benefited politically from the outcomes of the reform.

The literature on welfare politics suggests that party politics matters. Studies on welfare politics in emerging market economies also support this claim. For example, a study on welfare politics in Latin America concludes that the character of political parties, referring to a combination of factors including ideology and organisational structure, has a decisive impact on the direction and content of social policy reforms (Pribble 2013, p. 173). This chapter explores where the HTP fits into the AK Party's political programme and strategy, how the AK Party used the HTP to reach out to the public and how it generates consent and secures re-election.

It is argued here that the AK Party focused its energy on reforming healthcare because it was a key policy domain where the Party would be able to sustain its political alliances with various sectors of the society and create new ones. This chapter suggests that the HTP is a product of the AK Party's alliance with those who had been left out or marginalised by

V. Yılmaz, *The Politics of Healthcare Reform in Turkey*,
DOI 10.1007/978-3-319-53667-5_6

the previous healthcare system in Turkey and with an emerging group of entrepreneurs who owed their allegiance to the state-sponsored capital accumulation in the provision of healthcare services. Therefore, with respect to the future trajectory of Turkey's healthcare system, I argue conflicting political claims exist within the AK Party and in the new terrain of healthcare politics in Turkey.

6.2 Political Parties and the Society

Among the four approaches to the politics of healthcare – the pluralist, the power resources, the institutionalist and the new politics approaches – the first two in particular suggest that political parties represent the pre-defined interests of different social groups. In the pluralist approach, political parties are portrayed as brokers between civil society and the decision-making authorities (e.g. Truman 1951). The power resources approach assumes that political parties represent class interests and that social democratic/socialist parties represent working class interests in a capitalist democracy (e.g. Korpi 1980).

By contrast, Kirchheimer, in his thesis on the emergence of catch-all parties, suggests that political parties might not be representing the pre-defined sectors of the society with pre-defined interests (Kirchheimer 1990; Krouwel 2003, p. 30). Kirchheimer believes that catch-all parties appeal to all social classes (Kirchheimer 1990; Krouwel 2003, p. 30). Among the diverse factors that lead to the emergence of catch-all parties, one is an increasing tendency to attract voters to the personality of party leaders rather than to their ideological stances (Kirchheimer 1990; Krouwel 2003, p. 30). Kirchheimer explains the emergence of catch-all parties and their rise to power as the end product of a broader political transformation. The main tenets of the new political atmosphere include the following: the erosion of parliamentary democracy, the formation of a state-party cartel, the personalisation of electoral appeal and the undermining of the separation of powers (Kirchheimer 1990; Krouwel 2003, p. 31).

Kirchheimer's conceptualisation of catch-all parties can be useful in understanding the AK Party phenomenon in the politics of Turkey in the last decade. Military interventions into democratic politics in Turkey put pressure on the rise of class politics throughout the 1970s, which made populism in electoral politics the only way to engage in formal politics. Although earlier studies on the AK Party discussed in this chapter are helpful in understanding the original class basis of the Party and the political movement that gave birth to it, they fail to explain the latest form that the AK Party has taken. In the beginning of 2000s, the AK Party resembled a catch-all party in the sense that it appealed to all social classes at the same time. It then transformed into a state-party cartel, which increasingly led to the erosion of the separation of powers in the Turkish political system.

Adding to Kirchheimer's analysis of the transformation of political parties, Katz and Mair argue that the distancing of political parties from civil society and the convergence of political parties with the state give rise to a new form of political party, referred to as a 'cartel party' (1995, p. 14). A cartel party is characterised by its interpenetration with the state and its ability to prevent the success of external and internal dissent that would undermine its unity and authority (Katz and Mair 1995, pp. 17–23). Blyth and Katz suggest that major political parties in advanced capitalist societies have been transformed into cartel parties for two reasons: the limitations of catch-all parties and the limits that globalisation has imposed upon political systems (2005, p. 40).

The concept of a cartel party is helpful in explaining the form that the AK Party has taken in Turkey's political system. Turkey's political system was predisposed to the emergence of a cartel party owing to three factors. The first is that the political party funding structure is based on a model that favours political parties that capture enough votes to achieve the 10 per cent national threshold required for them to take seats in the Parliament. The bigger the share of votes a party gets in the general elections, the more financial resources it receives from the public budget in future elections. Second, Turkey's electoral system is clearly majoritarian. Third, the checks and balances in Turkey's political system are not strong enough to prevent the interpenetration of state and the governing party. As will be discussed later in this chapter, the AK Party's successive electoral victories and its political strategy, coupled with the lack of the necessary checks and balances in Turkey's political system to prevent the centralisation of power, paved the way for the transformation of this party into a cartel party.

6.3 The Influence of the AK Party's Political Ideology on the Content of the Reform

The AK Party was established 15 months before it came to power in the 2002 general elections. However, the leadership cadre of the AK Party was not a newcomer to parliamentary politics. It had separated from the major

Political Islamist movement, called the National Outlook movement, whose political parties had been closed down due to their allegedly anti-secular activities. In response, the AK Party presented itself as a 'conservative democratic' party that aimed to bring together the various streams of centrist and rightist politics. Coşar and Özman argued that the leadership cadres of the AK Party invented the conservative democracy label in order to avoid being seen as a religious fundamentalist party that would pose a threat to the Turkish political regime (2004, p. 65).

The AK Party's portrayal of itself as a centrist political party resonated in the conceptualisation of the party's political stance. For instance, Özbudun defined the AK Party as 'a moderate conservative democratic party' (2006, p. 543). While acknowledging the historical link between Political Islam and the AK Party, Özbudun suggested that the AK Party had less in common with the political parties that represented Political Islam (e.g. the RP) and more in common with the previous mainstream centre-right parties such as ANAP. The AK Party succeeded in rebuilding the former Motherland Party's centrist coalition that had brought together almost all components of the right and even a small segment of the centre left (Özbudun 2006, p. 546). In line with Özbudun, İnsel portrayed the AK Party not as the heir of Political Islam but as a pragmatic middle-class party within which the elements of the National Outlook movement would eventually become marginal (2003, pp. 300–1).

Both the AK Party programme and the public statements of its leadership cadre have been eclectic with respect to their approach towards social policies and healthcare policies in particular. On the one hand, the AK Party clearly adopted a pro-market approach in its major economic policies. Distinguishing itself from the National Outlook movement's Islamist 'third-worldism', the AK Party clearly aligned its economic policies with neoliberalism. In its party programme, the AK Party declares that it is 'in favour of a working market economy, with all its rules and institutions' (The AK Party 2014).

Whether or not the AK Party's neoliberal approach to the economy also influenced its perspective on social policies, including healthcare policy, is an open question. On the one hand, there is evidence that supports the claim that the AK Party's neoliberal approach also manifested itself in its healthcare policy, as evidenced in Erdoğan's public statement: 'I insist on this; free markets have to be formed in health, as there are free markets for all other things in the world' (Hürriyet 2006). On the other hand, the reform cannot be easily categorised as a purely pro-market reform due to its positive impact on citizens' access to healthcare services and its preference to keep the dominant role of the state intact, especially in healthcare financing.

The AK Party inherited the National Outlook movement's discursive and organisational expertise in appealing to and mobilising the urban poor, a group that had been left out of the political agenda of centrist parties of both the right and left sides of the political spectrum. The inheritance of the AK Party from the Political Islam of the 1990s found its echo in the party programme and in public statements of the leadership cadre, as both promised to expand public services, including healthcare services, for all citizens of Turkey, especially for those who had been left out or marginalised.

One of the seven main components of the AK Party's party programme is dedicated to social policies. In other areas such as education and social services, the programme lists healthcare under the heading of social policies and suggests that the AK Party acknowledges the responsibility of the social state to offer healthcare services to its citizens (The AK Party 2014).

Therefore, starting from its establishment, the AK Party's ideological stance has been 'a synthesis between the neoliberal context... and traditional-conservative values' (Coşar and Özman 2004, p. 67). The AK Party utilised a traditional-conservative political discourse to communicate its populist agenda to the general public which was based on the use of social policies, including healthcare policies, for electoral success. In other words, the AK Party simultaneously pursued both neoliberal economic policies and populist social policies based on a strange combination of pro-marketism and welfare expansionism. One of my informants who worked in the healthcare reform team of the AK Party government suggested:

> Three consecutive AK Party governments pursued liberal economic policies, but they also pursued serious social policies in education and health. In fact, these two policy sets are in conflict with one another. We have to see this.... This brought success.... If health is governed by the same liberal logic, the risk of the private sector becoming dominant might become reality. That is why this [the HTP] has to become state policy. (Interview no. 20)

The informant thus acknowledged a difference in perspective that informed the government's economic and social policies. In his opinion, the coexistence of the two logics in the discourse and practices of the AK

Party secured the government's political success. Similarly, an informant from the Revolutionary Health Workers' Union (*Devrimci Sağlık İşçileri Sendikası, DEV-SAĞLIK-İŞ*) who was critical of the government's healthcare reform stated:

> In order to prevent social opposition to these [neoliberal economic] policies, the AKP developed social policies to neutralise poverty. In this sense, it had a special mission. (Interview no. 31)

Therefore, it can be argued that representatives from both the pro-reform and anti-reform camps acknowledged the political success of the AK Party's two-tiered policy agenda, which included implementing neoliberal economic policies while pursuing expansionary social policies. As suggested by an informant who worked as a member of the AK Party's healthcare reform team, 'Healthcare was key in the AKP's quest for power. The AKP used healthcare to influence people' (Interview no. 8).

Öniş succinctly explained that the AK Party was arguably able to realise both of its main objectives, namely securing economic growth and mobilising formal and informal redistributive mechanisms (2012, p. 137). He suggested that the international political and the economic environment also enabled the AK Party's ability to realise these seemingly irreconcilable political objectives, which he conceptualises as 'controlled populism' (2012, p. 137). Another scholar conceptualises the policy mix of the AK Party as a representative of 'social neoliberalism' and presents it as part of a trend towards egalitarian capitalism in the Global South (Dorlach 2015).

However, the AK Party not only introduced social policies having a partly different logic when compared to its firm neoliberal stance on economic policy issues; it also initiated pro-market social policies. The HTP includes both pro-market and redistributive measures. Each set of measures has created conflicting dynamics within Turkey's healthcare system. On the one hand, the HTP actively supported the increasing role of the private sector in the provision of healthcare services and envisaged introducing user fees and supplementary private health insurance to top-up the public health insurance. On the other hand, the HTP established a general public health insurance scheme to cover all citizens without providing an opt-out option for those who might prefer purchasing private health insurance only. The HTP also made specific healthcare services such as emergency services and cancer treatment free of charge for all citizens in both public and private hospitals. I argue that, in doing so, the AK Party's synthesis of neoliberalism and populism also manifested itself in the HTP and rendered the reform process conducive to political conflicts within the AK Party and among different actors in healthcare politics.

6.4 The HTP as a Factor in the Consolidation of the AK Party Rule

The AK Party was established by a group of politicians who had resigned from the Political Islamist Virtue Party (FP) a little more than a year before the 2002 general elections. Following the economic crisis in 2001, the AK Party came first in the 2002 general elections. The AK Party was able take the majority of seats in the Parliament, which made it possible to form a single-party government. One of the most important results of the general elections in 2002 was the historic failure of the traditionally powerful political parties on the centre-right and centre-left (Çarkoğlu 2002, p. 131; Coşar and Özman 2004, p. 57). The AK Party's electoral victory in 2002 marked a turning point for Turkish politics, as the Party succeeded in consolidating and then expanding its constituency without leaving any chance for the success of another centre-right political party over the next decade.

Before the AK Party's rise to power in the 2002 general elections, Çarkoğlu defined the main characteristics of the Turkish party system as follows: 'the apparent lack of continuity, together with ever-increasing fractionalization and volatility of electoral support' (2002, p. 123). He then stated, 'The AK Party became the first political party in Turkish electoral history to gather behind it a uniform nationwide swing in its favour' (Çarkoğlu 2002, p. 139). After more than a decade of AK Party rule, the Party managed to increase its share of votes in three consecutive general and local elections. Most recently, the AK Party received more than 45 per cent of the votes in the March 2014 municipal elections.

Given the AK Party's electoral victories in the last decade, it is no longer possible to argue that the electoral support of the AK Party has been volatile. The AK Party's success in consolidating its constituency can hardly be explained on the basis of its ability to maintain its primary political coalition with the well-known centre-right politicians intact. Despite the heterogeneity of the AK Party's earlier parliamentary group, which included former members of centrist parties as well as former social democrats, Erdoğan's power over the Party consolidated gradually in its following two terms in power. Erdoğan's mandate over the AK Party proved to be strong, especially after the political conflict during 17–25 December 2013 between the AK Party's Erdoğan-led core cadre and the Gülenist organisation, which had supported the Party since its establishment. After the escalating political conflict, only 9 out of 326 members of Parliament (MPs) resigned from the AK Party (*Al Jazeera Turk Al Jazeera Turk* 2014a).

How could a political party dominated by a group of Political Islamists become the representative of the centre-right and secure the majority of the votes in three consecutive elections in a political context that was defined by volatility of electoral support? Academics have provided various reasons for the electoral success of the AK Party; these include the economic growth delivered during its rule, its increasing debatable ability to articulate democracy and Islam and its past willingness to introduce a peace process with the PKK, almost all of which had lost their appeal by the end of 2016.

I argue here that the HTP was one of the factors that contributed significantly to the electoral success of the AK Party. Pioneering scholars working on issue salience suggest that the public is generally concerned about specific policy developments in determining the political party for which they will cast their vote (e.g. Repass 1971, p. 400). Belanger and Meguid join those who claim that the political party or the candidate's ownership of the issue might affect voting behaviour, but only if the issue under question is salient in the eyes of the general public (2008, p. 489). Despite the fact that no studies are available on the issue salience of healthcare reform in Turkey so far, it can be suggested that the prevalent problems of the pre-reform healthcare system of Turkey possibly made the healthcare reform a salient issue for the general public throughout the 2000s. The AK Party had promised an important healthcare reform to its constituency in the 2002 general election campaign (Ağartan 2008), which indicated the Party's strong ownership of the healthcare reform.

Three sets of evidence substantiate the claim that the introduction of the HTP contributed to the electoral success of the AK Party in the general elections of 2002, 2007 and 2011. First, in a Turkish Statistical Institute survey, 39.5 per cent of the population stated that they were satisfied with public healthcare services in 2003, a figure that increased to 74.7 in 2013 (2014). Therefore, it can be said that this dramatic rise in the percentage of the population that was satisfied with public healthcare services might have affected voting behaviour.

Second, the success of the healthcare reform has remained part of the AK Party's election campaigns, even more than a decade after the launch of the reform. For example, before the municipal elections in 2014, Deputy Prime Minister Mr Bülent Arınç declared healthcare services as the most popular policy of the AK Party government (Anadolu Ajansı 2014). In an AK Party rally in the city of Yozgat before the March 2014 municipal elections, Erdoğan's address to the public cited the positive outcomes of the healthcare reform (Sorgun 2014).

Third, public opinion surveys indicate that the general public assesses the AK Party's performance in healthcare as the most important success among all other policy domains. For example, a report of the International Republican Institute indicates that respondents to the Institute's survey ranked the government's performance in the improvement of the healthcare system as 6.26 on a scale of 0 to 10 (where 10 is best), thus ranking improvements to the healthcare system as the best performance of the government (The International Republican Institute 2011, p. 8). In the same survey, 4 per cent of respondents suggested that improvement of the healthcare system would be the most important issue that they would consider in the next election (The International Republican Institute 2011, p. 9).

Given the evidence above, I argue that the AK Party's success in introducing and implementing the HTP contributed to its successive electoral victories. The AK Party, which first emerged as a by-product of a far-right Political Islamist National Outlook movement, managed to establish itself as a catch-all party especially in its first two terms by using formal and informal redistributive mechanisms, the most important of which has been the easing of access to healthcare services. As improvements in healthcare services affect the society as a whole, the AK Party's popularity increased.

The claim that the AK Party's social policies contributed to its electoral success might seem incompatible with the zeitgeist of the age of neoliberal globalisation. However, both the specific features of the development of the welfare state in Turkey and the political atmosphere in which the AK Party had to work created a context that was rather different from what scholars portrayed. Although Turkey's welfare system was established concurrently with Western European trends in social policy development in the post-WWII period, it was unable to provide social protection for all, mainly due to the absence of universal coverage and of social assistance and services components (Buğra and Keyder 2006, p. 212). As a result, the level of social expenditures in Turkey remained limited throughout the 1980s and 1990s when compared to other European countries and the overwhelming majority of OECD members (Buğra and Adar 2007).

Therefore, while the limits of neoliberal globalisation also applied to Turkey, there still was room for the Turkish government to increase the share of public social expenditures in the total public budget by changing the internal composition of the public budget. While public social expenditures increased during the AK Party period, this increase, however, did not change Turkey's position as a relatively low social spender. According to the OECD Social Expenditure Database, the share of public social expenditures in Turkey's GDP was 13.5 percentage in 2014, whereas the OECD average was 21 percentage.

Another factor that might explain why and how the AK Party did not pursue a radical pro-market healthcare reform is the political context within which the Party had to work. After the AK Party's rise to power in the 2002 general elections, it still had to demonstrate its political legitimacy to the general public and high-level bureaucrats to counteract its historical affiliation with Political Islam. Given the fact that all parties with a connection to Political Islam had been shut down, the AK Party's leadership cadre had to be politically cautious in order not to face a similar end (Ağartan 2015a, p. 992). In fact, the first public statement by Erdoğan after the AK Party victory included mention of his party's commitment to the EU accession process, his allegiance to the economic program of Turkey with the IMF and respect for the lifestyle of non-conservatives (Hürriyet 2002).

In addition, despite the victory of the AK Party, which allowed them to form a single-party government after the 2002 general elections, more than 50 per cent of the voters were not represented in the Parliament, mainly due to the 10 per cent national election threshold. In other words, as Sayarı suggested, 'the Turkish electoral system – proportional representation with multi-member districts under [the] d'Hondt formula and a 10 per cent national threshold that parties must exceed to qualify for seats – had a strong mechanical effect in translating votes into seats: the AKP won nearly two-thirds of the seats with about one-third of the vote' (2007, p. 200). Therefore, it can be safely argued that while the AK Party's first electoral victory brought it to power, its status as a single-party government did not come with strong political legitimacy (Çarkoğlu 2002, p. 152).

What is more striking about the AK Party's electoral success was its ability to increase its share of votes in the 2007 and 2011 general elections, which provided the Party with the political legitimacy it had not enjoyed in its first term. I believe that, among other factors, the introduction of healthcare reform was a sine qua non for the AK Party to become politically legitimate, at least for some sectors of society that did not vote for the AK Party in the 2002 general elections.

Ağartan suggests that the AK Party governments also considered the reform as an opportunity to reorganise healthcare bureaucracy through partisan patronage appointments (Ağartan 2015a, p. 992). In fact, a former MP from the AK Party, Mr Hüseyin Besli, declared that a religious sect called the Menzil had been setting up its own cadre in the MoH during the AK Party rule (Aksaç 2016), which evidences Ağartan's claim.

The HTP not only served the AK Party's quest for public legitimacy in Turkey but also helped it to impress global policy-making circles. The outcomes of the HTP increased the popularity of the AK Party at the global level and the 'new Turkey' to which it had given rise. Many international commentators appraised the successful implementation of the HTP, and even described it as a manifestation of the expansion of democratisation in Turkey (Horton and Lo 2013).

6.5 The HTP and the AK Party's Alliance with the Poor and the Rich

The AK Party's constituency increased from around 35 per cent of all voters in the 2002 general elections to approximately 50 per cent in the 2011 general elections. The AK Party also expanded organisationally. According to the data of the Supreme Court of Appeals Prosecutor's Office, as of 2013, the AK Party had the largest membership base with around 7.5 million registered members (of around 50 million citizens above the age of 18), whereas the main opposition, the CHP, had around 1 million in the same year (Hürriyet 2013).

Understanding the AK Party's social basis and its growth has been among the main paradoxes studied by social scientists in Turkey in the last decade. In order to understand the AK Party's social basis, it is important to note that the Party inherited a significant portion of the Political Islam votes. In fact, the FP, from whose leadership cadre of the current AK Party had resigned, had received around 15 per cent of the votes in the 1999 general elections. The new Political Islamist party that was established after the closure of the FP ran in the 2002 elections, but it received only around 2.5 per cent of the votes. Therefore, it is not surprising that about half of the votes for the AK Party in the 2002 general elections came from the Political Islamist constituency.

Given that the AK Party became heir to the previously existing Political Islamist parties, it is useful at this point to briefly discuss the core constituencies of these parties. Ayata suggested that the traditional petty bourgeoisie, consisting of artisans and shopkeepers, comprised the core of the Political Islamist constituency (1993b, p. 57). However, this group that Ayata describes constituted far less than a significant proportion of the AK Party voters.

The Nationalist Outlook movement gained pace throughout the 1990s as a result of its successful alliance with the urban poor. In the middle of the 1990s, the RP won the municipalities in key cities such as Ankara and Istanbul. The Party worked hard, both before and after the municipal elections, to organise and support the urban poor through the use of party and municipality resources during the time of Turkey's welfare system crisis (Akıncı 1999, pp. 76–8). The RP's endeavours to reach out to the urban poor through its 'just order' ideology, that is by offering social services to the urban poor and showing sympathy towards their everyday problems throughout the 1990s, strengthened its popularity (Ayata 1996, p. 52). Gülalp also links the popularisation of the Political Islam among the urban poor as a response to the lack of formal social safety nets in the age of a neoliberal transformation of Turkey's economy after the military coup d'état in 1980 (2001, p. 441). The National Outlook movement clearly benefited from the policy drift in social policies throughout the 1990s.

In addition to its strong links with the urban poor, the National Outlook movement also organised part of the business community throughout the 1990s. For instance, the Independent Industrialists' and Businessmen's Association (MUSİAD), known for its political affinity with Political Islam, was established in 1990. According to Ayata, the Islamist bourgeoisie 'grew as a result of the conscious efforts of Islamists in the ANAP governments who provided the Islamist bourgeoisie access to credit from official sources. They were also given preferential treatment in receiving government contracts' (1993b, p. 58). While the Islamist bourgeoisie did not constitute the strongest faction within the Turkish bourgeoisie at the time, its financial support for the Political Islamist parties proved to be especially important in assisting the urban poor in the days of the welfare system crisis.

As a result of the strengthening of Political Islam, and thanks to the alliance it created with the urban poor and the support it took from the Islamist bourgeoisie, the social base of Political Islam in Turkey became 'a vertical bloc comprising segments of different socio-economic classes', including the capitalists in the peripheral cities, the professional middle class and workers who were unable to secure formal employment (Gülalp 2001, pp. 444–5). In other words, the National Outlook movement started to gain the organisational capacity to form a catch-all party in the 1990s.

The AK Party inherited this organisational capacity from the earlier Political Islamist parties that had brought together the rich and the poor. Özbudun describes the core constituency of the AK Party as 'the rural population, artisans and small traders, urban slum-dwellers, and the rapidly rising Islamist bourgeoisie' (2006, p. 547). For İnsel, the AK Party emerged to represent 'the new middle class', the core of which was comprised of 'small and mid-range enterprisers who live mostly in midsize cities and some of whom are employer and employee simultaneously, and the young executives who have received university education, especially in technical fields' (2003, p. 297) and 'a good portion of the working class' (2003, p. 299). Finally, Sayarı describes the main alliance upon which the AK Party rested as follows: 'Backed financially by the country's growing Islamist business sector, the AKP did particularly well among the urban poor in major Turkish cities' (2007, p. 202). Finally, Tuğal argued that AK Party policies favoured the informally employed, which strengthened the popularity of the party among this section of society (2009, p. 56). A recent study demonstrated that the AK Party successfully kept the vertical bloc that it had inherited from its predecessors, which manifested itself in the form of a cross-class alliance at the neighbourhood level (Doğan 2016).

In line with the political legacy described above, it is argued here that the AK Party's healthcare reform was designed to cater both to the Islamist bourgeoisie and the urban poor at the same time. The AK Party's election platform evidenced the paradoxical appeal of the HTP among the business community and the poor. On the one hand, the AK Party's election platform included a section on healthcare that promised to abolish inequalities between the different public health insurance schemes and to expand the coverage of public health insurance to include all citizens (The AK Party 2002, p. 83). Public statements by the former Minister of Health remain as evidence of the AK Party's pro-poor discourse throughout the reform process. For instance, Minister Akdağ suggested that hospitals would be not be allowed to 'hold patients hostage' until they paid their debt to the hospital (Milliyet 2002). Similarly, Akdağ stated that AK Party was in favour of the poor and the middle class, so its healthcare reform was pro-poor (Demirkaya 2010). On the other hand, the AK Party promised private investors that it would allow them to have a part in healthcare provision (The AK Party 2002, p. 83). Erdoğan also suggested, 'Free markets should also be established in healthcare' (Hürriyet 2006).

The paradoxical appeal of the HTP among the business community and the poor and the AK Party's contradictory portrayal of the reform might be explained on the basis of their elective affinity with neoliberalism as an ideology. In addition, domestic context was also amenable to such political engineering. With regard to the inability of Turkey's welfare system to provide a safety net for all, Buğra argued that the relationship between the state and its citizens had been bifurcated (2008, p. 261). While Turkey's welfare system succeeded in offering a safety net for a considerable segment of the society through formal employment and social rights attached to the employment status, it failed to universalise this safety net for others who were unable to take up formal employment. These two broad social groups, therefore, had dissimilar experiences with the state and the welfare system in Turkey. Buğra argued that the AK Party government employed a polarising discourse, one that presented outsiders' interests as opposed to those who were benefiting from the formal social security system (2008, p. 263). Yoltar and Üstündağ substantiated Buğra's argument in the domain of healthcare services. According to their qualitative study, the majority of society, and Green Card beneficiaries and members of the SSK in particular, had been disillusioned with public health services before the AK Party came to power, while civil servants were generally satisfied (2007). Therefore, the AK Party's promises in the domain of healthcare were not sociologically unfounded.

A medical doctor who had worked in a public hospital and was a member of the Association for Human Health and Education explained an anecdote about how the poor felt empowered in the hospital setting after the AK Party's healthcare reform:

> The lower class feels more integrated into the system... They did this in health. For instance, we tell people in emergency services that if there are

> urgent cases, people without bona fide emergency health conditions will be denied services. This is something normal.... But their response to us was, 'we are now in the government, you have to examine us, you can't deny services to us'. (Interview no. 17)

As the quotation suggests, the poor felt empowered; they viewed the AK Party as the guarantor for access to healthcare service, even at times when they should have been procedurally denied. Another extreme manifestation of this feeling of empowerment among the citizens was an increase in violent physical attacks against medical professionals (Yılmaz 2012b).

6.6 Conclusion

In this chapter, I have argued that the AK Party's 'successful' synthesis of neoliberalism and populism manifested itself in the framing and content of the HTP in two ways. First, the AK Party succeeded in creating satisfaction among the poor with the healthcare reform, which strengthened and broadened the alliance with the urban poor that it had inherited from earlier Political Islamist parties. Second, the AK Party managed to use the healthcare reform process as a new contour of capital accumulation for its allied businessmen by integrating the private sector into the provision of healthcare services.

How long would the AK Party be able to continue reconciling the demands of the rich and of the poor in healthcare reform? Having established itself as a cartel party, would the AK Party be still interested in reconciling demands of both groups? These are questions we do not have enough information to answer. The future of the political alliance backing the reform is bleak. This is mainly due to inherent limitations of the pursuit of two incompatible strategies in the medium term and the uncertain future of the political system in Turkey. The very political strategy of the AK Party that made healthcare reform a success story in the first place may create hard-to-solve dilemmas in healthcare policies in the near future.

References

Ağartan, T. İ. (2008). *Turkish health system in transition: Historical background and reform experience*. Ph.D., State University of New York.

Ağartan, T. I. (2015a). Explaining large-scale policy change in the Turkish healthcare system: Ideas, institutions, and political actors. *Journal of Health Politics, Policy and Law*, 40(5), 971–999.

Akıncı, U. (1999). The Welfare Party's municipal track record: Evaluating Islamist municipal activism in Turkey. *The Middle East Journal*, 53(1), 75–94.

Aksaç, B. (2016, November 11). Eski AKP'li vekilden itiraf: Menzil tarikatı, Sağlık Bakanlığı'nda kadrolaştı (A confession from a former AKP MP: Menzil order staffed in the Ministry of Health), *Birgün*.

Anadolu Ajansı. (2014, March 7). En sevilen icraatımız sağlık hizmetleri (Our favourite policy is healthcare services). *Anadolu Ajansı*.

Ayata, S. (1993b). The rise of Islamic fundamentalism and its institutional framework. In A. Eralp, M. Tünay, and B. Yeşilada (eds.), *The political and socio-economic transformation of Turkey* (pp. 40–56). Westport: Connecticut and London: Praeger.

Ayata, S. (1996). Patronage, party and state: The politicization of Islam in Turkey. *Middle East Journal*, 50(1), 40–56.

Belanger, E., and Meguid, B. M. (2008). Issue salience, issue ownership and issue-based vote choice. *Electoral Studies*, 27(3), 477–491.

Blyth, M., and Katz, R. (2005). From catch-all politics to cartelisation: The political economy of the cartel party. *West European Politics*, 28(1), 33–60.

Buğra, A. (2008). *Kapitalizm, yoksulluk ve Türkiye'de sosyal politika (Capitalism, poverty and social policy in Turkey)*. Istanbul: İletisim Yayınları.

Buğra, A., and Adar, S. (2007). *Türkiye'nin kamu sosyal harcamalarının karşılaştırmalı bir analizi (A comparative analysis of Turkey's public social expenditures)*. Istanbul: Boğaziçi Üniversitesi Sosyal Politika Forumu.

Buğra, A., and Keyder, Ç. (2006). The Turkish welfare regime in transformation. *Journal of European Social Policy*, 16(3), 211–228.

Çarkoğlu, A. (2002). The rise of the new generation pro-Islamists in Turkey: The Justice and Development Party phenomenon in the November 2002 elections in Turkey. *South European Society and Politics*, 7(3), 123–156.

Coşar, S., and Özman, A. (2004). Centre-right politics in Turkey after the November 2002 general election: Neo-liberalism with a Muslim face. *Contemporary Politics*, 10(1), 57–74.

Demirkaya, N. (2010, December 3). Sağlık Bakanı Recep Akdağ, Başbakan Tayyip Erdoğan sonrasında AK Parti'de olacakları İnternethaber'e anlattı (Minister of Health Recep Akdağ explained to the İnternethaber what will happen in the AK Party after Prime Minister Tayyip Erdoğan). *İnternethaber*.

Doğan, S. (2016). *Mahalledeki AKP (AKP in the neighbourhood)*. Istanbul: İletişim.

Dorlach, T. (2015). The prospects of egalitarian capitalism in the global South: Turkish social neoliberalism in comparative perspective. *Economy and Society*, 44(4), 519–544.

Gülalp, H. (2001). Globalization and Political Islam: The social bases of Turkey's Welfare Party. *International Journal of Middle East Studies*, 33(3), 433–448.

Horton, R., and Lo, S. (2013). Turkey's democratic transition to universal health coverage. *The Lancet*, 382(9886), 3.

Hürriyet (2002). 6 güvence (6 guarantees). *Hürriyet*, 4 November 2002.
Hürriyet. (2006). Erdoğan: Sağlıkta da serbest piyasa olmalı (Erdoğan: Free markets should also be established in healthcare). *Hürriyet*, 17 March 2006.
Hürriyet. (2013). AK Parti üye sayısında fark attı (the AK Party outscored other parties on the number of members). *Hürriyet*, 13 February 2014.
İnsel, A. (2003). The AKP and normalizing democracy in Turkey. *The South Atlantic Quarterly*, 102, 293–308.
Katz, R. S., and Mair, P. (1995). Changing models of party organization and party democracy: The emergence of cartel party. *Party Politics*, 1(1), 5–28.
Kirchheimer, O. (1990). The catch-all party. In P. Mair (ed.), *The West European party system* (pp. 50–60). New York: Oxford University Press.
Korpi, W. (1980). Social policy and distributional conflict in the capitalist democracies. A preliminary comparative framework. *West European Politics*, 3(3), 296–316.
Krouwel, A. (2003). Otto Kirchheimer and the catch-all party. *West European Politics*, 26(2), 23–40.
Milliyet. (2002, November 28). Kimse hastanede rehin kalmayacak (Nobody would be put in pledge in hospitals). *Milliyet.*
Öniş, Z. (2012). The triumph of conservative globalism: The political economy of the AKP Era. *Turkish Studies*, 13(2), 135–152.
Özbudun, E. (2006). From political Islam to conservative democracy: The case of the Justice and Development Party in Turkey. *South European Society and Politics*, 11(3-4), 543–557.
Pribble, J. (2013). *Welfare and party politics in Latin America*. New York: Cambridge University Press.
Repass, D. E. (1971). Issue salience and party choice. *The American Political Science Review*, 65(2), 389–400.
Sayari, S. (2007). Towards a new Turkish party system?. *Turkish Studies*, 8(2), 197–210.
Sorgun. (2014, February 24). Başbakan Erdoğan Türkiye'ye Yozgat'tan seslendi (Prime Minister Erdoğan appealed to Turkey from Yozgat). *Sorgun Gazetesi.*
The AK Party. (2002). *Seçim Beyannamesi (The Declaration for Elections)*. Ankara: The AK Party.
The AK Party. (2014). *Parti Programı (The Party Programme)*. Ankara: The AK Party.
The International Republican Institute. (2011). *Turkish Public Opinion Survey.*
Truman, D. B. (1951). *The governmental process.* New York: Alfred A. Knopf.
Tuğal, C. (2009). *Passive revolution: Absorbing the Islamic challenge to capitalism.* California: Stanford University Press.
Türk, Al Jazeera. (2014a, February 7). AK Partili İşbilen istifa etti (İşbilen resigned from the AK Party). *Al-Jazeera Turk.*
Yılmaz, V. (2012b). A dangerous game to play in Turkey's health system: Medical doctors vs. patients and their relatives. *Centre for Policy and Research on Turkey*, I(4), 28–33.

CHAPTER 7

The Turkish Medical Association as an Actor in the Politics of Healthcare

7.1 Introduction

The literature on the role of the medical profession and its organisations suggests that their agendas generally reflect the short-sighted interests of the members of the profession. This chapter suggests that the role of the TTB during the launch and implementation of the HTP partly conflicts with the existing claims in the literature. Following the ideological change in the leadership cadre of the TTB in the 1970s, the TTB pushed the limits of working in the interest of medical doctors and developed a new political discourse that combines the medical doctors' rights with citizens' rights to healthcare to support a fully socialised universal healthcare system. This endeavour of the TTB underlies the emphasis that ideational institutionalism placed on the role and importance of ideas in welfare and healthcare politics.

While the AK Party's problem definition of Turkey's healthcare system is consistent with the definition of international organisations (especially that of the WB), the TTB advocated an alternative problem definition in its opposition to the reform (Ağartan 2016, p. 62). Countries with tax-funded universal public healthcare systems were the model for the TTB's approach (Ağartan 2016, p. 62).

During the reform process, however, the main contestation between the AK Party government and the TTB was the control over the labour of medical doctors. As a professional medical organisation, the TTB was

V. Yılmaz, *The Politics of Healthcare Reform in Turkey*,
DOI 10.1007/978-3-319-53667-5_7

unable to escape from its role as a special-interest group promoting the rights of a politically strong group of medical doctors during different periods of the healthcare reform.

7.2 The Literature on the Role of Medical Doctors and Professional Medical Organisations in Healthcare Reforms

The literature on the politics of healthcare acknowledges medical doctors and their professional organisations as pivotal actors in healthcare reforms (e.g. Walt et al. 2008) and rightly situates these organisations at the intersection of healthcare politics and professional politics.

It can be argued that the strength of medical doctors in the politics of healthcare originates from the moral authority of the medical profession and medical doctors' exclusive expertise. For instance, Hyde argues that the power and influence of the American Medical Association (AMA) originates from the professionalism of the medical community, its monopoly over the medical practice and its power of coercion in the form of medical ethics (1954, pp. 948–9). In addition, he suggests that the political power of the AMA can be attributed to the high social status of medical doctors in American society, its mastery over political tactics as an organised professional group, the increased activity of medical doctors in politics and its established relations with the administrative bodies (Hyde 1954, pp. 954–8).

The power of medical associations over healthcare reforms is debated in the literature. For some scholars, moral authority and expertise give medical doctors a significant power over healthcare reform decisions (Blank and Burau 2010, p. 4; Normand 1997, p. 223). While these scholars argue that the success of a particular healthcare policy requires at least tacit support from the medical community (Blank and Burau 2010, p. 4; Normand 1997, p. 223), others suggest that the power of medical doctors should not be overestimated, as it has been shown to be fragile in conflicts with stronger business interests and organised public interest in general (Arrow 2001, p. 1201).

It should also be noted that the power of medical associations vary according to the different dimensions of healthcare politics. In this respect, Moran's functional categorisation of the politics of healthcare can be helpful. Moran organises the politics of healthcare into three categories: the politics of consumption of healthcare, the politics of the production of healthcare and the politics of the medical profession (1999, p. 5). He suggests that the politics of consumption receives the greatest amount of attention from the general public due to its collective form of financing and access (1999, pp. 5–6), especially in state and societal healthcare systems. Governments are also highly involved in the politics of consumption for two reasons. First, they are in control of the largest portion of healthcare expenditures (Moran 1999, p. 175) and second, the politics of the consumption of healthcare may influence the electoral fortunes of the governing and opposition political parties (Moran 1999, p. 7). Political struggles over the consumption of healthcare have been carried out at the national level (Moran 1999, pp. 177–8). But a significant volume of the contemporary politics of production is organised at the international level (Moran 1999, pp. 177–8). Lastly, professional political activities generally take place at the national level between the organised medical profession and governments (Moran 1999, pp. 177–8). Therefore, medical associations generally enjoy greater power over the politics of the production of healthcare and professional politics than they do over the politics of the consumption of healthcare, where their power is relatively limited.

In the literature, there is a tendency to explain the political discourses and acts of medical doctors and their professional medical organisations in a uniform way. For instance, Navarro suggests that the impact of medical doctors on healthcare policy should be viewed on the basis of their class position in the society. According to Navarro, most medical doctors in the United States belong to the upper middle class (1976, p. 206), so he expects them to act in accordance with their class interests in political controversies over healthcare. Moran, however, suggests that the major objective of medical associations has been to 'appropriate public power to allow control over entry to, and competition within the market, while at the same time allowing the profession to control its own affairs' (2000, 144).

Nevertheless, Eckstein's study on the British case demonstrates the importance of the domestic political context and the healthcare system structure in shaping the political positions of the organisations of the medical profession with respect to healthcare policies. In his seminal work on the case of the British Medical Association (BMA), Eckstein suggests that the development of public health policies was closely correlated with the politicisation of the BMA, which had concentrated its activities mainly on the regulation of the medical profession after the introduction of the NHS (1960, p. 42). The ratification of the National Health Service Act in 1946, which made the state the main employer in healthcare services, led to the expansion of the membership base of the BMA to include the majority of medical doctors in Britain (Eckstein 1960, p. 44). Despite the fact that the BMA opposed the establishment of the NHS and had appeared as the chief enemy of the Ministry of Health before 1946, the establishment of the NHS in effect empowered the BMA organisationally and financially and transformed it into a corporatist body that eventually started cooperating with Ministry of Health (Eckstein 1960, p. 48). Eckstein's study also indicates that differences in the professional institutional context within which professional medical organisations operate do indeed matter in determining their power vis-à-vis other political actors. For instance, Eckstein notes that the BMA does not enjoy a monopoly over professional politics as the AMA does, due to the presence of the Royal Colleges. As a result, the Ministry of Health had the power in some cases to play the Royal Colleges against the BMA (1960, p. 48).

The political stances of medical professional organisations can reflect power imbalances among the members of the profession. Scholars note that power is not evenly distributed within the medical community. In a study on the AMA, Hyde suggests that urban practitioners and specialists, whose incomes are above the national average income of medical doctors, are in a better position to devote time and energy to professional politics (1954, p. 947). In a study on the BMA, Eckstein argues that the BMA has largely been a general practitioners' association which has an impact on the political positions it takes during conflicts (1960, p. 50). It can be, therefore, claimed that the level of organisation among the medical community, the internal coherency of the medical association and the powerful groups within the medical community might also have an impact on the political positions taken by medical associations.

Institutionalism situates medical associations within domestic political systems and suggests that the power of medical associations depends on the political system within which they are embedded. Immergut, in her analysis of healthcare reforms in Switzerland, France and Sweden, determined that while medical associations in all three countries opposed their government's efforts to introduce national health insurance, the policy outcomes were all different (1992, p. xxi). Therefore, Immergut argues that the power of medical associations derives not from their internal power resources but from a political system that either enables them to influence policy outcomes or prevents them from doing so. In her words, 'the political impact of a particular group is contingent on strategic opportunities stemming from the logic of political decision processes' (Immergut 1992, p. 11).

While these accounts provide insights for students of healthcare politics, it is argued here that the role of the medical community and medical associations in concrete healthcare reforms can be better understood by situating the medical community and the associations within the historical and political context of the country under consideration.

7.3 A Brief Political History of the Turkish Medical Association and Its Power Resources Within Turkey's Political System

The emergence of the medical profession in Turkey dates back to the late Ottoman period, when the first Western-type medical schools were established in the early nineteenth century. The graduates of the first medical schools, who then became the defenders of modern ideologies, had a significant impact on the late Ottoman politics and on the politics in the early Republican period.

The TTB was established in 1953 by law (The Republic of Turkey 1953) and was officially designated as a corporatist professional organisation that was expected to support the healthcare policies of the government, serve the medical community and act as an advisory body for the government and the MoH. Schmitter defines corporatism as follows:

> A system of interest representation in which the constituent units are organized into a limited number of singular, compulsory, non-competitive, hierarchically ordered and functionally differentiated categories, recognised or licensed (if not created) by the state and granted a deliberate representational monopoly within their respective categories in exchange for observing certain controls on their selection of leaders and articulation of demands and support. (Schmitter 1974, pp. 93–4)

In line with Schmitter's definition, lawmakers designed the TTB as a corporatist body that would represent the medical community at the policy level, while not offering it much power over policy outcomes.

In the 1970s, young medical doctors sympathising with the socialist ideology started to gain the upper hand with the executive board of the TTB, which resulted in the transformation of the TTB from a corporatist professional body into a dissenting civil society organisation composed of medical doctors who had a say on broader domestic political matters not limited to healthcare policy issues. The transformation of the TTB into a de facto dissenting civil society organisation proves that actual discourses and practices might push the predetermined limits that were imposed on organisations. While the military coup d'état in 1980 suppressed all forms of civil society organisations, including the TTB, the Association was one of the pioneering organisations in Turkey's civil society that succeeded in revitalising itself in late 1980s.

Today the TTB is officially a public corporate entity that works under the purview of the MoH. However, in practice, the TTB works independently from the MoH and still operates more like a non-governmental organisation. As a former head of the TTB argued, governments have acknowledged the Association as an opposing force since the second half of the 1970s (Interview no. 9), when the left-wing medical doctors assumed power in the executive board of the organisation. A former head of the TTB explained the current state of the Association as follows:

> With regard to the foundation law of the TTB, we are not fully a non-governmental organisation. We were founded by legislation. One way or another, we have a legal link to the Ministry of Health. That is why the Ministry of Health always wanted to keep the TTB in its backyard. (Interview no. 14)

However, as the TTB's ability to oppose the government's healthcare reform proposals indicates, the agency of the TTB leadership managed to restrict the influence of the MoH on the TTB. In the words of a former head of the TTB:

> The Ministry of Health wants to monitor the TTB. They also have a legal basis to do that. But we are against monitoring by the Ministry. We defend the position that professional organisations should be independent. We think this is the only way we can protect the values of the medical profession. (Interview no. 9)

As the above quote indicates, the agency of the TTB leadership cadre was determined to keep the organisation an independent professional organisation capable of promoting and protecting the values of the medical profession.

The TTB today has local chambers in 65 cities across Turkey. Membership is compulsory only for medical doctors working independently or in private healthcare institutions. It could be argued that non-compulsory membership in the TTB undermines its representative power. Nevertheless, the TTB states that its membership base included around 80 per cent of all practicing medical doctors in 2006 (TTB 2014).

Unlike most of its counterparts in other countries, the TTB defines the values of medical profession and professional autonomy broadly. In addition to defending autonomy against the political authority, the TTB does not accept sponsorship from private companies operating in the health sector. A former head of the Association explains the rationale behind this decision:

> We, as the TTB, are an organisation that can develop its own position independently when we get into a political conflict. Membership fees constitute the largest portion of the Association's total revenues. We reject sponsorship proposals from the pharmaceutical sector. We know that the pharmaceutical industry could make the Association rich. We are aware of that. But then we would lose the ability to develop our political position in line with our own values. (Interview no. 9)

As is seen in the quote above, the values of the medical profession and the professional autonomy have a central place in the political discourse of the TTB. The TTB bases its legitimacy on the universal values of the medical profession, which are defined on the basis of international human rights conventions, the Hippocratic Oath and medical ethics.

In fact, earlier studies on other medical associations indicate that recourse to ethics in opposing political reforms is not limited to the case of TTB. For instance, Hyde points out that the AMA substantiated its opposition to the state's attempts to control medical practice by referring to the ethical values of the profession. According to Hyde, in doing so, the AMA failed to address economic issues in the domain of healthcare politics realistically (1954, p. 976). Distinctiveness of TTB lies in its broader understanding of professional autonomy and its organisational success in defending it against the politically and economically powerful actors.

The representatives of the AK Party government, and especially the Minister of Health at the time, constantly accused the TTB of being 'too political' on healthcare issues and trespassing the boundaries of their identity as a professional organisation. For instance, the Minister of Health at the time, Mr Recep Akdağ, explained the major cause of contestation between the government and the TTB as follows:

> We are not in a struggle with the TTB as a professional organisation. It is an ideological battle. They are struggling with us on ideological grounds (Medimagazin 2011b).

On the one hand, the Minister acknowledges the political character of the TTB, but on the other, he does not consider an ideological battle with a professional organisation as legitimate. He continues:

> In this professional organisation, my esteemed friends represent 100 to 200 thousand people. I represent 74 million people. I am sorry, but I am not going to let anybody or any professional organisation trample the national will (Medimagazin 2011b).

Akdağ draws attention to the broader legitimacy of the government vis-à-vis the TTB, a legitimacy that originates from electoral victory and the greater representative power of the government. A member of the healthcare reform team also perceived the TTB as 'uncooperative' due to its pursuit of a hardliner position with respect to healthcare reform (Interview no. 20). Therefore, any political opposition of the TTB to the government position, according to Akdağ, was neither acceptable nor legitimate. This is because it would have implied an opposition to 'the national will', which is considered as almost sacred and clearly indivisible, especially after the AK Party's transformation into a cartel party. The AK Party thereafter used the notion of the national will against all forms of opposition, including those of the opposition parties in the Parliament.

A former head of the TTB explains how two different bases for legitimacy clashed during conflicts between the government and the TTB:

> The Minister takes a position against the TTB's proposals like this: He argues that they take their legitimacy from the populace. 'But', he says, 'you only do what your colleagues want you to do, you are not a political party'. He asks us to establish a political party and run in forthcoming elections, but we cannot seek recognition of universal values from the public. Of course, the government determines healthcare policies, but it is

> also our right to disagree with these policies. It should be possible to develop criticism as a matter of medical ethos. (Interview no. 9)

TTB was not only excluded from the preparation and implementation of the HTP. As is seen in the quote above, in addition to that, TTB representatives found themselves in an unenviable position to defend their right to disagree with the HTP in the context of shrinking democratic space in Turkish politics.

In practice, it can be argued that the TTB has been an outlier in the global scene of medical associations in terms of its overtly left-leaning political position and its broad interpretation of the universal values of the medical profession, through which they aim to reconcile the interests of medical professionals and patients and introduce a universal healthcare system funded by general taxation. The government side found the political character of the TTB a sufficient reason to justify the exclusion of a medical association from healthcare politics.

In response, TTB representatives have suggested that the following phrase from the founding law of the TTB provides them legitimate grounds to develop and voice criticisms against the healthcare reform under consideration so as 'to secure the progress of the medical profession in favour of the public and individual interest' (The Republic of Turkey 1953). To exemplify, a former head of the TTB states:

> Our objective is to protect the medical practice and its values for the good of society. For us, there is no distinction between the rights of medical doctors and the rights of patients. For us, there is only the right to healthcare. (Interview no. 9)

The holistic approach to the right to healthcare explained above is grounded in Marxian class analysis that the leadership cadre of the TTB had internalised since the 1970s. He argued:

> In the end, medical doctors are workers. They have a specialised labour, but it is still a form of labour. Medical doctors are increasingly part of the majority that does not have anything to sell except their labour.… Class conflict underlies the contestations in the domain of healthcare. (Interview no. 9)

The TTB has been active not only in professional politics but also in the politics of production and consumption. While the TTB does not have veto points concerning healthcare policy decisions, it has developed two main strategies to influence policy outcomes. The first of these strategies is legal activism. As a former head of the TTB stated, 'Legal activism is at the forefront of the TTB's opposition strategies, as it is a strategy that yield fast results. We use all legitimate means' (Interview no. 9). Once the government introduces a change in healthcare policy that is incompatible with the TTB political position, the TTB opens a case against the change, either at the Supreme Court or at the Constitutional Court, and puts forward its own interpretation of the public interest, opposing what is represented in the reform.

The second main strategy of the TTB is to organise press conferences and labour strikes by medical doctors, generally in collaboration with other organisations of health workers, including nurses and caregivers.

Politically speaking, the TTB has been acting in alliance with other left-leaning political parties, professional organisations, trade unions and non-governmental organisations. An interviewee explained the rationale behind this alliance as follows:

> The TTB is part of a broader labour struggle. It prioritises values. We do not prioritise medical doctors, we defend health workers as a whole. (Interview no.9)

The allied organisations of the TTB include but are not limited to the Turkish Nurses Association, the Health and Social Services Labourers Union (*Sağlık ve Sosyal Hizmet Emekçileri Sendikası, SES*), the Union of Chambers of Turkish Engineers and Architects, and the Revolutionary Health Workers Union. In addition, the TTB has been the leading organisation that informs and shapes the opinion of other allied organisations on healthcare issues. It can be argued that allied organisations of the TTB and all political parties, including today's main opposition party (CHP), the pro-Kurdish leftist People's Democratic Party (*Halkların Demokratik Partisi, HDP*) and organisations that place themselves on the left of the political spectrum, fall into its sphere of influence.

As a former head of the TTB states, the TTB keeps its distance from special interest-based lobbying strategies:

> We do not use lobbying strategies, using the word lobbying in a pejorative way. We do consult with other stakeholders, but we keep our distance. We

> do not have 'go-getter' skills. What we do instead is to prepare opinion statements, publications, press releases, labour strikes.... (Interview no. 9)

In fact, the TTB used judicial activism to annul critical changes in the healthcare reform by organising labour strikes and street protests against the reform,[1] especially on the Day of Medicine, which is celebrated every year in Turkey on 14 March to commemorate the introduction of modern medical training in the early nineteenth century.

The TTB holds general elections for its executive board. Despite the fact that the Active Democratic Group (*Etkin Demokratik Grup*) of left-leaning medical doctors has governed the Association since the 1970s, politics within the TTB has been vibrant. There are strong alternative groups seeking to come to power within the Association. These include but are not limited to the Turkish Physicians Platform (*Türkiye Hekim Platformu*), the Physicians Rights Group (*Hekim Hakları Grubu*) and the Medical Doctors Coalition (*Hekim Güçbirliği*).

As confirmed by a former head of the TTB, a major fault line between the three largest groups in the TTB echoes the broader political fault lines in the country (Interview no. 14). The Turkish Physicians Platform is ethnic nationalist, the Physicians Rights Group is neoliberal conservative and the Medical Doctors Coalition is Kemalist nationalist. To exemplify, the Medical Doctors Coalition calls for medical doctors to join their ranks, making these statements:

> Distinguished colleagues...We have been and are unified in our struggle against the trivialisation of all of our medical doctors and their labour and their enslavement; we have been defending our national values, and Mustafa Kemal Atatürk's principles and revolutions of the republic that are under threat.... (Hekim Güçbirliği 2012).

One of the major criticisms raised by the Medical Doctors Coalition against the Active Democratic Group is that the TTB prepared posters in minority languages (Kurdish and Armenian) under the administration of the Active Democratic Group (Güzelant 2012).

Interestingly, the socialists – represented by the Active Democratic Group within the TTB – are clearly a minority in parliamentary Turkish politics, but they have managed to remain in power in the TTB. In response to my question about how the socialists managed to remain in power in the Association, a former head of the Association gave the following response:

> With regard to the rights of medical doctors, people who are ideologically close to the government have recently established relationships with government officials, bypassing the TTB. They negotiated directly with the Ministry. They tried to improve the working conditions of medical doctors at the time. They worked to initiate some positive steps, but none of them succeeded. Therefore, they had to deal with this: those defend medical doctors' rights are us, those against privatisation. (Interview no. 14)

As the quote above suggests, one could argue that the legitimacy of the leadership cadre of the TTB originates from its know-how about legal and street activism, which can also mobilise campaigns against privatisation and for the amelioration of medical doctors' positions and working conditions. However, this source of legitimacy has always been elusive, as there is tension between the values and political causes of the leadership cadre and the reasons why the membership base of the TTB supports the leadership cadre.

7.4 The Turkish Medical Association Opposition to the Health Transformation Programme: Contestations with the AK Party Governments

The TTB bases its criticism of the healthcare reform on the universal values of the medical profession and a Marxian class analysis that sees medical doctors as part of the working class. In this respect, the TTB rejects the neoliberal idea that presents the interests of medical doctors and citizens as inherently incompatible. Instead, it aims to unify the struggles for the rights of medical doctors and the rights of citizens to healthcare. For the TTB, this can only be possible in a fully socialised universal healthcare system, with a strong preventive healthcare component that provides free and universal access to all citizens. There is also evidence that other healthcare professions and their organisations (e.g. the Turkish Nurses Association) share the pro-public stance of the TTB (Harmanci Seren and Yildirim 2013). Nevertheless, the AK Party's HTP had a rather different approach to healthcare – one that aimed to transform the healthcare domain into a quasi-market model.

The underlying conflict between the TTB and the AK Party governments was not limited to their opposing views on the general philosophy of the reform; it went beyond healthcare policy. As a secularist organisation that supported the rights of the Kurdish minority and has been part of a pro-labour rights alliance with professional organisations, trade unions and civil society organisations, the TTB were overtly critical of the AK Party's neoliberal economic policies and its conservative outlook. In fact, the TTB was an active participant in the Gezi protests in 2013. To exemplify the TTB's understanding of the AK Party rule, in the public statement issued jointly by the TTB, DİSK and Union of Chambers of Turkish Engineers and Architects (*Türk Mühendis ve Mimar Odaları Birliği, TMMOB*), these three organisations described the 'new regime' of Turkey established by the AK Party government in terms of three concepts: 'pro-market, reactionist, and pro-dependency' (TTB et al. 2012). In this respect, it can be argued that the relationship between the TTB and the AK Party started from almost irreconcilable political positions in the polarised political atmosphere that existed in Turkey at the time. It can be argued that the conflict about the HTP between the two actors was a manifestation of a deeper conflict between anti-communists vs. socialists, right vs. left, conservative vs. secular and pro-market vs. pro-state.

The conflict between the TTB and the AK Party government is explored in this book with a special emphasis on healthcare reform. The TTB criticisms of the reform included the following five main points: (1) the reform resulted in the privatisation of healthcare services, (2) it was a replica of neoliberal healthcare reforms the WB imposed on all emerging market economies, (3) it led to the deterioration of working conditions for medical doctors and other health workers, (4) it led to an increase in violence against health workers and (5) it resulted in the dissolution of teamwork between medical doctors and other health workers because it introduced performance-based payments and increased subcontracting and flexible employment within the sector (TTB 2011b).

7.5 The Clash Over the Role and Function of the Turkish Medical Association

The TTB does not enjoy an institutionalised veto power in the Turkish political system. However, the single-party government still took the TTB's opposition to the HTP seriously because the TTB plays a moral leadership role and therefore has the power to shape the opinion of other political actors as well as the popular perception of the healthcare reform. This is evident in public statements by the MoH that openly address TTB criticisms of the reform. To exemplify, in response to its criticism of the reform's call for the privatisation of healthcare services, the Minister of Health declared that the AK Party was not a neoliberal party but rather a proponent of social justice and cares for the general public (Medimagazin 2011b).

The ability of the TTB to evaluate the outcomes of the reform for the general public was challenged by the members of the reform team. According to a member of the reform team, despite the positive outcomes of the reform being made public evident over time, medical doctors working in public universities and those serving on the executive board of the TTB failed to change their views, mainly because they had limited contact with the public (Interview no. 20).

In the course of the AK Party's transformation from a single-party government with a shaky legitimacy to a cartel party, the AK Party government took steps to exclude all political activities from the scope of the TTB's activities. By issuing a statutory decree, the government removed the phrase 'to secure the progress of medical profession in favour of public and individual interests' from the foundational law of the TTB (The Republic of Turkey 2011a). With this change, the duties of the TTB as described in its foundational law (The Republic of Turkey 1953) were limited to catering for solidarity among the members of medical profession and pursuing the interests of medical doctors. While government representatives have accused the TTB of pursuing the private interests of medical doctors at the expense of the general public interest, this change affirms that the government, in fact, prefers the TTB to act merely as a special-interest organisation without claiming a broader responsibility to reconcile the interests of the medical professionals with the general public. Minister of Health's statement evidences the government position on this: 'Serving the public interest should not be a TTB mandate' (Hekim Postası 2012).

TTB opposition to the above-mentioned change found an echo among the ranks of the main opposition party, namely, the CHP. Two well-known MPs at the time, Ms Emine Ülker Tarhan and Mr Muharrem İnce, mobilised more than a hundred MPs to open a case at the Constitutional Court against the statutory decree that had removed the phrase 'to secure the progress of medical profession in favour of public and individual interest' from the foundational law. The petition included the following phrases:

> The statutory decree under consideration annuls the clause 'securing the progress of the medical profession in favour of public and individual interest', which is a reflection of the responsibility that is given to professional organisations by the 135th clause of the Constitution. The statutory decree aims at annulling the right and the authority given to the organisation by the 135th clause of the Constitution.
>
> ...
>
> In addition, the statutory decree aims at undermining the functions of the Turkish Medical Association by removing the clause 'securing the progress of the medical profession in favour of public and individual interest'. It is aimed at suppressing the pressure group character of professional organisations that do not comply with the policies of the Ministry of Health. Rather than adopting an approach that recognises and protects independent institutional identity, its aim to change the role and the character of professional organisations is against the democratic, social and constitutional qualities of the state. (The Constitutional Court of Turkey 2013, p. 67)

Finally, the Constitutional Court decided to annul the above-mentioned change in 2013 (TTB 2013). In a reasoned decision, the Constitutional Court declared:

> The Turkish Medical Association is a professional organisation with public institution status established in line with the 135th clause of the Constitution. It is not possible to make amendments to the professional organisations with public status within the scope of Empowering Law no. 622. (The Constitutional Court of Turkey 2013, p. 151)

Thus, the Constitutional Court acknowledged that the legitimacy of the TTB originates from the Constitution. Therefore, neither a simple majority in the legislative body nor a statutory decree is an appropriate means to amend the roles and functions of the TTB. This decision can be interpreted as the legal recognition of the constitutional status of the TTB and its official position, which claims to represent the universal values of the medical profession – values that may not necessarily reflect the popular will or the government position. The decision can also be read as the reinstitution of checks and balance mechanisms that restrict the power of the executive vis-à-vis civil society organisations and their political activities.

7.6 The Clash Over the Employment Status of Medical Doctors

The second key issue that sparked a conflict between the TTB and the AK Party government was the impact of the HTP on the employment conditions of medical doctors. This conflict was centred upon medical doctors' right to work in their own private clinics or private health institutions without quitting their positions in public sector hospitals.

Before the HTP, this 'dual commitment' of medical doctors – both to public hospitals and to their own private clinics – opened up the healthcare system to informality. It was common practice for patients to visit a medical doctor's private clinic to receive better and/or timely treatment in public hospitals than they would otherwise receive.

The clash between the government and medical doctors over doctors' employment conditions started just after the AK Party came to power. Mr Akdağ, the Minister of Health, made the following statement at the Congress of the TTB in 2003: 'Medical doctors should keep away from patients' wallets from now on' (Tıp Dünyası 2003). The government accused medical doctors of blocking citizens' access to healthcare services before the reform, thereby legitimising the HTP with its anti-medical doctor and anti-TTB discourse. One informant, a professor of public health, explained how the government gained the upper hand vis-à-vis TTB during the debate on the full-time work law, citing the deficiencies of the previous healthcare system:

> The government acted as if all guilt was on the medical doctor, as if there was no connection between medical doctors being caught up in these kinds of business and market mechanisms. Then the government attributed this mess to medical doctors and the TTB. As a solution, it proposed to unlink the private sector from the public sector. (Interview no. 13)

In the aftermath of the 2007 general elections, the AK Party government brought full-time work for medical doctors back onto the agenda. The government announced the draft law that included the introduction of a full-time work requirement for medical doctors in

2008. The draft law included clauses that prohibited all medical doctors working for both public and private hospitals from working outside the premises.

It is important to note that the full-time work requirement came onto the agenda in a context within which the HTP excluded the private clinics of medical doctors from the group of healthcare providers authorised to offer services to public insurees. The exclusion of private clinics from the new healthcare system was not a necessity. As the head of the Right to Health Association stated, 'they could have integrated private clinics into the new system. The new model permitted this integration' (Interview no. 15). However, the government's choice was to promote the establishment of large-scale private hospitals and their integration into the system. One informant, a professor of public health, examined the introduction of the full-time work requirement in the light of changes in the healthcare delivery market. He explained:

> Full-time work, in its current meaning, is a regulation that encourages the intensification of capital to the benefit of large corporations. It is the manifestation of a will that legally lays the ground for this intensification. Small enterprises were ruled out of the healthcare delivery by political intervention. (Interview no. 13)

The TTB has been traditionally in favour of a full-time work regulation for all medical doctors. But still the TTB strongly opposed the government's attempt to introduce a full-time work requirement for medical doctors. In explaining its contradictory position, the TTB made a distinction between 'real full-time work proposals' and 'fake full-time work proposals' and supported the former but not the latter (2012). The TTB called for a full-time work that would allow medical doctors to earn a salary that reflected the labour spent and their level of education. A former head of the TTB explained his position on the introduction of the full-time work requirement as follows:

> From my perspective, the full-time work principle is a rightful principle. In a public system, private clinics and public service should not go together. However, if you implement full-time work in a marketised privatised system like this, you cannot achieve the expected efficiency. I am against the full-time practice proposed by the Ministry, but I am for a rightful implementation of the full-time work. (Interview no. 14)

Parallel to the former head's position, the TTB suggested medical doctors should receive a salary that would eliminate the need to top-up their salaries with extra work and that salaries should be reflected in their prospective retirement pensions. The TTB released a draft law on full-time work (TTB 2011c) and declared that it was open to negotiation with the MoH for the implementation of 'real full-time work' (TTB 2012).

The TTB released a report on the draft law. The report suggested that the government's proposed full-time work requirement was different from the full-time work proposal of the TTB. While the TTB was in favour of full-time work in public hospitals, the intended context was a state healthcare system. However, the new healthcare system of Turkey was increasingly dependent on private healthcare providers, for which reason the attempt to regulate doctors' labour and employment status was unjustified; it aimed at strengthening the control of private sector healthcare providers over the labour of medical doctors. This type of full-time work requirement, according to the TTB report, would eventually result in the devaluation of medical doctors' labour (TTB 2008). The TTB presented three principles in this report: 'No' to the devaluation of medical doctors' labour, full-time work is not possible with a merchant's logic, and so-called full-time work of the MoH is actually flexible work (TTB 2008). A former head of the TTB explained why they expected decrease in medical doctors' salaries in the near future as follows:

> In the pro-market system I mentioned before, a full-time work requirement inevitably leads to the weakening of the negotiation power of medical doctors.… You increase the private sector, you want medical doctors to work there, but you don't provide them union rights, and you don't enforce a standard employment contract as a precondition, while the TTB is fighting for it. (Interview no. 14)

In response, the Minister of Health drew the attention of the public to the high income of a minority of medical doctors who were running private clinics. The Minister stated: 'All this uproar is because of 1,200 professors. They are insistent on earning more' (Yalçın 2009). This statement can also be read as evidence that the government portrayed medical doctors as greedy in order to create legitimacy for the healthcare reform by generalising the income of a small number of high-earning medical doctors to the profession as a whole.

A senior economist from the WB supported the Minister's analysis of the opposition of medical doctors to the introduction of a full-time work requirement:

> Those who oppose the reform are the pro-status quo camp. These were the medical doctors who benefited from the old system. These were civil servants working in public universities, teaching and using the bed capacity of university hospitals and who also had their own private clinics. A specialist academic group... I even received hate messages from this group. (Interview no. 25)

The government passed the law in 2010 (The Republic of Turkey 2010), marking a success for the pro-reform camp composed of the government and the WB. The law aimed to put an end to the historical privilege of medical doctors, which caused a political uproar from the doctors.

In response, the TTB, in collaboration with MPs from the CHP, applied to the Constitutional Court to stop the law. The Constitutional Court annulled the articles of the law that prohibited the private practice of medical doctors employed in public university hospitals and set a time limit for other medical doctors to decide in which sector they wanted to work for full-time (The Constitutional Court of Turkey 2010). The Court based its decision on a procedure violation.[2]

Despite the decision of the Constitutional Court, the MoH issued a statement announcing that medical doctors working for public hospitals would not be allowed to open private clinics after the deadline determined in the law. The TTB applied to the Council of State to annul the ruling of the MoH and won the case (*CNN Türk CNN Türk* 2010). The Council of State declared that all medical doctors have the right to open private clinics. In response, the MoH contested the earlier decision of the Council of State. In its new decision, the Council of State accepted the objection of the Ministry and decided that medical doctors, with the exception of professors of medicine in universities, would not be allowed to open or operate private clinics without quitting their position at the public sector hospital (Sabah 2011).

Then the Council of Ministers once again issued a statutory decree that introduced a full-time work requirement for all medical doctors in 2011 (The Republic of Turkey 2011b). Following the promulgation of this statutory decree, 1,157 doctors resigned from the public sector and 246 retired (Medimagazin 2012). The Constitutional Court once again annulled the statutory decree (The Constitutional Court of Turkey 2012) on the basis of a procedure violation. In response, the TTB announced that the government should respect both the decision of the Constitutional Court and the professional autonomy of medical doctors (TTB 2012). In a press release published after the Constitutional Court had annulled the law on full-time work in 2012, the TTB made the following statement:

> The insistence of the AKP government on the full-time work law is neither for the good of medical doctors nor for the good of the patients. It is a regulation for the good of private hospital bosses. The aim is not to encourage medical doctors to provide better service in public facilities or to give patients easy access healthcare services, but to devalue the labour of the medical doctor (TTB 2012).

However, the government did not lose its determination to regulate the labour market for medical doctors. Instead of issuing a statutory decree, this time using its parliamentary majority it introduced a new law that prohibited those working for public sector providers, including public universities, from operating private clinics, yet under certain conditions it allowed them to work for private hospitals and for the public provider (The Republic of Turkey 2014a).

By allowing medical doctors working in public universities to also work for private sector providers, while prohibiting them from operating private clinics, it can be argued that the government made a conscious political choice in the reconfiguration of the healthcare delivery structure at the expense of private clinics. This decision was also in line with the prior decision of the government to exclude private clinics from the portfolio of SGK healthcare providers. The circular that followed the law set a new time limit for medical doctors to make their decision: three months (The Republic of Turkey 2014b).

The TTB met with the President of the Republic and the Head of the Constitutional Court to express their criticisms of the new law (Mayda 2014; Öngel 2014). In response to an application of MPs from the CHP, the Constitutional Court decided to stop the execution of the time limit, after which point university professors would be prohibited from running private clinics unless they left their university position (The Constitutional Court of Turkey 2014). However, the Court did not annul the article prohibiting university professors employed in public university hospitals from running private clinics unless they left their university position. With this ruling, TTB lost the case over full-time work.

In fact, medical doctors who own clinics have been a strong special-interest group within the community of medical doctors. Private clinics are not financially sustainable investments for all specialties. As a former head of the TTB suggested, the majority of doctors that own clinics are obstetricians, organ transplant specialists, haematologists and oncologists. He added, 'They are a group with relatively high incomes and who do not pay much in taxes. Their number does not exceed 1,000–2,000' (Interview no. 14). The total number of specialists in Turkey in 2010 was 63,563 (The Ministry of Health 2011). If the higher estimation of the informant is accepted, medical doctors who owned clinics constituted only 3 per cent of all specialists in the country.

A former head of the TTB openly expressed the challenge of convincing doctors with clinics to work for a salary in either the public or the private sector. He stated:

> The TTB conducted a survey on full-time work. Medical doctors who owned clinics refrained from specifying a certain salary that would convince them to work full time for the public sector. I asked if it was 10 thousand (approx. 5,500 Euros), 15 thousand (approx. 8,250 Euros), 20 thousand (approx. 11,000 Euros), and they answered by asking me if I wanted them to starve. It is impossible to satisfy this group – their expectations are that high. (Interview no. 14)

As the quotation above suggests, the leadership cadre of the TTB has been aware of the fact that doctors who own clinics constitute a privileged minority within the medical community and are not likely to support the TTB's ideal type of universal healthcare system.

I argue here that the political opposition of the TTB against the government's full-time work proposal is a synthesis of the medical doctors' self-interest – coupled with their strong position within the TTB – and an expression of the leadership cadre's opposition to the growing importance of private sector healthcare providers. The broad scope of the conflict originated from the issue at hand, which was the issue of the ownership of doctors' labour in a marketised healthcare sector. While the government attempted to tie doctors' labour to either public or private sector providers without leaving them room to run private clinics, the TTB defended doctors' right to work independently, which in practice served only a minority. The leadership cadre's emphasis on the ills of the privatisation of healthcare neither sounded convincing nor was it widely heard.

But many of the leadership cadre's predictions have been proved. The devaluation of doctors' salaries and a labefaction of the position of medical doctors in healthcare delivery have been taking place. A manager of a nationwide hospital chain argued:

> People now come to X Hospital. They used to go a specific medical doctor. They used to visit a specific medical doctor in public hospital.... Now they come directly for our brand. Recognition of our brand is more important than the recognition of [individual] medical doctors now. (Interview no. 3)

This statement shows that the full-time work requirement for doctors might have contributed to their being marginalised in healthcare delivery and their proletarianisation. In addition, as a former head of the TTB suggested, the new healthcare delivery model subjugated the salaries of medical doctors to the profit margins in the private sector. He argued that after the SGK introduced cost containment measures in 2008, private healthcare providers decreased the salaries of medical doctors (Interview no. 9).

Despite the proven appropriateness of the TTB criticisms of the full-time work law, it should also be stated that this conflict left the TTB in a defensive position and, in the eyes of the general public, reduced its political power to simply the defence of the rights of medical doctors. Given the fact that the government framed the introduction of the full-time work requirement as the only way to eliminate unjustified informal out-of-pocket payments –which did not come true – the defensive position of the TTB has been perceived as the defence of the previous status quo from which patients suffered. A politically active professor of public health criticised the TTB as follows:

> The TTB should not oppose the loss of the privileges of doctors who own clinics. Instead, it should popularise the idea of 'full public' rather than full-time work in its current meaning...The TTB chose to explain itself to medical doctors only, and failed to explain itself to the general public. (Interview no. 13)

As the criticism above suggests, the TTB failed to popularise the rationale for its opposition to the full-time work requirement. It is important to note, however, that it had very limited resources to do so, and its capacity to reach out to the mainstream media and the willingness of the mainstream media to listen to the TTB was already quite limited.

7.7 Conclusion

The literature on the role of medical associations in healthcare politics tends to assume that professional medical associations are organisations that aim only to represent the interests of medical doctors and that these interests are similar across countries (e.g. Moran 2000). However, the case of the TTB challenges these assumptions. Despite the fact that protecting and promoting the interests of medical doctors is part and parcel of the TTB, the TTB's self-description, its political stance with respect to healthcare policy issues and its broader political discourse transcends the ideal medical association that the literature suggests. Drawing on a particular historical experience and situated within a specific healthcare and political system, the TTB aspires to promote a holistic approach to the right to health and works for the establishment of a universal public healthcare system. The Turkish case thus demonstrates that the direction of the influence of medical associations on healthcare reforms is context-specific and historically grounded.

Second, institutionalist approach, explaining the influence of medical associations in the process of healthcare reform on the basis of opportunities that a given political system provides to these associations, partly accounts for the Turkish case. Turkish political system limited TTB's opportunities to influence the reform. However, as the government's attempts to change the TTB mandate demonstrates, political system might not remain stable over time. Political system might well become a locus of political conflict among different actors.

Studying TTB arguments against the introduction of a full-time work requirement for medical doctors as part of the HTP and examining how the government responded to the TTB's opposition is critical to an understanding of the limits of the TTB political position to defend the right to healthcare without separating the rights of medical doctors from the rights of patients. The complexity of the TTB position with respect to the introduction of the full-time work requirement and the responses it has given is telling, especially when examining, to what extent it is possible for the TTB to keep a distance from interest-based professionalism in an increasingly marketised healthcare environment, facing with a strong pro-market and populist political actor and an institutional history within which medical doctors with private clinics played key roles.

In an increasingly marketised healthcare scene, the TTB's mission to act both as a professional organisation and as a dissenting civil society organisation with the aim of establishing a universal public healthcare system for all has its limits. These limits include the opportunities the TTB has to appeal to the general public, especially when compared to the government, and the responsibility that the leadership cadre of the TTB has towards its constituency. Given these constraints, the TTB may face difficulties in reconciling the rights of medical doctors with the rights of citizens to healthcare in its political strategies and in making its holistic approach convincing to and widely heard by the parties involved.

Notes

1. For example, labour strike on 5 November 2003, protest on 24 December 2003, protest on 10–11 March 2004 and protest on 13 March 2011.
2. In Turkey's political system, the Parliament is authorised to promulgate an Empowering Act that permits the Council of Ministers to pass a statutory decree that has the power of law. In this case, the Constitutional Court decided that the Empowering Act did not authorise the Council of Ministers to make regulations on the labour of medical doctors.

References

Ağartan, T. I. (2016). Learn, frame and deploy? Cross-national policy ideas and comparisons in Turkey's health reform. *Journal of Comparative Policy Analysis*, 18(1), 54–69.

Arrow, K. J. (2001). Reflections on the reflections. *Journal of Health Politics, Policy and Law*, 26(5), 1197–1203.

Blank, R. H., and Burau, V. (2010). *Comparative health policy*. Hampshire: Palgrave Macmillan.

CNN TÜRK (2010, July 2010). Tam Gün Yasası'nda yeni karar (New decision on Full Time Work Law). *CNN Türk*.

Eckstein, H. (1960). *Pressure Group Politics: The Case of British Medical Association*. London: George Allen & Unwin Ltd.

Güzelant, M. (2012). *Demokratik katılımcı hekim grubunu açık ve dürüst olmaya davet ediyoruz! (We are asking Democratic participatory medical doctors' group to be open and honest!)*. Izmir: Hekim Güçbirliği (Medical Doctors' Union of Forces.

Harmancı Seren, A. K., and Yıldırım, A. (2013). Nurses' perceptions about health sector privatization in Turkey. *International Nursing Review*, 60(3), 320–327.

Hekim, Güçbirliği. (2012). Hekim güçbirliği (Medical doctors' union of forces). http://www.hekimgucbirligi.org. Accessed 12 July 2012.

Hekim Postası. (2012, January 16). Akdağ: 'Kamu yararı' TTB'nin işi değil (Akdağ: Public interest is not a TTB mandate). http://www.hekimpostasi.org.tr/2012/01/16/bakan-akdag-ttb-tabipligi-kamu-yararina-uygulayarak-amacini-asiyor/.

Hyde, D.R. (1954). The American medical association: Power, purpose, and politics in organized medicine. *Yale Law Journal*, 63, 937–1022.

Immergut, E. M. (1992). *Health politics: Interests and institutions in Western Europe*. Cambridge, New York and Melbourne: Cambridge University Press.

Mayda, M. (2014, March 26). TTB Anayasa Mahkemesi başkanı ile görüştü (The president of Turkish Medical Association talked to the head of the Constitutional Court). *Evrensel*.

Medimagazin. (2011b, December 5). Akdağ'dan "ideolojik" suçlama ("Ideological" accusation from Akdağ). *Medimagazin*.

Medimagazin. (2012, January 21). Bin 157 hekim istifa etti (Thousand 157 medical doctors resigned). *Medimagazin*.

Moran, M. (1999). *Governing the healthcare state: A comparative study of the United Kingdom, the United States and Germany*. Manchester and New York: Manchester University Press.

Moran, M. (2000). Understanding the welfare state: The case of healthcare. *British Journal of Politics and International Relations*, 2(2), 135–160.

Navarro, V. (1976). *Medicine under capitalism*. New York and London: Prodist and Croom Helm.

Normand, C. (1997). Health insurance: A solution to the financing gap?. In C. Colclough (ed.), *Marketizing education and health in developing countries: Miracle or mirage?* (pp. 205–221). Oxford: Clarendon Press.

Öngel, İ. (2014, January 10). Gül TTB'yi haklı buldu (Gül recognised Turkish Medical Association to be right). *Cumhuriyet*.

Sabah. (2011, January 13). Danıştay'dan 'Tam Gün'e onay (The Council of State approved "the Full Time"). *Sabah*.

Schmitter, P. (1974). Still the century of corporatism?. *The Review of Politics*, 36(1), 85–131.

The Constitutional Court of Turkey. (2010). *5947 sayılı üniversite ve sağlık personelinin tam gün çalışmasına ve bazı kanunlarda değişiklik yapılmasına dair kanunun iptali ve yürürlüğünün durdurulması Anayasa Mahkemesi Kararı (Constitutional court decision on the stay of execution of law on full time work for medical doctors). 2010/29.*

The Constitutional Court of Turkey. (2012). *The ruling of the Constitutional Court. 2011/113.*

The Constitutional Court of Turkey. (2013). *The ruling of the Constitutional Court. 2011/150.*

The Constitutional Court of Turkey. (2014). *The ruling of the Constitutional Court. 2014/61.*

The Ministry of Health. (2011). *Sağlık istatistikleri yıllığı 2010 (Health statistics yearbook 2010).* Ankara: Ministry of Health.

The Republic of Turkey. (1953). *Türk Tabipleri Birliği Kanunu (Turkish medical association law). 6023.*

The Republic of Turkey. (2010). *Üniversite ve Sağlık Personelinin Tam Gün Çalışmasına ve Bazı Kanunlarda Değişiklik Yapılmasına Dair Kanun (Law on full time work for medical doctors). 5947.*

The Republic of Turkey. (2011a). *Sağlık Bakanlığı ve Bağlı Kuruluşlarının Teşkilat ve Görevleri Hakkında Kanun Hükmünde Kararname (Statutory decree on the organisation and duties of the ministry of health and its subsidiary institutions). KHK/663.*

The Republic of Turkey. (2011b). *Adalet Bakanlığı'nın Teşkilat ve Görevleri Hakkında Kanun Hükmünde Kararnamenin Değiştirilerek Kabulü Hakkında Kanun ile Bazı Kanun ve Kanun Hükmünde Kararnamelerde Değişiklik Yapılmasına Dair Kanun Hükmünde Kararname (Statutory decree on the promulgation of the law changing the organisation and responsibilities of the ministry of justice and statutory decree changing other statutory decrees). 650.*

The Republic of Turkey. (2014a). *Sağlık Bakanlığı ve Bağlı Kuruluşlarının Teşkilat ve Görevleri Hakkında Kanun Hükmünde Kararname ile Bazı Kanunlarda Değişiklik Yapılmasına Dair Kanun (statutory decree on the organisation and responsibilities of the ministry of health and affiliated institutions and law changing other laws). 6514.*

The Republic of Turkey. (2014b). *Tam gün yasası uygulaması (Implementation of full time law). 2014/8.*

Tıp Dünyası. (2003, July 15). TTB'nin 53. Büyük Kongresi'ne katılan Sağlık Bakanı Akdağ: "Hastanın cebinden elinizi çekin" (Minister of health akdağ participated in Turkish medical association's 53rd congress: "Stay away from patients' pockets"). *Tıp Dünyası*, 108.

TTB. (2008). *Sağlık Personelinin Tam Gün Çalışmasına ve Sağlıkla İlgili Bazı Kanunlarda Değişiklik Yapılmasına Dair Kanun Tasarısı Taslağı Hakkında Türk Tabipleri Birliği Görüşleri (Views of Turkish medical association on the draft law on full time work for the health personnel and changing other laws related to health).* Ankara: TTB.

TTB. (2011b, May 25). AKP sağlık politikası: Yalanlar ve gerçekler (Health policy of the AKP: Lies and truths). *Bağımsız İletişim Ağı.*

TTB. (2011c). *Saggĝlık Personelinin Tam Suĝre Cĝalısĝmasına ve Bazı Kanunlarda Deggĝisĝiklik Yapılmasına Dair Kanun Tasarısı Oĝnerisi*

(Proposal for draft law on the full time work for medical professionals and on making changes in certain laws). Ankara: TTB.

TTB. (2012, July 20). *Anayasa Mahkemesi (bir kez daha) iptal etti (The constitutional court rescinded once again). Ttb.org.tr.*

TTB. (2013, February 15). *Anayasa Mahkemesi'nin 663 sayılı KHK'nin iptal ettiği maddeleri (Clauses that the Constitutional Court annulled in the* Statutory Decree *no. 663). Ttb.org.tr.*

TTB. (2014). *Türk Tabipler Birliği: Nedir? Ne yapar? (Turkish medical association: What is it? What does it do?).* http://www.ttb.org.tr/index.php/bilgi.html. Accessed 10 July 2014.

Walt, G., Shiffman, J., Schneider, H., Murray, S.F., and Brugha, R. (2008). 'Doing' health policy analysis: Methodological and conceptual reflections and challenges. *Health Policy and Planning*, 23(5), 308–317.

Yalçın, Z. (2009, June 8). Bütün gürültü 1200 hoca için çıkarılıyor (All this mess is because of 1200 university professors). *Sabah.*

CHAPTER 8

Private Healthcare Provider Organisations as New Actors in the Politics of Healthcare

8.1 Introduction

Successive governments and the TTB dominated the healthcare politics scene until the end of the 1980s, when the WB entered as another major actor. The HTP then generated other strong political actors: private healthcare provider groups and their business associations.

The Private Hospitals and Health Institutions Association (*Özel Hastaneler ve Sağlık Kuruluşları Derneği, OHSAD*), established as a voluntary business organisation one year after the launch of the reform, emerged as a pioneering actor representing private healthcare providers in healthcare politics. OHSAD consolidated sectoral interests and began functioning as a pressure group to persuade the government to increase the role of the private sector in healthcare provision. The relationship between OHSAD and the government can be better understood when examined within the peculiar political and historical context of state-business relationships in Turkey.

The chapter examines the following: the emergence of and the role played by private healthcare provider organisations as actors in the politics of healthcare in Turkey, the discourse they employed in influencing the reform, the content of their demands and their concerns about the reform, and the strategies they used to reach out to members of the government and the healthcare bureaucracy.

V. Yılmaz, *The Politics of Healthcare Reform in Turkey*,
DOI 10.1007/978-3-319-53667-5_8

8.2 The Literature on the Relationship Between the State and Business Organisations in Healthcare Politics

With regard to the liberal perspective that naturalises free markets, Polanyi responded that 'the road to the free market was opened and kept open by an enormous increase in continuous, centrally organised and controlled interventionism' (2001, p. 146). The HTP is a quintessential example of the market-constituting role of the state. It effectively created a new market, a quasi-market, in healthcare provision by including private healthcare providers in the public health insurance plan and by providing incentives for the establishment of private hospitals. The increasing marketisation of healthcare services had a substantial impact on healthcare politics, namely the diversification of the political actors in the healthcare politics landscape and reshuffling the power distribution among these actors.

While the increase in the role of the private sector in healthcare delivery is part of a global trend, the form it takes in different local contexts differs. Arguing against the proposition that economic globalisation leads to the convergence of economic and social welfare policies, Hall and Soskice have introduced an approach called the varieties of capitalism to demonstrate that responses of national economies to globalisation are path-dependent (Hall and Soskice 2001). Following in the footsteps of this approach, I believe it is important to contextualise and historicise the relationship between private health provider organisations and the state in order to understand the influence of the former on healthcare policies.

Bennett notes that the literature on the role of private healthcare providers in contemporary healthcare systems in emerging market economies has been underresearched (1991, p. 50). While the healthcare reform literature on emerging market economies successfully addresses the influences of international financial institutions, national governments, healthcare bureaucracy on reforms leading to marketisation of healthcare services (e.g. Batley 2004; Armada et al. 2001; Berman and Bossert 2000), international epistemic communities (e.g. Freeman 1999) and 'peer dynamics' between similar countries (e.g. Brooks 2005), it only rarely examines private healthcare provider organisations as potentially important actors in healthcare reforms in these countries.

Giaimo and Manow's comparative study of healthcare reforms in Britain, Germany and the United States (1999) and Giaimo's follow-up study in the same countries (2005) are two studies that have examined the relationship between states and private healthcare providers in their analysis of healthcare politics in advanced capitalist societies. Giaimo argues:

> The reasons for these different reform outcomes lay in the specific constellation of actors and institutions in the political and healthcare systems of each country that underpinned the capitalist settlement in healthcare. Together, they created distinct reform politics in each nation that produced different mixtures of governance instruments and that proved more or less amenable to market solutions. Formal institutions and the balance of political forces in the political arena either granted or denied healthcare stakeholders entry to the policy process to shape reform and thus affected the capacity of governments to formulate and enact a radical market programme. (Giaimo 2005, p. 4)

Giaimo thus successfully contextualises the politics of healthcare; she invites students of healthcare politics to appreciate the diversity of political actors, examine the power dynamics between these actors and situate them within a political system.

While Giaimo draws strictly institutionalist conclusions such as that single-party governments in centralised political systems are free to unilaterally decide the terms of the healthcare reform (2005, p. 195), she also underlines the agency of special-interest groups that may challenge the institutional barriers that block access to decision-making mechanisms (Giaimo 2005, p. 196). Similarly, Giaimo and Manow questioned the static analysis of institutionalism and asserted that arguments based on the power of political systems to shape each political actor's influence on policy outcomes (e.g. Immergut 1992) do not help scholars examine the exact direction that healthcare systems take after the reform (Giaimo and Manow 1999, p. 993).

Therefore, they urge students of healthcare politics to consider the pre-existing institutional context that shapes the politics without underestimating the power of existing actors to effect change. Their position is as follows:

> Policy makers have had to anticipate the views of key healthcare actors in the reform debates and have tailored their reform policies to fit the existing institutional configuration of their given healthcare system. In addition, sectoral institutions may provide or deny government actors leverage over, and links to, healthcare providers and payers. These linkages, in turn, affect state capacity to intervene in the health sector, to shape market forces in

> healthcare, and to take a leading role in the project of reform. (Giaimo and Manow 1999, pp. 993–4)

The merit of Giaimo and Manow's perspective lies in its ability to relativise the power of policymakers and situate them within a set of other political actors including actors representing strong business interests.

Despite its emphasis on the multiplicity of political actors in healthcare politics, Giaimo's approach does not call for an analysis based on a pluralist understanding of politics. When actors gain economic power in the healthcare market, their economic power can translate into political power in healthcare politics. Giaimo maintains that it is crucial to examine the inter-linkages between the health sector and healthcare politics in order to understand the power basis of each political actor. She explains this inter-linkage between the health sector and healthcare politics as follows:

> However, the political arena tells only part of the story of healthcare reform. A full explanation requires that we look also at the health sector itself and its interplay with the political arena. Thus, existing policies and institutional arrangements in the health sector both created and reinforced certain expectations on the part of the public and stakeholders as to the appropriateness of state intervention in the health sector. (Giaimo 2005, p. 4)

Another of Giaimo's contributions to the study of healthcare politics is her emphasis on ongoing political conflicts in the post-legislative process of healthcare reforms, even after the failure of a reform effort (2005, p. 196). This insight is in line with the position of historical institutionalist scholars in terms of the emphasis they place on the impact of policies on politics, or the notion of 'policy feedback' (Pierson 1993). While most political scientists focus only on legislative victories and failures in investigating the politics during healthcare reforms, Giaimo underlines the fact that political contestations continue after the promulgation of key legislations and that these contestations can be as powerful as pre-legislative ones in terms of their impact on policy outcomes. Jacobs and Skocpol's study on healthcare politics during President Obama's healthcare reform also indicates that a legislative victory in a healthcare reform is not the finish line for political contestations between different political actors. Instead, a victory can ignite new contestations, which may have the power to fundamentally change the future direction of the healthcare system (Jacobs and Skocpol 2010, p. 7).

8.3 The Literature on the Relationship Between the State and Business Organisations in Healthcare Politics in Turkey

One has to look closely at the historical and political structures of the state-business relationship in Turkey in order to understand the actual contestations and negotiations that have taken place between private healthcare providers, their organisations and the government during the HTP.

Relationships between the state, the government, and business in Turkey are complex. Historically, Turkey's bourgeoisie has been a product of the nation-state making process. One of the major objectives of the newly founded Republic of Turkey was to give birth to a 'national bourgeoisie' that would replace the non-Muslim and non-Turkish bourgeoisie of the late Ottoman period (Keyder 1987). It can therefore be argued that Turkey's bourgeoisie owes its very existence to the state.

After the establishment of the Republic, the bureaucracy contributed to the emergence of domestic manufacturing bourgeoisie, which then made it possible to pursue import-substituting industrial developmentalist policies (Keyder 1987, pp. 129–137). As the state had the upper hand, the ability of the business community to formulate its interests independent of the state was limited. In line with the corporatist ethos of the first three quarters of the twentieth century, Heper suggests that all business community organisations in Turkey were established either directly by the state or with the support of the state (1991, p. 15). For example, the establishment by law of the Turkish Union of Chambers and Commodity Exchanges (TOBB) in 1950 proved Heper's suggestion.

The fact that business organisations were closely associated with and controlled by the state did not mean that the business community did not negotiate in favour of its own interests. As Heper indicates, negotiations between the business community and the state did not operate through institutional channels: '*Individual* members of the private sector often by-passed their interest group associations and attempted establishing *clientele* relations with government officials' (1991, p. 17). Therefore, clientelism and particularism were the main characteristics of the relationship between the state, the government and the business community.

While the government supported the capital accumulation of the business community, they never welcomed the participation of business organisations in public policy-making processes (Buğra 1997, p. 324) or embraced the use of an interest-based discourse by business organisations (Buğra 1997, p. 355). In response, Buğra argues, while Turkish businessmen perceived the state as the main source of uncertainty in the growth of the private sector, they were also well aware that they owed their acquired social status to the state. Therefore, businessmen in Turkey did not call for a 'free market' economy but rather always asked the state for close cooperation with the private sector (Buğra 1997, p. 176).

There were attempts from the business community to formulate its own class interests by coming together under the umbrella of voluntary organisations. Established in 1961, TİSK was the first voluntary organisation of the business community. Big industrialists, however, were not content with the representation structure of TİSK, which distributed power in favour of small- and medium-sized companies in the way the TOBB did. As a result, TÜSİAD was established in 1971. TÜSİAD is 'the first example of an explicit interest group that is voluntary' (Esmer 1991, p. 132). Esmer suggests that big industrialists established TÜSİAD because they felt that power distribution in TOBB and TİSK did not reflect their market shares (1991, p. 133).

While TÜSİAD proved to be politically effective in developing a class agenda that could be more confrontational than corporatist business organisations such as the TOBB, Esmer underlines the fact that TÜSİAD always sought public legitimacy by reconciling its own interests with general social interests (1991, p. 133). Similarly, Buğra states that the narratives of Turkish businessmen were almost apologetic with respect to their quest for capital accumulation, and even businessmen themselves felt uneasy about the social legitimacy of working for material gains (1997, p. 42).

The birth of TÜSİAD did not suffice to break the clientelistic relationship between individual businessmen and the state. The state steadfastly refused to recognise TÜSİAD as mediator between the state and big business. Instead, the state continued to deal with businessmen individually, which in turn disempowered the legitimacy and representative power of TÜSİAD within the business community (Buğra 1997, p. 349). Buğra and Savaşkan explain the nature of state-business relationship in Turkey before 1980 as follows:

> The Turkish business environment was characterised, first and foremost, by the nature of the relations between the government and big business, which were carried outside the frame of organised interest representation. The relations of the latter with the government were characterised by particularism and clientelism, but were also rife with tensions. To the extent that one can see these two parties as partners in development, the dominant partner was surely the one holding the political power. (Buğra and Savaşkan 2014, p. 10)

Yalman questions Buğra and Savaşkan's claim that those holding political power had more power than the business community. He contends that the fact that the state in Turkey always acted in favour of the business community in its economic policies might well prove the strength of the bourgeoisie rather than its relative impotency (2009, p. 344). While Yalman's theoretical argument might be valid in understanding the relationship between the state and the business in the long term, it is hardly useful in an empirical analysis of interactions between the state and the business community, of conflicts within the business community and of the formulation of business interests in a specific sector and within a particular historical and political context.

In response, Buğra and Savaşkan proposed a perspective that enabled an empirical yet historically grounded analysis of the state-business relationship and demonstrated how market actors might define the political interests that transcend their short-term market interests:

> Individual economic gain does not seem to be a sufficient motive to explain the broader scope and underpinnings of the relations among the actors involved. In the Turkish case, these relations were part of a politically guided process of class transformation that reshaped and influenced the configuration of business interests and the interface between economic power and the political influence of the private sector. The interaction was situated in networks that brought business actors together with the government and operated according to a logic that extended beyond economic concerns and, in certain cases, even conflicted with efforts to maximise short-term private economic interests. (Buğra and Savaşkan 2014, p. 77)

Buğra and Savaşkan note that individual economic gain, which is apparently crucial for the sustainability of the business, is not the only motive that drives the business community. However, the inter-linkages between the business community and the state might require the business community to go against its immediate economic gains for achieving a greater goal, which

Buğra and Savaşkan conceptualise as 'the politically guided process of class transformation' (2014, p. 12). Therefore, rather than searching for the dominant partner in state-business relations, scholars advise investigating 'a form of interaction that involves a mutual dependency between the government and the business' (Buğra and Savaşkan 2014, p. 12).

In their analysis of the state-business relationship in the AK Party period, Buğra and Savaşkan draw significant conclusions. First, they argue that particularism is still salient in government-big business relations (Buğra and Savaşkan 2014, p. 109), which are hardly mediated by business associations (Buğra and Savaşkan 2014, p. 12). Second, voluntary business associations, however, have gained power, which should be taken into consideration (Buğra and Savaşkan 2014, p. 109). Third, they suggest that 'the state might not only form the market, but also the market actors themselves through the processes of politically supported capital accumulation and business development' (Buğra and Savaşkan 2014, p. 170). Fourth, scholars underline that the privatisation of healthcare services (referring to the privatisation of healthcare provision) has been one of the sectors where the state created markets and gave rise to new market actors (Buğra and Savaşkan 2014; Yılmaz 2013; Adıyok 2012).

8.4 Private Healthcare Providers in Turkey's Healthcare System Before the Reform

Before the HTP was launched in 2003, healthcare provision in Turkey had been dominated by public hospitals and public health centres. Private clinics owned by medical doctors also played an important role in the structure of healthcare provision before the reform. Medical doctors had the right to open and work in their own private clinics alongside their duties in public hospitals. In a healthcare system that failed to provide sufficient services for all and that offered relatively low salaries for medical doctors, the dual practice laid the foundation for a system where patients made informal payments to medical doctors and where healthcare services were implicitly commodified. People willing to cut into the waiting line or to receive more attention from their doctor, went to private clinics before and during their treatments in public hospitals and made payments under the table to medical doctors before undergoing an operation. Therefore, Turkey's healthcare provision structure before the HTP could be categorised as a public-dominated one that had strong informal elements of commodification.

In the early days of the Republic, private hospitals were established and operated by non-Muslim minorities and foreigners, which constituted only a marginal element of healthcare delivery. The promulgation of the Private Hospitals Act provided them a legal status and introduced regulations they had to comply with (The Republic of Turkey 1933). During the 1960s and 1970s, private sector healthcare provision was comprised of private clinics and small-sized laboratory and radioscopy services (Temel 2003, p. 4). In the aftermath of the military coup of 1980, which oppressed political opposition to the neo-liberalisation of the Turkish economy, the economy began a march towards neoliberalisation and an externally oriented growth strategy.

The change in the country's macroeconomic policy was reflected in the trajectory of social policies, which manifested themselves in the commencement of a political agenda that promoted more private sector involvement in education and healthcare services. In line with the global wave of healthcare reform, governments started to adopt a new language within which health services began to be referred to as 'the health sector' after the 1980s (Ersoy 1998). Governments introduced economic incentives for the private sector to invest in healthcare provision (Günal 2008). This policy started to yield results in 1990s with an increased private sector presence, first in outpatient and then in inpatient services (Temel 2003, p. 4; Belek et al. 1998). At a time when public investment in healthcare was at a low level, the share of the private sector in the total volume of investment exceeded that of the public sector in the early 1990s (Soyer 2005). Despite the emergence of private hospitals in the 1980s, it should be noted that the scope of private healthcare provision was quite limited until the implementation of the HTP. Private hospitals established between the 1980s and the early 2000s were limited in number and service capacity, based in metropolitan areas and primarily served well-to-do citizens.

One interviewee, who had established a medium-sized private hospital in the early 1990s and still runs it, succinctly summarised the state of private hospitals before the mid-2000s:

> There was almost no connection between private hospitals and the public sector before 2000. We generally catered to those who were not covered by public social security and who had money. I am talking about the situation in Istanbul. There was really a very powerless structure in Anatolia[1] anyway. (Interview no. 24)

Against this background, the HTP symbolised a new era for the private sector in the provision of healthcare services. First of all, the Urgent Action Plan of the first AK Party government declared that one of the government's main objectives in healthcare was to provide incentives for the private sector to invest in healthcare (The Republic of Turkey 2003, p. 11). The language of the Urgent Action Plan was generally vague, but the HTP explicitly stated that the Programme would deliver 'competition in service provision' and that the MoH would be restructured so as to assume responsibility for planning and monitoring (The Ministry of Health 2003, pp. 26–7). Similarly, the WB project, which aimed to support the success of the Programme, was responsible for the transformation of the MoH role from that of a provider body to a controlling and planning agency, which was hailed as the first indicator of success of the project (World Bank 2010, iii). Finally, then Prime Minister Erdoğan openly declared, 'Free markets should also be established in healthcare' (Hürriyet 2006). In practice, as scholars suggested, the market direction of the HTP has been most visible in the provision dimension of the Programme (Ağartan 2012; Yılmaz 2013).

Second, the government began to use a public-private partnership (PPP) model in the construction and operation of public hospitals (The Republic of Turkey 2005b).[2] With the objective of finding an alternative way to finance the extension of healthcare services (rather than increasing public expenditures), the government sought private investment in healthcare provision through the introduction of PPP in the establishment of large hospital complexes referred to as 'city hospitals' (*şehir hastaneleri*). In return for private company investment in the construction of the hospital complexes, the government offered these companies the right to operate all non-medical services for 49 years. Construction companies expressed interest in these projects. Potential tensions may arise between investors of private hospitals in the AK Party period and the partners of the government in PPP projects in healthcare delivery in near future.

More importantly, the government decided to integrate private hospitals[3] into the public health insurance plan in 2005, which was the next step after the purchaser and provider functions were split in the healthcare system. Before the reform, the SSK functioned as an insurance body for blue-collar workers that also owned and operated hospitals serving this constituency. Once all public hospitals had been transferred to the MoH with the objective of eventually granting them financial and administrative autonomy, the government began to implement one of the key objectives of the HTP: fostering private sector involvement in the provision of healthcare services.

The integration of private hospitals into the public health insurance plan works in the following way: The SGK annually sets and announces fees for services to be provided by private hospitals in the form of Health Implementation Statements. If they are interested, private hospitals sign a Service Procurement Agreement with the SGK. Once agreements are signed, citizens (assuming they have no premium debts to the public health insurance fund) have the option of receiving healthcare services from private hospitals. There is no referral system in Turkey's healthcare system, so citizens are not required to apply first to general practitioners (or family physicians, as they have been called in Turkey's healthcare system since the reform) for a referral to specialists. Furthermore, no other restriction (e.g. geographical) is imposed on citizens in choosing a hospital.

Citizens may be required to make payments to top-up their public health insurance if they apply to private hospitals. Private hospitals have the legal authorisation to charge patients. Two factors influence the rate of such additional payments. The first is that the SGK determines a cap on additional payments. Second, the level of this cap varies according to the specific hospital's ranking in the MoH system that identifies the quality of healthcare services provided. Therefore, one has to make additional payment to access private hospitals, and larger payments are required in order to access the better quality ones. As a result, the introduction of additional payments and the inclusion of private hospitals into the public health insurance plan exacerbated income-based inequalities in access to healthcare services (Yılmaz 2013).

Similar to the integration of private hospitals into the public health insurance system, the HTP also aimed to turn the MoH into a stewardship agency rather than a provider of healthcare services. With the transfer of all publicly owned health facilities to the MoH,[4] the Ministry became the owner of the overwhelming majority of public healthcare providers in the country, the only exception being public university hospitals. Finally, as the new legal changes were enacted, the transformation of the Ministry's role from that of provider to steward began, and public hospital unions were established (The Republic of Turkey 2011a).[5]

8.5 The Position of the Private Sector in Healthcare Provision After the Reform

The HTP redrew the boundaries of the private sector in the delivery of healthcare services in Turkey. In addition to the inclusion of private hospitals into the public health insurance plan, which was the most generous incentive, government incentives for the establishment of private hospitals continued. The IFC also financially supported selected large hospital chains from the beginning of the reform process (IFC 2012a, 2007; Joseph 2006; Albawaba 2003). This section demonstrates how and to what extent the role of the private sector has changed in healthcare delivery in the last decade.

The HTP clearly led to an increase in the number of private hospitals. The number of private hospitals nearly doubled after the launch of the HTP, as shown in Table 8.1. This dramatic increase was not paralleled by a similar increase in other hospital types.

Another indicator of the increasing role of the private sector in the provision of healthcare services is the increasing number of beds in private hospitals. Table 8.2 presents the figures.

The bed capacity of private hospitals almost quadrupled with the healthcare reform. The bed capacity of public and university hospitals also increased during the same timeframe, yet the rate of increase in these hospital types remained far below that of private hospitals.

Table 8.3 shows the changes in the number of beds in different hospital types in relation to the total number of beds.

The largest change in the share of bed capacity occurred in private hospitals. While the share of bed capacity in private hospitals has almost tripled since the launch of the healthcare reform, the share of bed capacity in public hospitals has experienced a decrease of roughly 7 per cent. University hospitals, a category that includes the hospitals of private universities, has increased their share of bed capacity in this time period, yet with a small increase of approximately 2 per cent. Tables 8.1, 8.2 and 8.3 indicate that privatisation – though this does not occur in the form of a direct transfer of public hospitals into the private sector – has been increasing in the provision of healthcare services.

Figures on the number of hospitals, bed capacity and the share of bed capacity provide an indication of major trends in healthcare delivery structure, but it is also important to look at the number of applications that different hospital types receive. Table 8.4 indicates this change.

Private hospitals received almost one-fifth of all applications to health institutions in 2015. While the private hospital sector established in the pre-reform period was concentrated in a few major cities and served only the top quintile of the income distribution, new private hospitals substantially increased the capacity, spread throughout the country and began to serve middle-income patients.

Table 8.1 Number of hospitals, in terms of ownership of hospitals, 2002–2015

	2002	*2006*	*2007*	*2008*	*2009*	*2010*	*2011*	*2012*	*2013*	*2014*	*2015*
Public	774	767	848	847	834	843	840	832	854	866	865
University	50	56	56	57	59	62	65	65	69	69	70
Private	271	331	365	400	450	489	503	541	550	556	562
Other	61	49	48	46	46	45	45	45	44	37	36
Total	1,156	1,203	1,317	1,350	1,389	1,439	1,453	1,483	1,517	1,528	1,533

Table 8.2 Bed capacity in different hospital types, in terms of ownership of hospitals, 2002–2015

	2002	*2006*	*2007*	*2008*	*2009*	*2010*	*2011*	*2012*	*2013*	*2014*	*2015*
Public	107,394	110,819	112,037	114,428	115,443	120,180	121,297	122,322	121,269	123,690	122,331
University	26,341	31,193	30,978	29,912	30,112	35,001	34,802	35,150	36,056	36,670	38,361
Private	12,387	14,639	17,397	20,983	25,178	28,063	31,648	35,767	37,983	40,509	43,645
Other	18,349	17,691	17,588	17,905	17,905	16,995	6,757	6,833	6,723	5,967	5,311
Total	164,471	174,342	178,000	183,228	188,638	200,239	194,504	200,072	202,031	206,836	209,648

The Ministry of Health (2012, p. 64, 2016, p. 93)

Table 8.3 Share of bed capacity/total bed capacity for different hospital types, in terms of ownership of hospitals, 2002–2015

	2002	*2006*	*2007*	*2008*	*2009*	*2010*	*2011*	*2012*	*2013*	*2014*	*2015*
Public	65.3	63.6	62.9	62.5	61.2	60.0	62.4	61.1	60.0	59.8	58.4
University	16.0	17.9	17.4	16.3	16.0	17.5	17.9	17.6	17.8	17.7	18.3
Private	7.5	8.4	9.8	11.5	13.3	14.0	16.3	17.9	18.8	19.6	20.8
Other	11.2	10.1	9.9	9.8	9.5	8.5	3.5	3.4	3.3	2.9	2.5

Calculated by the author based on The Ministry of Health (2012, p. 64, 2016, p. 93)

Table 8.4 Distribution of total applications to hospitals by type of healthcare providers, in terms of ownership of hospitals, 2002–2015

	2002	*2013*	*2014*	*2015*
Public sector	88.3	73.3	73.7	73.3
University	7.1	7.9	8.1	8.3
Private sector	4.6	18.8	18.2	18.4

Calculated by the author based on The Ministry of Health (2016, p. 139)

As the HTP made the SGK the single payer of healthcare services and included private hospitals into the public health insurance plan, the SGK began to transfer financial resources for these hospitals in return for the services they provided. As a result, the share of public expenditures for private provision of healthcare services has been on the rise since 2002. Table 8.5 shows the changes in the breakdown of SGK expenditures according to hospital type.

The largest increase in the share of SGK funds transferred to different hospital types occurred in private hospitals. While 14 per cent of the total SGK expenditures went for healthcare services in private hospitals in 2002, the share had increased to 28.2 per cent by 2011. Despite a more than 10 per cent decline in the share of expenditures made for public hospitals, these expenditures still constitute more than half of SGK total expenditures for healthcare services.

The breakdown of total investment figures in healthcare according to sector suggests a potential for the private sector to increase its role in healthcare delivery in the future. The share of the private sector in the total volume of investment in healthcare services exceeded that of the public sector since early 1990s (Soyer 2005). The share of private investments

Table 8.5 Breakdown of the share of SGK expenditures according to different hospital types, 2002–2011

	2002	*2006*	*2009*	*2010*	*2011*
Public sector	64.2	64.0	51.8	52.1	52.3
University	21.8	15.6	19.1	20.3	19.5
Private sector	14.0	20.4	29.1	27.6	28.2

Figures of 2002 and 2006 were calculated by the author based on Sönmez (2011, p. 60). Figures of 2009, 2010 and 2011 were calculated by the author based on SGK (2012)

Table 8.6 Sizes of private hospitals, 2011

Bed capacity	*No. of hospitals*	*No. of beds*	*Share of hospitals*	*Share of beds*
200–600	10	2,791	2	9.9
100–199	58	7,374	11.8	26.2
50–99	137	9,215	28	32.7
0–49	285	8,767	58.2	31.1
Total	490	28,147	100	100

Sönmez (2011, p. 75)

in healthcare provision between 2006 and 2010 roughly constituted two-thirds of total investments made in healthcare provision (Sönmez 2011, pp. 71–2).

One should note that private healthcare providers constitute a heterogeneous group. Three types of variation within private hospitals can be identified, which can be of importance in understanding healthcare politics within the delivery sector today. The descriptors of these variations are when they were established (before or after the reform), size and investors (foreign or domestic).

In terms of when they were established, private hospitals can be categorised into two ideal types: those serving public insurees and those serving individuals with private health insurance plans or with high incomes. These two groups differ on the basis of the source of their main revenues. While the major source of revenue for most of the second group is out-of-pocket payments from high-income individuals and private health insurance companies, the major source of revenue for the first group is the public health insurance fund.

Second, there are different sizes of private hospitals in the sector. Table 8.6 illustrates the diversity in the size of private hospitals on the basis of their bed capacity for the year 2010.

The private hospital sector is a diverse one in terms of bed capacity. Private hospitals with a capacity of up to 49 beds constituted more than half of the sector. Their bed capacity constituted approximately 31 per cent of the total bed capacity of private hospitals. At the top end of the spectrum, only 10 private hospitals had a bed capacity of more than 200 in 2010. While the share of hospitals in this cluster stood at only 2 per cent, the share of bed capacity in these hospitals constituted almost 10 per cent of total bed capacity in private hospitals.

Table 8.7 FDI in healthcare, 2006–2011

	2006	*2007*	*2008*	*2009*	*2010*	*2011*
Total FDI in healthcare services	265	177	149	106	111	232
Total FDI (million dollars)	17,639	19,137	14,747	6,252	6,238	15,703
Share of FDI in healthcare	1.5	0.9	1.0	1.7	1.8	1.5

The Ministry of Economy of Turkey (2012, p. 14)

The table offers only a snapshot of the sector. News stories (e.g. Doğu 2010) reveal a concentration tendency in the private hospital sector. This sector has become home to private hospital groups such as the Acıbadem Health Group, which started as a domestic company and sold to international investors (Milliyet 2011). Many private healthcare provider companies are listed on the Istanbul Stock Exchange (Sönmez 2011, p. 74). Given that the economic rationale of the SGK's current pricing system for private hospitals depends on the logic of profiting from high demand, chain hospitals are in an advantageous position, as they have the ability to use economies of scale. If the current pricing system remains intact, this will further increase pressure on most private hospitals to form hospital chains or to join one of the existing ones.

Foreign direct investment in private hospitals sector might result in a variation within the sector. Table 8.7 indicates the total amount of foreign direct investment in the healthcare sector as a whole.

The share of foreign direct investment in Turkey's healthcare sector (both the pharmaceutical and private hospital sector) in total foreign direct investment (FDI) per year oscillated between 0.9 per cent and 1.8 per cent between 2006 and 2011. While $111 million was invested in the healthcare sector in Turkey in 2010, investment increased to $232 million in 2011 (The Ministry of Economy of Turkey 2012, p. 4). A breakdown of this substantial amount into the various sectors of healthcare is required in order to arrive at sensible conclusions about the increase.

Interviewees had conflicting views on the potential of the private hospital sector to attract foreign direct investment. For instance, a professor of public health stated:

> It is logical to expect a flow of foreign direct investment in the hospital sector in the upcoming period. If health complexes with thousands of beds are established as promised by the government, I think it will be impossible for the domestic capital in Turkey to operate these hospitals by itself, and such a scale in the hospital sector will whet foreign hospital chains appetite for profit. (Interview no. 13)

In fact, in line with this expectation, mergers between domestic hospital groups and international hospital groups are now being carried out. For instance, one of the best-known mergers in the healthcare delivery sector was the International Heath Care Holding's purchase of 75 per cent of the stock of Turkey's Acıbadem Group at the end of 2011 (Habertürk 2011).

An overview of the private hospital sector after a decade of healthcare reform suggests that the reform clearly resulted in the expansion of the role of the private sector in healthcare provision. Once a marginal component of the healthcare delivery structure, private hospitals have reached a significant capacity. This is evident, as they receive roughly one-fifth of all applications to healthcare institutions. In return for their services, the SGK transfers more than one-fourth of its total expenditures for healthcare services to private hospitals. Higher level of private investment in healthcare provision might increase the rate of private sector expansion in Turkey's healthcare provision and accelerate passive privatisation.

Domestic capital has dominated the private hospital sector until today. Owing to the SGK pricing policy, there was a tendency towards capital concentration in the sector. However, with the exception of a small number of mergers between domestic hospital groups and international hospital groups, there is still no significant change in the share of inflow in the healthcare sector in the total FDI.

Finally, the analysis of the impact of the reform on private healthcare providers in this section demonstrates that the reform led to the emergence of a new cluster of private healthcare providers that constitute the majority of the private sector capacity today and that depend on revenues from the SGK. This dependency relationship between the state and the new business created by the reform echoes the insights of scholars working on state-business relations in Turkey, which will be discussed in the following sections.

8.6 The Birth of New Actors in Healthcare Politics: Private Healthcare Provider Organisations

After the expansion of the private sector's role in the delivery of healthcare services, private healthcare providers started to organise, which was necessary if they were going to negotiate with the government (the Council of Ministers) and the two strong state institutions, the SGK and the MoH. In fact, private hospital owners established working groups within national business organisations and founded their own sectoral business organisations, which have become increasingly involved in debates in the domain of healthcare policy.

However, institutional channels for institutionalised dialogue with non-governmental stakeholders, including private healthcare provider organisations, are limited in policy-making in Turkey. Even in cases where non-governmental stakeholders are included in policy-making mechanisms, their representation remains symbolic. The interaction between private healthcare providers and the government is no exception to this rule.

Among the organisations of private healthcare providers, three stand out as key players: the Health Sector Committee of TÜSİAD, the Health Sector Union of The Union of Chamber and Commodity Exchanges and OHSAD.

The TOBB was founded by law in 1950. In the corporatist structure of Turkey's previous political system, the TOBB served as the highest representative of the private sector. The Health Sector Union of the TOBB was established in 2008. In line with the corporatist legacy of the TOBB, the membership of the Union is composed of leading private hospitals in Turkey, related high-level state officials and representatives of voluntary organisations of private healthcare providers. In addition, the Health Sector Union of the TOBB represents private healthcare providers with one seat in the Planning of Human Resources Committee in the MoH and an another one in the Classification Committee in the Ministry of Labour and Social Security. As explained by an interviewee who served as head of the Health Sector Union of the TOBB, the Union uses all legal channels for lobbying in order to influence the drafting of laws on the health sector. They arrange meetings with bureaucrats from key ministries, share their opinions with the Council of Ministers, present their views in parliamentary committees and work with MPs in order to effect necessary changes to the upcoming legal regulations in the General Assembly of the Parliament (Interview no. 10).

TÜSİAD is Turkey's most powerful voluntary business association and represents the largest enterprises in Turkey's economy. It has a Commission on Social Policies, under which the Health Sector Committee operates. However, this Committee does not work as a representative body. Instead, it functions as an expert group that prepares and publishes reports on healthcare policies, including policy recommendations. One of these, entitled *Charting the Way Forward: Healthcare Reform in Turkey* (TÜSİAD 2005), argued for the introduction of compulsory public health insurance for the entire population but with an opt-out option for those with an income above a specified threshold. The report also supported a stronger role for private healthcare providers and the recognition of greater financial and administrative autonomy for public hospitals (TÜSİAD 2005, pp. 19–35). Other than TÜSİAD's call for an opt-out option in the public health insurance plan, all other recommendations of TÜSİAD were realised as part of the HTP.

In addition to the growing interest in healthcare and the establishment of committees within national business organisations, private hospital owners and hospital managers began to establish their own voluntary sectoral associations (e.g. the Association of Health Managers of Turkey and the Aegean Health Institutions Association) and to revitalise other organisations that had existed before the reform (e.g. OHSAD). All of these business organisations can be classified as interest groups in the classical meaning of the concept.

Among these organisations, OHSAD has been the most active. The product of a working group dating back to 1991, OHSAD was formally established as an association in 2004. The Private Hospitals Association, the Health Institutions Association, the Touristic Regions Health Institutions Association and the Southeastern Anatolia Private Health Business Association joined forces and founded OHSAD. Today it represents roughly 80 per cent of the private hospital sector and has been quite active in developing a common position for private healthcare providers and voicing the demands of the private hospital sector.

The composition of the OHSAD executive board reflects the distribution of power within the private healthcare provision market.[6] Along with the large hospital chains, midsized hospitals and hospital groups also have seats on the executive board, one of whom has served as the head of the executive board.[7] In line with the distribution of power in the executive board, OHSAD's honorary committee is composed of pioneers of the private healthcare provision sector.[8]

The OHSAD decision-making structure gives more power to the largest private healthcare providers. In the OHSAD general assembly, the vote of each hospital is weighted according to its number of beds. The OHSAD charter stipulates that hospitals with more than 75 beds will have seven representatives, hospitals with 50–75 beds will have five, hospitals with 20–49 beds will have three, hospitals with 10–19 will have two and all other health institutions will have a single representative in the general assembly. In addition, the charter states that the number of representatives of groups that own more than one hospital will not increase linearly as the number of hospitals in the group increases. The increase in the number of hospital group representatives will therefore be less than the sum of each hospital's number of representatives, as if each one were owned by different individuals or companies (OHSAD 2004).

In this way, while the voting structure of OHSAD favours large hospital groups more than does the structure of the TOBB, it still restricts the direct translation of the market power of the largest healthcare providers on the decision-making structure of OHSAD. Given a tendency for particularism in relationships between government and big business, this might not altogether eliminate incentives for the largest healthcare providers to engage in particularistic relationships with the government.

The executive board and the honorary committee of OHSAD included members who worked for the healthcare bureaucracy and/or served as members of the leadership cadre of the AK Party. For instance, Mr Tahsin Güney, who sat on the OHSAD executive board in 2014, had served as head of the SGK between 2008 and 2009. In addition, Mr Mehmet Nil Hıdır, also a member of the OHSAD executive board in 2014, served as an MP from the AK Party between 2007 and 2011, worked for the healthcare bureaucracy as head of North Izmir Public Hospitals Union and then as the head of the Public Health Department in Izmir. Finally, Mr Süleyman Soylu, who was vice chairman of the AK Party and the Minister of Interior, was also the member of the honorary committee of OHSAD in 2014. These connections between OHSAD and the healthcare bureaucracy and the government challenge the artificial distinction made between the business community and the bureaucracy as well as between the business community and the government in the pluralist approach to welfare politics.

Formulating a common political position for the sector is a complicated task for private healthcare provider organisations. In response to my question of how and to what extent the Health Sector Union of the TOBB has been able to accommodate the demands of private hospitals with quite different scales of investment and different clientele, a former head of the Health Sector Union stated:

> I can't tell you that we are confident about that. After 2002 a significant imbalance emerged in the sector. On the one hand, you have chain hospitals established by important investors. On the other hand, you have small and medium-sized hospitals.... I don't think it is easy to find a solution that will satisfy all. (Interview no. 10)

As the quote above suggests, the head of the Health Sector Union of the TOBB acknowledges the complexity of reconciling the interests of private healthcare providers, which are diversified in terms of the scale of their investments and the market shares. While the decision-making structure of the Health Sector Union of the TOBB does not provide an easy solution to this, the dominance of the larger private healthcare providers in OHSAD eases the task of developing a common sectoral discourse, most likely favouring the larger private healthcare providers. The current pricing policy of the SGK already favours chain hospitals, as it allows them to benefit from economies of scale. This policy, as part of the reform, not only changed the distribution of power among different players in the market, it also transformed healthcare politics by undermining the legitimacy of the TOBB vis-à-vis private healthcare providers, paving the way for the emergence of OHSAD as the strongest actor to represent the private sector in healthcare provision and possibly sustaining the particularistic relations between state and business.

8.7 Private Healthcare Provider Organisations at Work: Discourses, Demands and Strategies

Increasing the role of private hospitals in healthcare delivery in Turkey has never been a popular political promise in Turkish politics. Public opinion has been averse to the withdrawal of the state from the provision of healthcare services. For instance, in a nationwide survey, researchers found that only 19.1 per cent of respondents agreed with the following statement: 'the government should provide only limited basic healthcare services' (Çarkoğlu and Kalaycıoğlu 2012, p. 11). In other words, an overwhelming majority of Turkey's population favoured the dominance of the state in healthcare provision including specialty medical services.

In spite of their limited political power and lack of institutional veto power, organised labour and the TTB strongly resisted all governmental attempts to increase the role of the private sector in healthcare provision. In a society that has been overwhelmingly in favour of public provision of healthcare services, the opposition has always had the potential to become popular in the event the government were to fail to absorb public demand. These political and cultural values, therefore, had a major impact in framing the discourse of both the government and the private healthcare provider organisations on healthcare reform. Neither the government nor private healthcare provider organisations explicitly called for the privatisation of healthcare services.

The HTP did not adopt direct privatisation, but another form of privatisation arose during the implementation of the Programme. This form of privatisation – passive privatisation – allowed the private sector to increase its share in healthcare delivery. Many scholars perceived the reform as an attempt to privatise healthcare services (Belek 2012; Civaner 2011; Sönmez 2011; Soyer 2007). Among those, Soyer successfully addresses the distinctive feature of privatisation in the Turkish case: the privatisation of healthcare services was implemented by integrating private hospitals into the public health insurance plan. In addition, he claims, the state transferred public resources to finance the private sector, which increased the pace of privatisation (Soyer 2007, pp. 90, 105).

Belek argues that privatisation and marketisation trends became clearer in Turkey's healthcare system in the aftermath of the implementation of the HTP and that these trends have given way to the monopolisation and centralisation of the healthcare sector. Taking these developments into account, he concludes that the HTP has been perfectly aligned with the interests of the bourgeoisie. Indeed, there is also evidence that the bourgeoisie has been in charge of implementing the Programme (Belek 2012, p. 11). As Belek's line of argumentation indicates, this form of analysis has a tendency to treat the private sector as a homogenous group with a clear political prospect of full privatisation of healthcare services provision and does not differentiate between the power resources and interests of the government and those of the private healthcare provider organisations. Thus, their analysis has become short of explaining disagreements within the sector and between the sector and the state, and omits the question of what balance the government would like to strike between public and private healthcare delivery. This line of analysis has the potential to underestimate the role of politics in making predictions for the future.

In fact, without underestimating the political affinity between successive AK Party governments and private healthcare provider organisations, the next part of this section discusses a diverse set of issues that caused controversies between these actors during the preparation and implementation of the HTP. While the two parties were in agreement on some issues, they were in open contestation on others.

First, the HTP has been a double-edged sword for AK Party governments from the beginning. On the one hand, the Programme's positive impact on access to healthcare services was clearly one of the main factors that led to the popularity of the governing party, especially among the low-income constituency. On the other hand, the government had been keen to foster private sector involvement and to make healthcare one of the main sectors within which it would create its allied bourgeoisie. Despite its success in delivering both promises at the same time in the early years of the reform process, pursuing this conflicting political strategy started to put the governing party in an ambivalent political position. Therefore, in order to understand the future direction of Turkey's healthcare system, one has to examine the negotiations and contestations between private healthcare provider organisations and the government.

The HTP did not come into existence as a result of long discussions between government representatives and important stakeholders in the healthcare domain. MÜSİAD, a business organisation that has a political affinity with the AK Party, stated that there had been an 'insufficient exchange of ideas with stakeholders...during the reform process' (MÜSİAD 2009, p. 17). An interview with a former head of the WB team assisting the reform process (Interview no. 22) also provides sufficient evidence for this. The HTP was instead a product of a small reform team (Ağartan 2008). The government constituted the team and backed most of its proposals politically. The WB supported the team financially and, more importantly, provided know-how support.

Members of the reform team clearly were not averse to increasing the role of the private sector in healthcare delivery. The content of the resulting reform, the discourse of the reform team and their professional career paths both before and after the reform provide sufficient evidence for this thesis. However, they disassociated their positions from the private healthcare provider organisations when they were being interviewed. Feeling accountable to the government, they spoke on behalf of the state and presented the direction of the reform in a way that differed from the way private hospital representatives generally did. For instance, one member of the reform team argued:

> One of the important objectives of the Health Transformation Programme was this: Serving the people with all resources in the country, regardless of their ownership [public or private]. (Interview no. 20)

This member of the reform team presented both public and private hospitals as national resources that the state could use in order to provide services to its citizens. Another member of the reform team made a similar statement:

> For citizens, rather than the ownership of healthcare service providers, it is more important whether service is being provided or not. (Interview no. 32)

Both statements indicate that portraying private hospitals as 'national resources', which might imply a corporatist understanding, was common among the members of the reform team.

A member of the reform team noted that private healthcare providers that existed before the reform did not share this approach in the early days of the reform:

> We have seen that once groups who defend their commercial interests realised that the political power was indeed going to implement this reform and that the reform was inevitable, they declared themselves as actors in this process. But we have also seen that they were generally not very supportive of what was being done. (Interview no. 20)

In his view, the government was powerful enough to initiate the reform without regard for commercial interests. Therefore, he suggested, private healthcare providers and their organisations had no choice but to secure a place within the process.

In contrast, a former head of OHSAD argued that they had been willing to collaborate with the government from the beginning. He explained the position of the private hospital sector vis-à-vis the government's stance as follows:

> We asked them (the government) to purchase services from us. We constitute a significant capacity. This capacity should not be left idle. We told

> them to benefit from us, and we signed an agreement with the public social security in 2005. This was an agreement that the private sector was extremely enthusiastic about. (Interview no. 24)

Both the government (and its reform team) and the private sector seemed to share the same discourse: private hospitals are no different from public ones, and the state could and should use these resources in delivering healthcare services to its citizens. This common discourse seemed to work well in resolving possible conflict scenarios and thus in satisfying both parties for a fresh beginning without challenging the public aversion to the privatisation of healthcare services.

After the SGK started to purchase healthcare services from private hospitals in 2005, the HTP served the private hospital sector well until 2008. During this period, more than a hundred new private hospitals were established, and the bed capacity of private hospitals nearly doubled. The first three years after the inclusion of private hospitals into the public health insurance plan is referred to as a laissez-faire period during which the state provided strong incentives for the expansion of private sector healthcare provision without making an effort to regulate the expansion. One member of the healthcare reform team succinctly summarised the state of the private sector in the laissez-faire period of the reform:

> The private sector found a significant opportunity here. The Ministry of Health had failed to respond in a timely way to this process before 2008. It was not against this process, but it was able to control the process and it could have instituted a controlled competition. The Ministry of Health was late in transforming the free market atmosphere into a regulated competitive one. That's why there was an explosion in the number of private hospitals at the time. (Interview no. 20)

This free market atmosphere in private hospitals sector did not last long. A historic moment that changed the relationship between the state and the private hospital sector occurred in February 2008 when the MoH issued a bylaw that introduced significant limitations to the further expansion of the role of the private sector in healthcare provision (The Ministry of Health 2008). This bylaw ruled that the private hospital sector would not be able to extend the range of the services it provided, hire new health professionals or establish new private hospitals without the permission of the MoH. In other words, it allowed only for the establishment of new private hospitals in locations specified by the Ministry and obliged already established private hospitals to comply with the central planning of the Ministry. In the bylaw, the MoH defined its planning role as follows:

> In accordance with the mentioned objectives, the Ministry is authorised to develop plans covering both public and private sectors with respect to health institutions needed for their services, health workforce in these institutions, the medical service branches and qualities of these institutions, and the distribution of technologically-intense medical devices. (The Ministry of Health 2008, clause 9)

Private hospitals were caught unprepared for this sudden change (Güneş 2008). I argue that the shared discourse of the government and private hospital organisations – which conceptualised private hospitals as 'national resources' – broke down with this change. Some private healthcare provider organisations even applied to the Turkish Competition Authority, claiming that the bylaw created a double standard for private hospitals (Coşkun 2008). In response to the strict regulation of private hospitals after the promulgation of this bylaw, some scholars criticised the process by coining the term 'étatisation of private hospitals' and argued that the MoH had overstepped the boundaries of its stewardship role assigned in the healthcare reform (Aksoy 2008).

Despite the fact that private healthcare provider organisations levelled harsh criticisms against this bylaw, they failed to make a difference. This was due to two main factors. First, the private healthcare provider organisations did not have the option of turning to the constituency. In a recent national survey, researchers found that public trust in public hospitals was greater than in private hospitals: 72.3 per cent of the respondents expressed trust in public hospitals, 13.9 per cent said they neither trusted nor distrusted public hospitals and 13.8 per cent expressed distrust in public hospitals. Meanwhile, 45.5 per cent said they trusted private hospitals, 17.7 per cent responded that they neither trusted nor distrusted private hospitals and 36.8 per cent said they did not trust private hospitals at all (Konsensus Araştırma 2011). In a political context where private hospitals were not trusted, private healthcare provider organisations had no choice but to continue the dialogue with the government.

The second factor that impeded the capacity of private healthcare provider organisations to take a politically effective step against the MoH dominance in healthcare delivery is that the majority of private hospitals had already become dependent on the SGK – and therefore on the government, in the Turkish context – for their financial sustainability. One interviewee, a high-level representative of the private hospitals sector, succinctly made this dependency clear in his statement as follows:

> More than 60 per cent of the revenues of private hospitals with signed agreements with the SGK come from the SGK. We have no choice but to live with public social security. (Interview no. 24)

The dependency of the majority of private hospitals on revenues from the SGK forced private healthcare provider organisations to concentrate their efforts on seeking alternative ways to increase their profit margins. One way was to pressure the SGK to increase the prices it set for the services. In this regard, the Health Implementation Statement, issued annually by the SGK, has become one of the most important regulatory tools in the hands of the government. Almost all interviewees from private hospitals expressed their displeasure with the SGK pricing of their services. They argued that these price levels do not match their costs, especially in large cities, as they claimed that private hospitals in metropolitan areas generally pay higher rent and higher salaries for specialist medical doctors.

Although the representatives of private healthcare provider organisations met several times with high-level public officials, they failed to secure an increase in the level of prices in the Health Implementation Statement. This failure can be explained by two factors. First, because any increase in the prices for services would automatically translate into a burden on the public budget, the interests of the private hospitals sector were in direct conflict with that of the government on this issue. Second, the government had a strong weapon in its hands, as an interviewee from the WB pointed out:

> If there were more private health facilities to deal with, the government would not be able to avoid working with medical associations or private hospital associations. Here they can implement the reforms and avoid all these people, so this is again a reflection of the specifics of your heath sector. (Interview no. 22)

As the quote implies, while the private sector is dependent on the government for its revenues, the government is not yet totally dependent on the private sector for delivering healthcare services. This is mainly because the government has the power to directly control more than half of the healthcare delivery structure. The promulgation of the 2008 bylaw can be considered the government's resistance to giving up this effective power resource. From an institutionalist angle, it might well be argued that the dominance of public hospitals in healthcare provision created a 'lock-in effect' during the reform process.

The government also took additional steps to protect its dominance in the healthcare delivery structure. In doing so, the SGK ruled that patients willing to access outpatient services of private hospitals would have to pay a 15 TL (roughly 5 GBP) contributory payment on the spot, while the rate in public hospitals would be 8 TL (~2.75 GBP) for patients willing to use outpatient services (SGK 2010b, Clause 3.2.1). In response, one of the private healthcare provider organisations applied to the Competition Authority:

> Patients coming to our hospitals pay 15 TL, but patients going to public hospitals pay 8 TL. We applied to the Competition Authority.... [who] replied that it could not intervene. Why? They declared that this is public, and you are private. The relationship between the public and private sectors is not a horizontal relationship. The rules of competition cannot be applied to this kind of relationship. This is a vertical relationship, so one cannot talk about competition here. (Interview no. 24)

The decision of the Competition Authority can be interpreted as evidence that the idea of free competition between public and private entities in public services, which formed the backbone of the changes planned in healthcare delivery as part of the HTP, has not become mainstream in the Turkish judiciary.

The Council of State, however, made a decision in the opposite direction in a case filed by the Association of Health Corporations in Turkey against the SGK claiming that the introduction of higher rates for contributory payments for private hospitals was not legal. The Council of State decided to grant a stay of execution (NTVMSNBC 2009). In its decision, the Council of State declared that there is no legal basis for the introduction of different levels of contributory payments for public and private hospitals (The Council of State of Turkey, 2009). Despite the fact that this decision was later repealed by another circle of the Council of State and therefore not implemented, the partial success of private healthcare provider organisations in legal advocacy efforts may yield results in future cases and signal shifting perspectives amongst the judiciary on competition in healthcare delivery.

Legal dimension of political contestations over healthcare policies is of key importance that will have an immense effect on healthcare system in Turkey. The treatment of public healthcare delivery as part of the public law might limit commodification, while the inclusion of healthcare delivery into the realm of the competition law might lead to a de jure end to public sector dominance.

The government also framed private hospitals as 'national resources'. Taking advantage of the private sector's dependence on the government, they prohibited private hospitals from charging patients for emergency healthcare services. Citizens are entitled to use emergency services in private hospitals free of charge. The SGK pays for these services in accordance with the rates it has set. In fact, this was to the detriment of private hospitals, as this regulation prevented them from selling services at a higher price than the amount they would receive from the SGK. However, it was not easy for private healthcare provider organisations to challenge the government's position on this issue, mainly because the public would perceive such an opposition as illegitimate. The head of OHSAD explained how prohibition of private hospitals from charging patients for emergency healthcare services put them in an awkward position: 'Do you think it is possible to go out and tell people that you want to charge for emergency healthcare services?' (Akdağ 2012).

This no-charge policy was extended to intensive care services, burn injury treatment services, neonatal care, organ, tissue, stem cell transplantation, cardiovascular surgery, dialysis, surgery to correct congenital anomalies and oncology (SGK 2010b, Clause 3.3.3).[9] Private healthcare provider organisations did not publicly express their discontent with these responsibilities but decided to take advantage of the situation to argue for the lifting of the cap on additional payments in other healthcare services.

Another controversial issue in the relationship between the private healthcare provider organisations and the government was the assigning of specialist doctors to public and private healthcare providers. The government chose to serve the interests of private healthcare providers instead of those of medical doctors by putting an end to the dual commitment of medical doctors and by refusing to include private clinics into the public health insurance plan. In response, the TTB strongly opposed the government's attempts to put an end to doctors' private practice, which essentially forced medical doctors to work either for public or for private healthcare providers. Owing to a shortage of specialists, private healthcare provider organisations had to compete with public healthcare providers to attract doctors. While they had succeeded in attracting a significant share of medical doctors to work for the private sector before 2008, the government intervention that prohibited the further migration of doctors from the public sector to the private sector restricted the ability of private healthcare providers to increase their share of specialists.

In response to the growing discontent with this restriction among private healthcare providers and the active lobbying of OHSAD, the government and OHSAD signed a memorandum in 2011 (OHSAD 2011) three years after the end of laissez-faire period. The memorandum recognised the government's sole authority over the employment of medical doctors. However, with this memorandum, the government agreed to allocate a thousand additional specialist positions to private hospitals. Therefore, once again private healthcare provider organisations failed to challenge the government regulation – this time in the employment of medical doctors – yet they succeeded in improving their relative position in the new configuration.

Another government regulation of private healthcare delivery regards the cap on the level of additional payments that private hospitals were allowed to charge patients (SGK 2010a). The SGK sets this cap as a percentage of the SGK prices for services. The cap varies according to the quality category that each hospital falls under in the classification of the MoH. Since increasing the SGK prices increases the burden on the public budget, private healthcare provider organisations had to focus their strategies on lifting the cap on additional payments. In other words, shifting the burden to patients has become the best strategy both for the government (as it appeases the private sector without putting a burden on the public budget) and the private sector providers, because it increases their profit margins. Two interviewees from private healthcare provider organisations claimed that their reason for accepting all other government conditions was their hope that the cap on additional payments would be lifted:

> The SGK would pay part of the charges and we would top it up with our prices.... Because we thought we would top it up by charging patients, we didn't really evaluate whether the prices offered by the public social security

> for our services were realistic or not. We were free to opt out of the system as well. (Interview no. 24)

> If caps were lifted, our demand to increase prices in the Health Implementation Statement would cease. (Interview no. 10)

In fact, the Health Sector Union of the TOBB concentrated its energy on lifting the cap on additional payments that they could charge patients with public health insurance plans, because if they were successful in doing so, it would mean the introduction of a free market. While the government did not accept this demand, the Health Sector Union of the TOBB did succeed in increasing the ceiling for the rate of additional payments from 20 per cent of the SGK prices at the time to 100 per cent (Interview no.10). The interviewee explained how this process unfolded:

> In the draft law, there was a clause allowing private hospitals to charge 20 per cent of the prices set in the Health Implementation Statement. Our demand was to remove this clause. Our lobby succeeded in changing the clause, which thus gave the Council of Ministers the authority to determine the cap on additional payments as 100 per cent. The final law included this clause. While we were trying to negotiate the rate, we learnt that the Ministry of Health was insisting that the clause should specify the ceiling as 20 per cent. The change in the clause that we had pushed for offended the Ministry, so in order to appease them, the Council of Ministers determined that the level of contributory payments would be 30 per cent. (Interview no. 10)

As the quote above shows, the Health Sector Union of TOBB had the power to challenge the proposed cap on additional payments by using its connections with the members of the Council of Ministers. While the original proposal of the Health Sector Union of TOBB was not accepted, it succeeded in increasing the cap.

While policy level contestations over the cap on additional payments shapes the future trajectory of marketisation, there is also evidence that points to the failure of the state regulation of monetary transactions between patients and private hospitals. There have been many cases where private hospitals have required additional payments from patients that were above the stipulated level. This illegal practice became increasingly widespread, and newspapers published stories of how excessive payments had been unlawfully requested from patients who used the outpatient services of private hospitals with contracts with the SGK (e.g. Sonay 2012; Tezel 2009).

In response, public institutions began to impose more regulative and punitive measures. For instance, the Court of Accounts imposed a record fine on private hospitals that had charged patients more than the legally permitted amount (Avcı 2012), and the SGK introduced new procedures to thwart attempts by private hospitals to overcharge. These procedures included obliging private hospitals to have their patients sign a printed statement that indicates their agreement to pay a specific amount. The hospitals then had to issue an invoice for any additional payments exceeding a specific amount (100 TL, ~35 GBP), hand the invoice to the patient and inform the patient and accompanying relatives about possible fees once the patient is no longer an emergency case (SGK 2011).

Representatives of private hospital organisations argued that private hospitals, especially those in large cities, argued that they had no other option but to charge patients more than the legally stipulated amount in order not to go bankrupt (Interview no. 10; Interview no. 24). As private healthcare providers searched for informal ways to circumvent the regulations, state institutions responded by implementing even stricter ones.

Although the SGK did not increase the prices it set for the private healthcare providers over the years, the increasing number of patients applying to private hospitals increased the financial burden on the state budget. For this reason, the SGK took a further step and introduced a legal basis for regulating patients' use of their public health insurance to access private hospitals. With the new regulation, the SGK declared:

> The [SGK] Institution may set up procedures and principles regarding the direct use of services of private health providers on the basis of the following factors: the province where the service is provided, whether or not the provided service is of vital importance, *whether the service may be given in public healthcare service providers* [my italics] and the quality of service. (SGK 2010b, Clause 4.2)

With this regulation, the SGK indicated that it might put restrictions on the use of private healthcare services when public healthcare providers offer the same services. This was a significant divergence from the original objective of the HTP, which clearly fostered competition. This SGK regulation can be read as a form of 'institutional inertia'.

Private sector providers are not totally powerless vis-à-vis the government when their interests conflict. After the relationship between the private healthcare provider organisations and the government became tense after the regulations imposed in 2008, one of the representatives of OHSAD made a controversial statement to the public just before signing the Service Procurement Agreement with the SGK in 2012: 'Two thousand patients would die tomorrow unless we didn't sign the agreement' (Vatan 2012).[10] It could be argued that this statement symbolised the power that private healthcare providers had gained with the healthcare provision, which manifested itself in the fact that the total number of patients that private hospitals served in 2011 was more than 3 million (The Ministry of Health 2012, p. 92). However, even during this conflict, the OHSAD representative was unable to refrain from expressing the private sector allegiance to the state, which he perceived as sine qua non to the sustainable growth of private healthcare providers. He stated, 'We established these hospitals by trusting the state's word. We [still] trust the state's word' (Vatan 2012). Therefore, private healthcare providers, while opposing the policy, continued to ask the state to intervene on their behalf, rather than calling for non-intervention.

The current direction of healthcare policies in the domain of healthcare provision might imply that the alliance established in the early years of the reform between the government and private healthcare providers is disintegrating. The former head of OHSAD argued that the government has come to a turning point:

> The state has to decide at this point. Will the private sector exist in this sector or not? To what extent will it exist? To what extent will the state allow the private sector [to exist]? Where will the planning go?... These are all open questions. People's votes will determine the result. I don't believe that this has been done as part of a long-term plan. (Interview no. 24)

The head of OHSAD did not believe that the government had already decided the future direction of Turkey's healthcare system. In fact, the government's preference for a public–private mix in healthcare provision would be important in determining its future direction.

While the ongoing political contestations, including those within the AK Party, will shape the future direction of Turkey's healthcare system, recent developments offer a few hints about what is to come. The government did not increase the prices set by the SGK, but they did offer an increase in the number of specialist medical doctors that private healthcare providers were permitted to hire, allowing private healthcare providers to shift the financial burden to patients. In 2013, the Council of Ministers increased the cap on additional payments from 90 to 200 per cent (*NTVMSNBC* 2013). This change is clearly in line with the demands of private healthcare provider organisations, yet it does not conflict with the government's plans.

In responding to the increase in the cap on additional payments from 90 to 200 per cent, OHSAD representatives declared their discontent with this increase, citing three reasons. First, the cap calculated on the basis of prices set by the SGK was lower than they expected. Therefore, from their perspective, the increase in the cap did not substantially improve the financial situation of private healthcare providers. Second, competition between private healthcare providers on additional payments is high, which limits the ability of each provider to increase additional payments up to the limit of the cap. Third, exempting key services such as oncology and emergency services from additional payments limits the revenues of private hospitals. OHSAD representatives therefore suggested that the government should provide incentives for citizens to buy private health insurance plans (*Al Jazeera Turk* 2014b). It can be argued that OHSAD had opened up a new battlefield for further marketisation, which expanded its boundaries to cover healthcare financing. In fact, this might be the way for private healthcare providers to free themselves from reliance on the state and thus lift obstacles to the full-scale privatisation of healthcare.

It is important to note that the government had various options for solving this crisis with the private healthcare providers, including increasing the prices set by the SGK and providing incentives for patients to choose public healthcare providers. With this policy, the government appeased private healthcare providers but did not openly prevent patients from using their public health insurance plans to access private healthcare providers. However, in practice, the policy shifted the financial burden to patients and further encouraged the marketisation of healthcare services.

8.8 Conclusion

This chapter examined the scale of the privatisation of healthcare provision in Turkey's healthcare system after the HTP and evaluated its impact on the politics of healthcare. In the light of Giaimo and Manow's insights, it focused on the period that followed the legislation of the original reform and examines the political contestations between different actors as well as the impact of these contestations on the direction that the reform took as a result.

As a result of the HTP, the role of private healthcare providers has increased substantially in the last decade. From a negligible share in the total bed capacity and patient applications, private healthcare providers started to constitute around 20 per cent of the country's total hospital bed capacity and receive roughly one-fifth of all applications for healthcare providers annually.

Given the general population's support for the dominance of the public sector in healthcare provision, the government pursued a passive privatisation policy. The main mechanism through which the government fostered private sector involvement in healthcare provision was to incorporate private healthcare services into the public health insurance plan. Drawing on insights from the literature on state-business relations in Turkey, it is argued here that healthcare has been selected by the AK Party as one of the sectors through which the Party would create and strengthen its own business community. Linkages between private healthcare provider organisations and the government as well as the healthcare bureaucracy demonstrate the intricate relationship between the state and the business in Turkey's politics.

The privatisation of healthcare provision led to the emergence of new strong political actors, namely the private healthcare provider organisations. The emergence of private healthcare provider organisations and their integration into healthcare politics can be understood through the concept of 'institutional conversion', which refers to the idea that 'the adoption of new goals or the incorporation of new groups into the coalitions on which institutions are founded can drive a change in the functions that these institutions serve or the role they perform' (Thelen 2004, p. 36). The incorporation of private healthcare providers and their organisations into healthcare politics made it possible to construct an alliance for gradual marketisation in the future. As a brilliant analysis of the post-retrenchment welfare politics in Chile suggests, increase in private sector involvement and the organised interests of private sector actors could restrict the future government's ability to reverse the marketisation dynamic (Kay and Ewig 2011).

OHSAD and the Health Sector Union of TOBB emerged as the strongest actors representing private healthcare providers. It is important to note that private healthcare providers do not constitute a homogenous group, as they differ in terms of size. The government's healthcare policy, which favoured the big players in the healthcare provision market, found its echo in the interest representation of private healthcare providers. In addition to maintaining particularistic relationships between the government and individual businessmen, the big players preferred to work for the common demands of the sector under the umbrella of OHSAD. This preference derives from its decision-making structure, as it offered more weight to big players in comparison to the Health Sector Union of the TOBB.

While OHSAD generally took the lead, both of these organisations focused on three key issues: the prices set by the SGK for private healthcare services, the cap on additional payments that private healthcare providers were allowed to charge patients and the distribution of specialist medical doctors between public and private healthcare providers. In all these issues, private healthcare provider organisations lobbied the government and related public institutions to make changes in favour of their constituency. Because private healthcare provider organisations had depended on the state for the overwhelming portion of their revenues and because of the political impossibility of mobilising the public in favour of privatisation, these organisations had been modest in their demands and avoided direct confrontation with the government.

While the conflict of interest between the government and private healthcare providers over the optimal balance of public and private sectors in delivery will continue to exist in the foreseeable future, the two parties seem to have agreed on a temporary win-win solution. Rather than increasing the SGK set prices to be paid for private healthcare services, the government and private healthcare providers agreed to shift this financial burden to patients by increasing the cap on additional payments. This illustrates how private healthcare provider organisations are able to influence the government when their interests conflict with those of medical doctors and patients, but they fail when their interests are in conflict with those of the government.

It can be claimed that the government serves the further marketisation of healthcare services without always serving the short-term economic interests of private healthcare providers. The government's ability to act with relative autonomy originates from its dominance in healthcare provision, despite the drastic increase in the role of the private sector. Nevertheless, it is not clear whether the government can retain its bargaining power vis-à-vis private healthcare providers in the future if the pace of privatisation in healthcare provision and the oligopolisation tendency continue. Further research is needed to understand the emerging tensions between investors of private hospitals in the AK Party period and the new partners of the government in 'city hospitals' (PPP projects in healthcare delivery) in near future. The increase of private involvement in healthcare provision and its translation to the politics of healthcare appears to further strengthen the marketisation tendency in Turkey's healthcare system, which may infiltrate healthcare financing in near future.

Notes

1. Anatolia here refers to the greater part of Turkey outside Istanbul.
2. In Turkey, PPPs have been increasingly used since the 1980s in various sectors, ranging from highway construction to electricity production and distribution. Earlier forms of PPP in Turkey had been in line with the build-operate model and the build-operate-transfer model. In the aftermath of the promulgation of the memorandum allowing public hospitals to purchase non-medical services from the market by the Ministry of Health in 1985, the first use of PPPs in Turkey's healthcare sector was in the procurement of non-medical services in public hospitals, including catering, maintenance, security and so on. Following this, PPPs have been extended to diagnostic services in public hospitals. In the form of a setup-transfer-operate model, private investors have been allowed to set up diagnostic machinery – computed tomography, magnetic resonance imaging – in public hospitals and operate the diagnostic services for a specific period of time, and later transfer the ownership of the machine to the hospital. Please see Tekin, P. Ş. 2012. Public–private partnerships and the healthcare sector. *Turkish Review*, 2, 48–55.
3. Hospitals associated with 'private' universities constitute a grey area in the study of the role of private hospitals in Turkey's healthcare system. In the Turkish higher education system, it is legally prohibited to establish private universities and therefore private university hospitals. Alternatively, the Turkish higher education system allows the establishment of 'foundation' universities, which are essentially private, and thus foundation university hospitals. In theory, these universities and their hospitals are not allowed to operate for profit. The legal status of foundation universities and their hospitals is vague since it provides some privileges to foundation hospitals that public institutions have, but without endowing them with all privileges of the public institutions. On the one hand, hospitals of foundation universities are not under the direct control of the state but instead are administered by the private foundation's board of trustees. On the other hand, these institutions, which are affiliated with the Higher Education Council, enjoy privileges that public institutions traditionally enjoy. From the perspective of patients, however, hospitals of foundation universities are private hospitals because they charge additional payments in the same way that

private hospitals do. Therefore, for the purpose of this book, hospitals of foundation universities are considered a type of private hospital. However, in the official data, hospitals of foundation universities are categorised under the same category of 'university hospitals' as public university hospitals are categorised. Due to this problem, the official categorisation used in the data presented in the following section should be treated with caution.

4. Despite the dominance of the insurance-based social security system in Turkey, social security institutions (the Social Insurances Institution for blue-collar workers, the Retirement Fund for civil servants and the Pension Fund for the Self-Employed for farmers and the self-employed) did not, in practice, enjoy financial and administrative autonomy. Despite the resistance of trade unions to the transfer of health facilities owned by these pension and health insurance funds as a part of the Health Transformation Programme, the government was able to make the transfer possible without receiving much criticism from the general constituency.
5. According to the new configuration, all public hospitals are transformed into autonomous 'public hospital unions' in order to foster competition between private hospitals and public hospital unions as well as among these unions. The TKHK was founded as a new department of the Ministry of Health in charge of establishing new public hospitals and administering the healthcare services in public hospitals. While this configuration did not provide full autonomy to public hospitals, as the head institution was still directly part of the Ministry, this step can be considered the first step in experimenting with autonomy for public hospitals. The main difference between public hospitals and newly established public hospitals unions was in their management structures. While it was chief medical doctors who had previously administered state hospitals, professional managers were employed on contract for two or three years to administer public hospital unions. Unlike life-long positions of medical doctors working for public hospitals, these managers could be fired and replaced by a new manager.
6. The executive board of OHSAD was composed of but not limited to the following persons affiliated with largest hospital chains in the market as of 2014: Fahrettin Koca from the Medipol Group, Sema Akgün from the Memorial Group, Ahmet Şah Kolan from Kolan Hospitals, Muharrem Usta from Medical Park and Liv Hospitals, Hüseyin Bozkurt from the Medicana Group, Azmi Ofluoğlu from the Universal Group, Erhan Kamışlı from Medline, Nurettin Demirkol from the Hisar Hospitals.
7. The executive board of OHSAD also included the following representatives of midsized hospitals as of 2014: Yusuf Ziya Yıldırım from Konukoğlu Hospital, Reşat Bahat from Bahat Hospitals, Hayreddin Yekeler from Emsey Hospital and Abdurrahman Külünk from Erdem Hospital.

8. The honorary committee of OHSAD is composed of but not limited to the following: Mehmet Ali Aydınlar from the Acıbadem Group, Turgut Aydın from the Memorial Group, Cemşid Demiroğlu from the Florence Nightingale Group, Doğan Birgül from Doğan Hospital, Hüseyin Urlu from Avrasya Hospital, Ömer Güzel from Biruni Laboratories and Yusuf Elgörmüş from the Medicine Hospital Group.
9. For these specified services that private hospitals provide free of charge, the SGK makes payments according to the Health Implementation Statement.
10. He referred specifically to patients in intensive care units in private hospitals.

References

Adıyok, M. (2012). Turkey's healthcare: A bad prognosis. *Turkish Review*, 2(4), 26–31.

Ağartan, T. İ. (2008). *Turkish health system in transition: Historical background and reform experience*. Ph.D., State University of New York.

Akdağ, E. (2012, May 28). SGK'lıya kaç, özel hastanelere tut! (Run public insuree, catch private hospitals!) *Aksiyon*.

Aksoy, B. (2008, February 5). Özel hastanelerin devletleşmesi ya da Sağlık Bakanlığı'nın haksız rekabeti (Etatisation of private hospitals or Ministry of Health's unfair competition). *Sağlık Düşüncesi ve Tıp Kültürü Platformu Dergisi (Journal of Health Thoughts and Culture of Medicine)*.

Al Jazeera Türk. (2014b, January 29). Hastanın şikayeti fark ücreti (Additional payment is the complaint of patients). *Al Jazeera Turk*.

Albawaba Business. (2003, July 22). IFC makes first investment in Turkey's health sector. *Albawaba Business*.

Armada, F., Muntaner, C., and Navarro, V. (2001). Health and social security reforms in Latin America: The convergence of the World Health Organization, the World Bank, and transnational corporations. *International Journal of Health Services*, 31(4), 729–768.

Avcı, Ç. (2012, September 14). Sayıştay'dan özel hastanelere 300 milyon liralık ceza şoku! (Court of Account's shocking fine of 300 million TL for private hospitals). *Zaman*.

Batley, R. (2004). The politics of service delivery reform. *Development and Change*, 35(1), 31–56.

Belek, İ (2012). *Sağlıkta dönüşüm: halkın sağlığına emperyalist saldırı (Transformation in health: Imperialist attack on people's health)*. Istanbul: Yazılama Yayınları.

Belek, İ, Onuroğulları, H., Nalçacı, E., and Ardıç, F. (1998). *Sınıfsız toplum yolunda Türkiye için sağlık tezi (Health thesis for Turkey marching towards a classless society)*. Istanbul: Sorun Yayınları.

Bennett, S. (1991). *The mystique of markets: Public and private healthcare in developing countries.* London: London School of Hygiene & Tropical Medicine-Department of Public & Health Policy-Health Policy Unit.

Berman, P. A., and Bossert, T. J. (2000). Decade of health sector reform in developing countries: What have we learned?. In *Data for decision making project-Appraising a decade of health sector reform in developing countries.* Washington, DC: Harvard School of Public Health.

Brooks, S. M. (2005). Interdependent and domestic foundations of policy change: The diffusion of pension privatization around the world. *International Studies Quarterly*, 49(2), 273–294.

Buğra, A. (1997). *Devlet ve işadamları (State and businessmen).* Istanbul: İletişim.

Buğra, A., and Savaşkan, O. (2014). *New capitalism in Turkey: The relationship between politics, religion and business.* Cheltenham and Northampton: Edward Elgar.

Çarkoğlu, A., and Kalaycıoğlu, E. (2012). *Türkiye'de sağlık: toplumbilimsel bir değerlendirme (Health in Turkey: A sociological analysis).* Istanbul: Koç Üniversitesi, Sabancı Üniversitesi.

Civaner, M. (2011). "Transforming" our health by privatisation-Response to Baris et. al. *British Medical Journal*, 342.

Coşkun, N. (2008, December 26). Özel hastaneler 'hak' arayacak (Private hospitals will claim their 'rights'). *Milliyet.*

Doğu, N. (2010, November 6). Özel hastanede el değiştirme rüzgarı (A wave of handover among private hospitals). *Radikal.*

Ersoy, T. (1998). *Türkiye tıp tarihi için materyalist notlar (Materialist notes for Turkey's medical history).* Istanbul: Sorun Yayınları.

Esmer, Y. (1991). Manufacturing industries: Giants with hesitant voices. In M. Heper (ed.), *Strong State and Economic Interest Groups: The Post-1980 Turkish Experience* (pp. 119–134). Berlin and New York: Walter de Gruyter.

Ewig, C., and Kay, S. J. (2011). Postretrenchment politics: Policy feedback in Chile's health and pension reforms. *Latin American Politics and Society*, 53 (4), 67–99.

Freeman, R. (1999). Institutions, states and cultures: Health policy and politics in Europe. In J. Clasen (ed.), *Comparative social policy: Concepts, theories and methods* (pp. 80–94). Oxford and Massachusetts: Wiley-Blackwell.

Giaimo, S. (2005). *Markets and medicine: The politics of healthcare reform in Britain, Germany, and the United States.* Ann Arbor: The University of Michigan University Press.

Giaimo, S., and Manow, P. (1999). Adapting the welfare state: The case of healthcare reform in Britain, Germany, and the United States. *Comparative Political Studies*, 32(8), 967–1000.

Günal, A. (2008). *Health and citizenship in Republican Turkey: An analysis of the socialization of health services in Republican historical context.* Ph.D. Istanbul: Boğaziçi University.

Güneş, S. (2008, February 23). Özel sağlık sektöründe 15 Şubat depremi (15 February earthquake in private health sector). *Ntvmsnbc.com.*

Habertürk. (2011, December 14). Acıbadem devleşiyor (Acıbadem grows in size). *Habertürk Ekonomi.*

Hall, P. A., and Soskice, D. (2001). *Varieties of capitalism: The institutional foundations of comparative advantage.* New York: Oxford University Press.

Heper, M. (1991). The state and interest groups with special reference to Turkey. In M. Heper (ed.), *Strong state and economic interest groups: The post-1980 Turkish experience* (pp. 3–23). Berlin and New York: Walter de Gruyter.

Hürriyet. (2006). Erdoğan: Sağlıkta da serbest piyasa olmalı (Erdoğan: Free markets should also be established in healthcare). *Hürriyet,* 17 March 2006.

IFC. (2007). Financing private healthcare in Turkey: Acibadem Healthcare Group. Reducing poverty, improving lives. http://www.ifc.org/wps/wcm/connect/9522e0004970c18b9f3edf336b93d75f/Reduce%2BPoverty%2BAcibadem.pdf?MOD=AJPERES. Accessed 21 July 2012.

IFC. (2012a). Investing in private healthcare in emerging markets. *ICF in Turkey.* http://www1.ifc.org/wps/wcm/connect/region__ext_content/regions/europe+middle+east+and+north+africa/ifc+in+europe+and+central+asia/countries/turkey+country+landing+page. Accessed 10 February 2012.

Immergut, E. M. (1992). *Health politics: Interests and institutions in Western Europe.* Cambridge, New York and Melbourne: Cambridge University Press.

Jacobs, L. R., and Skocpol, T. (2010). *Healthcare reform and American politics: What everyone needs to know.* Oxford and New York: Oxford University Press.

Joseph, L. (2006, March 8). IFC invests in Turkish healthcare company. *International Finance Corporation.*

Keyder, Ç. (1987). *State and class in Turkey: A study in capitalist development.* London and New York: Verso.

Konsensus Araştırma. (2011). *En güvenilen kurumlar araştırması (Survey on the most trusted institutions).* Istanbul: Konsensus Araştırma.

Milliyet. (2011, December 23). Acıbadem Sağlık Yatırımları Holding'in devir sözleşmesi imzalandı (Transfer contract signed for Acıbadem Health Investments Holding). *Milliyet.*

MÜSİAD. (2009). *Sağlık sektörü 2008 yılı değerlendirmesi ve sağlık sektörünün geleceği (Analysis of health sector in 2008 and the future of health sector).* Istanbul: Ofset Basım Yayın.

NTVMSNBC (2009, April 23). Özel hastanede katkı payına yargı freni (Judiciary granted a motion for stay of execution in the case on contributory payments in private hospitals). *NTVMSNC.*

NTVMSNBC. (2013, October 14). Özel hastanelerin fark ücreti 2 kat arttı (Additional payments of private hospitals doubled). *NTVMSNBC.*

OHSAD. (2004). The Charter of the Association. http://ohsad.org/hakkimizda/tuzuk/. Accessed 5 March 2012.

Pierson, P. (1993). When effect becomes cause: Policy feedback and political change. *World Politics*, 45(4), 595–628.

Polanyi, K. (2001). *Great transformation: The political and economic origins of our time.* Boston: Beacon Press.

SGK. (2010a). *Özel hastanelerin puanlandırılması ve ilave ücret alınması hakkında yönerge (Directive on the categorisation of private hospitals and receiving additional payments).* Ankara: SGK.

SGK. (2010b). *Sosyal Güvenlik Kurumu Sağlık Uygulama Tebliği (Social Security Institution Health Implementation Statement). 27532.* Ankara: SGK.

SGK. (2011). *Sosyal Güvenlik Kurumu Sağlık Uygulama Tebliğinde değişiklik yapılmasına dair tebliğ (Statement of changing the Health Implementation Statement). 28159.* Ankara: SGK.

SGK. (2012). *Sosyal güvenliğe ilişkin temel parametreler (Basic parameters of social security).* Ankara: SGK.

Sonay, N. (2012, June 10). Özel hastanelerde fark vurgunu (Sack of additional payments in private hospitals). *Bugün.*

Sönmez, M. (2011). *Paran kadar sağlık: Türkiye'de sağlığın ticarileşmesi (Healthcare as much as you have money: The commercialisation of health in Turkey).* Istanbul: Yordam Kitap.

Soyer, A. (2005). *Bir muhalefet odağı olarak tabip eylemleri, bir eylem biçimi olarak beyaz eylemler (Protests of medical doctors as a node of opposition, white protests as a form of opposition).* Istanbul: Sorun Yayınları.

Soyer, A. (2007). *AKP'nin sağlık raporu (Health report of the AKP).* Istanbul: Evrensel Basım Yayın.

Temel, T. (2003). *Özel hastaneler sektör profili (Private hospitals sector profile).* Istanbul: Istanbul Ticaret Odası (Istanbul Chamber of Commerce.

Tezel, A. (2009, September 9). Özel hastaneler SGK'yı hala iplemiyor (Private hospitals still don't care about the SGK). *Habertürk.*

The Ministry of Economy of Turkey. (2012). *Uluslararası doğrudan yatırım verileri bülteni (International direct investment figures bulletin).* Ankara: Teşvik Uygulama ve Yabancı Sermaye Genel Müdürlüğü (Directorate General for Incentive Implementation and Foreign Capital).

The Ministry of Health. (2003). *Transformation in health.* Ankara: The Ministry of Health.

The Ministry of Health. (2008). *Özel hastaneler yönetmeliğinde değişiklik yapılmasına dair yönetmelik (Bylaw on the changing of the bylaw of private hospitals). 26788.*

The Ministry of Health. (2012). *Sağlık istatistikleri yıllığı 2011 (Health statistics yearbook 2011).* Ankara: Ministry of Health.

The Ministry of Health. (2016). *Sağlık istatistikleri yıllığı 2015 (Health statistics yearbook 2015).* Ankara: Ministry of Health.

The Republic of Turkey. (1933). *Hususi Hastaneler Kanunu (Private Hospitals Act). 2219.*

The Republic of Turkey. (2003). *T.C. 58. Hükümet Acil Eylem Planı (58th Government of Republic of Turkey Urgent Action Plan).* Ankara: The Republic of Turkey.

The Republic of Turkey. (2005b). *Sağlık Hizmetleri Temel Kanununa Bir Ek Madde Eklenmesi Hakkında Kanun (Law on the Addition of a Clause to the Principal Law on Health Services). 5396.*

The Republic of Turkey. (2011a). *Sağlık Bakanlığı ve Bağlı Kuruluşlarının Teşkilat ve Görevleri Hakkında Kanun Hükmünde Kararname (Statutory Decree on the Organisation and Duties of the Ministry of Health and its Subsidiary Institutions). KHK/663.*

Thelen, K. (2004). *How institutions evolve: The political economy of skills in Germany, Britain, the United States, and Japan.* Cambridge: Cambridge University Press.

TÜSİAD. (2005). *Charting the way forward: Healthcare reform in Turkey.* Istanbul: TÜSİAD Publications.

Vatan. (2012, February 6). 'İmzalamasaydık yarın 2 bin kişi ölürdü' ('2 thousand would die tomorrow unless we signed the agreement'. *Vatan.*

World Bank. (2010). *Implementation completion and results report on a loan in the amount of Euro 49.40 million to the Republic of Turkey for a Health Transition Project.* Human Development Unit, Turkey Country Unit, Europe and Central Asia Region: The World Bank.

Yalman, G. L. (2009). *Transition to neoliberalism: The case of Turkey in the 1980s.* Istanbul: Istanbul Bilgi University Press.

Yılmaz, V. (2013). Changing origins of inequalities in access to healthcare in Turkey: From occupational status to income? *New Perspectives on Turkey,* 48, 53–75.

CHAPTER 9

Conclusion

Healthcare reforms are products of political processes, which can hardly be reduced to an automatic response of national healthcare systems to economic growth, demographic change, lack of insurance coverage or deficiencies in citizens' ability to access services. How healthcare policies are organised, which form of healthcare financing is used, how access to services is determined and who provides the services are distribution questions that lie at the centre of healthcare politics. The power dynamics between diverse actors within the institutional and political-cultural constraints determine whether – and in which direction – healthcare systems are reformed. Both the viability of a reform and its content are dependent on the interplay of global and domestic political dynamics.

Healthcare today is both a commodity and a human right. The contemporary understanding of healthcare, which lost significant transformative power with the marginalisation of the public health perspective, limits healthcare politics to a distributional question concerning a set of curative services and medications. Despite its limitations, this elusive state of healthcare today still makes it a locus of political contestations at both global and domestic levels.

Viewed from another angle, healthcare is a sizeable economic sector with powerful corporate interests and is a significant area of social policy in which there has been significant public investment in meeting the demands and expectations of citizens. The peculiar situation of healthcare today makes it an excellent domain from which to observe the changing

V. Yılmaz, *The Politics of Healthcare Reform in Turkey*,
DOI 10.1007/978-3-319-53667-5_9

balance between market relations and institutionalised forms of social solidarity.

With the increasing acceptance of the neoliberal perspective as the modus operandi of neoliberal economy and society, political and economic pressure on state and societal healthcare systems also increased. In the domain of healthcare, neoliberalism manifested itself in an extension of the commodification of healthcare services, particularly in healthcare financing and delivery, and in the adoption of private sector management techniques by public sector healthcare delivery institutions.

This historically grounded single-country case study is situated within a comparative framework. It examined the political dynamics that led to the legislation and implementation of Turkey's HTP between 2003 and 2013 and explored how it reconfigured the particular distribution of power that formed the basis of Turkey's healthcare system. In other words, it is an analysis of the political dynamics that enabled the introduction and implementation of the reform, the political dynamics that the HTP generated and the impact of these dynamics on the direction of change that the reform engendered.

At the empirical level, the study examined the interplay between the direction of change in healthcare financing and delivery and various key political actors' subjective interpretations of the reform, their interests and their strategies to pursue their interests throughout the reform process. Actual political conflicts between different actors – such as the struggle over the introduction of a full-time work requirement for medical doctors and the struggle over a cap on additional payments that publicly insured patients were required to make to private hospitals – were explored so as to understand the power relationships between these actors and the different impact each had on the reform. Finally, the book provides an analysis of how and to whose benefit these political conflicts were resolved, demonstrates the direction of change in Turkey's healthcare system and describes the new configuration of power on which it rests.

This study was inspired by the historical institutionalist perspective, which called for a careful examination of the political system, the policy context and the political culture of the country under consideration in explaining institutional change. The use of the historical institutionalist perspective, however, was restricted to taking into consideration history and political systems, rather than arguing for a purely institutionalist explanation for the reform. Ideational institutionalism in particular was used to account for the role of subjective interpretations of political actors in their strategies throughout the reform process.

Comparative analysts of healthcare reforms successfully trace the cross-border migration of reform ideas and explore how domestic actors use these global ideas to frame their reform initiatives. An investigation of domestic healthcare politics scenes with a bottom-up approach, however, yields a much more complicated picture, the analysis of which has to address interactions among existing political actors in healthcare politics and investigate their subjective perspectives on the reform at hand as well as their strategies to influence the reform for their self-defined benefit. This book, therefore, draws on different approaches to healthcare politics – pluralism, the power resources approach, and the new politics approach – without discounting the insights that policy diffusion literature has provided so far.

International organisations, especially the WB, and international epistemic communities of health economists have been the harbingers of neoliberalism in the domain of healthcare policies. These actors pioneered the translation of healthcare policy issues into a health economics discourse. Starting from a radical privatisation in healthcare carried out in Chile under Pinochet, the WB popularised a pro-market 'policy paradigm' in healthcare policies and made it available to emerging market economies, despite significant changes in the intensity of its discourse over time.

The growing popularity and availability of the pro-market approach to healthcare policies worldwide has not yet led to the convergence of healthcare systems into private healthcare systems. This makes it more interesting to study the interplay between global influences and domestic political dynamics in shaping healthcare reforms in different country cases.

This book puts forward a set of reasons why the presence of a uniform pro-market approach to healthcare reform – that is one promoted by dominant international organisations – did not immediately lead to the convergence of healthcare systems with private healthcare systems. One reason is that in some countries, including Turkey, domestic political actors operate within a political culture that accepts citizens' access to healthcare as part of citizenship rights. This clearly limits their ability to initiate radical pro-market healthcare reforms. Second, the presence of state and societal healthcare systems accounts for a clear policy feedback effect on healthcare reforms that are initiated. Third, the existence of political competition – in its electoral form as well as in the form of a broader quest for legitimacy – restricts the introduction of radical pro-market healthcare reforms. Fourth, despite the 'technocratisation of politics' – referring to Silva's concept (1991) – in healthcare at the global level, various domestic political actors still have fundamentally different perspectives on healthcare policy which diverge considerably from that of the global pro-market reform blueprint. While experts who are part of global epistemic communities pushing for pro-market healthcare reforms may find all but one of these different perspectives outdated and ideological, we – as students of healthcare politics – can still treat these diverse perspectives on healthcare policies as equally legitimate alternatives for reform.

In line with historical institutionalist insights, understanding the state of Turkey's political system and culture before and during the introduction and the implementation of the HTP is crucial in deciding which approach or combination of approaches to healthcare politics best explains the political dynamics that formed the basis of the reform. Turkey's political system, prior to recent changes, could be considered a form of 'state corporatism', as defined by Schmitter (1974). In this model, both medical doctor organisations and business organisations were state-created bodies that lacked veto points. While this model did not totally exclude them from policy-making bodies, their presence in policy-making bodies had been merely symbolic.

Contrary to the assumption of historical institutionalism, however, Turkey's political system was not stable over the course of the HTP. In fact, the political system in Turkey was undergoing a significant transformation at the time the HTP was being implemented. As Somer suggests, Turkey has been witnessing the rise of a new authoritarian regime that relies partly on popular support originating from the AK Party's social policies (2016). Akkoyunlu and Öktem argue that this new regime, however, can be identified as a weak and contested one due to the existential insecurity it faces due to widespread domestic and international power struggles (2016). This transformation of the political system manifests itself in the AK Party's proposal to transition from a majoritarian parliamentary democracy to a strong presidential system without an effective system of checks and balances. The impact of this proposed transition on social policy-making in general and in healthcare policies in particular is unclear at this point.

A technocratic turn in healthcare policy and politics literature, along with an increasingly teleological interpretation of healthcare reform processes, limit the explanatory power of the literature. After this turn, the literature downplays the role of politics in healthcare, the significance of value conflicts in healthcare politics, the availability of alternatives to pro-market reforms, and strong links between healthcare politics and broader politics. As a result, the literature fails to consider the immense impact that the erosion of checks and balances in a democratic system and the weakening of political actors with alternative views on healthcare policies would have on the content and the direction of changes in healthcare systems.

For example, a qualitative study on the politics of the HTP conceptualises four institutions – allegedly with veto points – that might have created an obstacle to the HTP, namely the Ministry of Finance and Treasury, the Ministry of Labour and Social Security, the Office of the President and the Constitutional Court (Sparkes et al. 2015). Scholars argued that their analysis of the HTP points to the limitation of the institutionalist approach, as it suggests that a willing and powerful Minister of Health could successfully override the institutional veto points. Thus, they concluded, 'institutional veto points were not binding obstacles to the reform' (Sparkes et al. 2015, p. 264). They suggested that the Minister of Health's 'skillful use of political strategies' succeeded in overcoming institutional veto points (Sparkes et al. 2015, p. 265).

When democratic politics is narrowly defined as a struggle between an elected government and a bureaucracy (including the judiciary), an elected government's ability to circumvent bureaucratic actors might be lauded as a victory for democracy. But this narrow definition of democratic politics loses sight of all other political actors – including but not limited to opposition political parties, professional organisations, business groups and NGOs. More importantly, equating bureaucracy – and especially the judiciary – with obstacles to much needed policy change can be misleading, as it may be providing significant opportunities to political actors with alternative views on healthcare policies.

Healthcare politics is embedded in domestic politics and should be analysed accordingly. Otherwise, scholars may fail to notice how the implementation of the HTP coincided historically with the consolidation of power in the hands of few in Turkey, which led to the erosion of bureaucratic veto points in particular and parliamentary democracy in general. Especially after its victory in the constitutional referendum in 2011, the AK Party established itself as a cartel party in the sense that Katz and Mair define the concept (1995). Forgetting the strong historical link between democracy and pro-public healthcare policies, healthcare policy scholars ended up appreciating the manifestations of the rise of a cartel party or the emergent new authoritarianism, as Somer suggests, if it successfully delivers a healthcare reform in the 'right' direction.

The HTP arrived when Turkey had already established a state healthcare system according to Wendt et al.'s typology of healthcare systems (2009). From the first half of the twentieth century to the introduction of the HTP in 2003, Turkey's healthcare system had developed in two directions: the introduction of social health insurance schemes and the establishment of a relatively strong institutional capacity for preventive and curative healthcare services delivery. The development of a state healthcare system in Turkey was the product of populist attempts by a series of governments in power after the bifurcation of the ruling group that established the Republic and the electoral competition between the two (Keyder 2007b, p. 147).

Before the launch of the HTP in the first half of the 2000s, social insurance-based financing, coupled with a tax financed non-contributory scheme for the very poor since 1992, was the main financial source for healthcare. Public sector healthcare providers, combined with the private clinics whose specialists also worked in public hospitals, dominated the provision of healthcare services. Despite institutional fragmentation in healthcare financing and provision, Turkey's healthcare system before the reform most resembled state healthcare systems, as the government and the bureaucracy were in charge of these fragmented institutional structures. Pressing issues affecting Turkey's healthcare system before the reform included the vertical and horizontal expansion of services, admitting the outsiders to the social insurance-based system, the problem of medical doctors' dual commitment to public hospitals and their own private clinics, a relative lack of human resources capacity in healthcare and increasing fiscal deficits in social security institutions.

Turkey's healthcare system witnessed a series of reform attempts throughout the 1990s, but their failure was not only due to the political instability of the various governments that were unable to tackle oppositions to their reform proposals but also due to the power of those opposed. Most of these reform proposals had strong pro-market components. Those opposed to a pro-market healthcare system reform were able to block these reform initiatives to an extent.

Two conflictual developments in healthcare system occurred during the 1990s: the introduction of revolving funds into public hospitals and the establishment of the Green Card scheme, a means-tested social assistance program that provided the poor with free access to inpatient services in public hospitals. While the introduction of revolving funds into public hospitals was a move towards marketisation, the launch of the Green Card scheme extended health insurance coverage and marked an increase in the responsibility of the state to offer financial protection from catastrophic health expenditures for a growing body of citizens who had no social health insurance. Apart from these two developments, which can be regarded a form of policy layering, the general trend in healthcare policy between the 1980s and the 2000s can be categorised as policy drift.

With the AK Party's rise to power as a single-party government in the 2002 general elections, a significant transformation in Turkey's healthcare system and a fundamental policy revision began. The first political dynamic that paved the way to the introduction of the HTP was the electoral victory of the AK Party in the 2002 general elections and the formation of a single-party government. The AK Party, which came onto the scene less than a year before the 2002 general elections, was an inheritor of the Political Islamist National Outlook movement. This inheritance was both a curse and a blessing for the AK Party. It was a curse in that all forebears of the AK Party had been closed down because of their anti-secular activities, which obliged the AK Party to seek broader consent from the masses to stay in power. It was also a blessing for the AK Party, as it was thus able to acquire the social networks and political alliances that the Political Islamist National Outlook movement had built with small- and medium-sized conservative entrepreneurs and the urban poor.

While the AK Party relied primarily on social networks and the political alliances that it inherited from the National Outlook movement, it aspired to become a catch-all party using state power. In its quest for broader public legitimacy, the AK Party decided on healthcare reform as a viable way to strengthen its ties with the urban poor and to create consent among the broader public. Despite the common assumption that the AK Party relied on non-state actors in social provision (as claimed by Somer 2016), healthcare reform and the related political implications that this book analyses provides evidence to the opposite. While this assumption might partly explain the incorporation of private healthcare providers to public health insurance plan, the AK Party, as its healthcare reform demonstrates, overwhelmingly relied on the state infrastructure in social policy financing and provision.

The political framing of the HTP in its early phase included a promise to make healthcare services accessible for all and a commitment to equality among citizens in their access to healthcare services, with a special emphasis on those outside the formal social security system. The AK Party's appeal to those outside the formal social security system, which, according to a concept defined by Alfred (1975), had 'repressed structural interests' on healthcare policies, was a prominent feature: the Party then consolidated its popularity among the urban poor. At the same time, the AK Party called for the marketisation of healthcare and promised to open healthcare to private sector involvement. While the AK Party's use of these opposing approaches to healthcare reform suffers from a contradiction in terms that manifests itself slowly but surely, it also reflects its ability to appeal to different social classes with a single reform in the early stages of the reform.

Historically, major political parties in Turkey have not been organised along class lines, and working-class politics has always been under state pressure. As Keyder suggests, due to political-economic factors such as late industrialisation and the suppression of class-based political actors since the establishment of the Republic, neither farmers nor workers were organised enough to exert a strong influence on mainstream politics (Keyder 2007b). This scenario limits the applicability of the power resources approach in understanding social policy reform in Turkey.

The low level of organisation among workers and farmers and state pressure on working-class politics, however, does not make class irrelevant in welfare politics in Turkey. Alternatively, one could investigate how and to what extent catch-all parties have been able to integrate different social classes into their hegemonic projects. Van Kersbergen's analysis of the Christian democratic political party influence on social policies, for example, can be useful in understanding the role of the AK Party in the healthcare reform. Finally, while the new politics approach (Pierson 1996) might explain the continued public support for the dominant role of the state in healthcare provision and delivery, it fails to explain the rationale behind the increase in public spending for healthcare services in Turkey in the age of neoliberalism or how this increase managed to fund privatisation of healthcare services without fostering a public debate.

On the one hand, given the AK Party's ownership of the healthcare reform and the saliency of the issue for the general public, it is argued here that the success of the HTP in generating public satisfaction contributed to the consecutive electoral successes for the AK Party. These victories are especially noteworthy in a context where electoral support, as Çarkoğlu suggests (2002), has traditionally been volatile. Therefore, the HTP can be considered an AK Party investment in the sustenance of its alliance with the urban poor, as it equalised the benefit package of the non-contributory tax-financed Green Card scheme with other contributory public health insurance schemes. To use Öniş's conceptualisation, the increase in the rate of citizen satisfaction with healthcare services in this context might symbolise the success of the AK Party's 'controlled populist' (2012) strategy. On the other hand, the HTP created a quasi-market in healthcare delivery and introduced NPM tools to public hospitals. The AK Party redefined healthcare as an economic growth sector with the HTP, especially in the areas of healthcare delivery and health tourism.

The HTP eased access to healthcare services while creating a strong commodification and marketisation dynamic at the same time. Inherent contradictions in the early political framing of the HTP that combined a pro-market approach with egalitarian discourse translated into actual inconsistencies within the healthcare system.

The distribution of power in Turkey's political system made it possible for the government to introduce the reform without seeking the consent of other domestic political actors. While political contestations between different political actors over the direction of the HTP did not cease after the legislation of the reform, combined with the cartelisation of the AK Party and the suppression of dissenting actors, welfare politics has been increasingly confined within the party boundaries; they have almost become an endogenous affair. The shrinkage of welfare politics leaves the fate of the healthcare system to AK Party internal politics in the context of its cartelisation.

The second political dynamic that made it possible to introduce the HTP was the involvement of the WB. The influence of the WB on the HTP is twofold: a long-term influence on how bureaucrats understand healthcare policy issues, which originated from its historical partnership with the governments of Turkey, and the impact of direct hands-on involvement in the preparation and implementation of the HTP.

The WB was the international organisation that pioneered neoliberal healthcare reforms in emerging market economies. In practice, the WB offers loans to carry out comprehensive healthcare reforms and provides empirical data and know-how to governments of emerging market economies on reforming their healthcare systems. While the WB experts I interviewed disagreed with the idea that the WB has a healthcare reform blueprint, they acknowledged that what the WB does offer is a 'loose jacket'. This jacket, which changed colour with the transition from roll-back to roll-out neoliberalism, still has distinctive pro-market components, including a purchaser-provider split in healthcare systems, the necessity of user fees and the transformation of the role of the state from provision to stewardship – hence, the privatisation of healthcare provision. I argue that the looseness of the jacket refers mainly to the flexibility in the implementation of these components in different domestic contexts. The WB experts present their pro-market perspectives in healthcare policies as scientific, evidence-based and beyond politics, which implies a technocratisation of healthcare reform processes in emerging market economies in the age of neoliberalism.

The partnership between the WB and the Turkish government on healthcare policies started in the 1990s. While this partnership was unable to initiate a reform for more than a decade, I argue that it had a moulding effect for a pro-market healthcare reform. Indeed, WB involvement in Turkey's healthcare system equipped the organisation with critical knowledge about healthcare policies and policy-making in Turkey. More importantly, with this partnership, the WB succeeded in exporting its globally hegemonic approach to healthcare reforms to MoH bureaucrats, some of whom later joined the AK Party's reform team that prepared the HTP. The WB influence on the perspective of bureaucrats to healthcare policies had already manifested itself in the presence of a pro-market approach in the five-year development plans of Turkey since the mid-1980s, which was then reflected in the design of the HTP.

The WB influence on the HTP was not limited to its success in promoting a pro-market approach to healthcare at the global level and in popularising this approach among the healthcare bureaucracy throughout the 1990s. The WB also collaborated with the AK Party government in preparing and implementing the HTP. The preparation of the HTP was a closed process that excluded the TTB and healthcare worker unions; it also left out opposition political parties and business organisations. The key role played by the government's reform team was a manifestation of the victory of the technocratic approach to healthcare reform. The reform team worked closely with WB experts throughout the reform. Given their generally shared perspective on the direction of healthcare reform, which could be attributed partly to the previous integration of these experts into the WB-created epistemic community, their collaboration was conflict-free for the most part.

In some emerging market economies, factors such as economic crises, a lack of public resources to carry out a reform, and lack of know-how among the bureaucracy and politicians made governments susceptible to the influence of the WB. The Turkish case evidences an alternative mode of collaboration between the WB and a government in an emerging market economy, one which was built on a more symmetrical relationship between the two parties. Contrary to the WB's expectation, the AK Party government, for instance, took rather hesitant steps to completely privatise healthcare provision and to transform the MoH into a stewardship body. In fact, a stakeholder analysis conducted at the end of 2008 and the beginning of 2009 argued that stakeholders perceived the transformation of the MoH into a stewardship body as the component of the HTP that moved the slowest (Akinci et al. 2012). The AK Party government was allowed to pick and choose from WB proposals, mainly due to favourable domestic economic and political conditions, not to mention the importance of the healthcare reform in the AK Party's aim to appeal to society. Rather than rapidly creating a profitable healthcare market at the expense of public dissatisfaction, the AK Party government highlighted the success of the reform in order to secure electoral victories in the early stages of the reform.

The third political dynamic that helped shape the direction of the HTP was the involvement of the TTB as a contending party to the government, especially in the struggle over control of the labour of medical doctors. The TTB occupied a special place in healthcare politics in Turkey that originated from the privileged status of their profession in the history of the nation-state making process, their central position in the practice of medicine, the previous corporatist political structure that gave the TTB a monopoly over the representation of medical doctors' interests – although without a veto power – and its pro-public approach to healthcare policies.

While the TTB performed its corporatist function until the end of the 1970s, the democratic takeover of the TTB executive board by a socialist group in 1977 led to its transformation into a professional organisation fighting for a strong preventive healthcare approach to healthcare policy planning and for a universal healthcare system that would provide free and quality healthcare for all citizens. The TTB based its political stance on the universal values of the medical profession and pursued organisational strategies to secure its autonomy from the private sector as well as from the MoH. While the autonomy of medical associations is not uncommon in most advanced capitalist countries, the TTB's funding policy, which prohibits financial contributions from the private sector, is an exception.

This feature of the TTB is noteworthy, given that scholars criticise the lack of stringency in the policies of professional medical associations that concern conflicts of interest in their relationship with the private sector (Rothman et al. 2009, p. 1367). In the light of its broader understanding of the right to health that aims at reconciling interests of medical doctors and patients, the TTB engaged not only in professional politics but also in the politics of production and consumption throughout the reform process.

The AK Party government, in collaboration with the reform team and the WB, carried out the preparation of the reform as a closed process. Given the fact that the TTB lacked a veto point on healthcare reform decisions, the TTB used the only available checks and balance mechanisms that could have an impact on the decisions of a single-party government: street protests and legal activism. While street protests could arguably serve the consolidation of the TTB constituency over common goals, they did not have an observable impact on the reform. However, TTB legal activism centred on stopping the government plan to introduce a full-time work requirement for all medical doctors – an action that would have virtually eliminated private clinics and would have led to proletarianisation and the loss of their professional autonomy – proved to be successful in delaying the government's policy for a long time. While the TTB's political stance aimed to unify the interests of medical doctors and the general public under the broader demand for a universal public healthcare system, the political system and the marketised healthcare domain left no room for the TTB to succeed in its political strategies on the politics of consumption to the extent that it had done so on professional politics.

The reform had an impact on professional politics within the TTB. While the TTB had favoured the full-time work requirement as part of a state healthcare system prior to the introduction of the HTP, it had to revise its political stance during the HTP. On the one hand, this revision can be attributed to the fact that the introduction of a full-time work requirement would lead to the weakening of the position of medical doctors vis-à-vis private hospitals. On the other hand, here it is argued that that the leadership cadre was squeezed between its values, which centred on a demand for a universal healthcare system for Turkey and the expectations of its constituency, who wanted them to protect and promote the interests of medical doctors. The TTB failure to produce a discourse that combined the interests of medical doctors and the interests of the general public, in a context where government representatives portrayed medical doctors as greedy for money in legitimising the reform, restricted the TTB's influence over the politics of consumption.

The fourth political dynamic that partially shaped the direction of the reform in the post-legislative process is a combination of the birth of private healthcare provider organisations (OHSAD in particular) and their involvement in the reform process. The HTP opened up a new area for capital accumulation by including private hospitals into the public health insurance plan and excluding the private clinics of medical doctors. In fact, the most visible market direction of the HTP has been in healthcare delivery (Ağartan 2012; Yılmaz 2013). The share of bed capacity in private hospitals among all hospitals tripled between 2002 and 2015, and private hospitals received almost one-fifth of all applications to health institutions in 2015.

In line with Polanyi's insights (2001) and with the application of those insights in the healthcare domain, it is argued here that this partial privatisation of healthcare delivery, was a result of state intervention to create a market in this domain. This state-led market making in healthcare delivery had a significant impact on healthcare politics by giving rise to new actors, namely private healthcare provider organisations.

The Health Sector Union of the TOBB (the corporatist body) and OHSAD emerged as the strongest parties representing private healthcare providers in healthcare policy-making. It is argued here that the OHSAD structure of representation, which gave more weight to larger private hospital groups in making decisions, resulted in OHSAD's emergence as the strongest and most active representative of the private sector in healthcare provision. Despite the fact that the private hospital sector is heterogeneous in terms of the size of private hospitals, the pricing policy of the SGK strengthens an oligopolisation tendency in the sector by favouring larger hospitals that can use economies of scale (Akdağ 2012). This oligopolisation tendency in provision that originated from the HTP shapes private healthcare delivery politics. It disempowers the Health Sector Union of the TOBB and puts OHSAD in a more favourable position in the eyes of large entrepreneurs.

While the research that led to this book relies on data of interactions between private healthcare provider organisations and the government, particularistic relationships between healthcare business and the government in Turkey might be left uncaptured. The analysis of the composition of the executive board and the honorary board of OHSAD, however, is sufficient to demonstrate the interpenetration of the business organisation and the healthcare bureaucracy as well as the governing political party.

Both the interest formation of private healthcare provider organisations and their interaction with the government diverge from a pluralist understanding of healthcare politics that treats politics and markets as mutually exclusive domains. Historically, the relationship between the state and business was not conflict-ridden in the Turkish context. In fact, successive Turkish governments used the state capacity to create a national bourgeoisie that was politically allied with the party in power (Buğra 1997). Against this background, Buğra and Savaşkan suggest that the AK Party followed the historical path of state-business relations in Turkey and initiated a politically guided process of class transformation with healthcare as a significant component of this project (2014). While this book demonstrates how this trend manifested itself in the incentives provided for investment in private healthcare delivery with the HTP, this has not been the AK Party government's only strategy. Recent establishment of PPP model 'city hospitals' introduces a new dimension to healthcare politics that is yet to be fully understood.

As a result of the above-mentioned historical structure and its contemporary manifestations, and drawing on the discourses and strategies used by private healthcare provider organisations throughout the reform process, it is argued here that these organisations did not engage in open conflicts with the government, even in cases where their economic interests were in direct conflict with existing policies. Instead, they adopted closed-door lobbying strategies and employed a discourse that defined private healthcare provision as a growth sector. Both the government and the healthcare bureaucracy were thus open to listening to their demands.

From 2005 to 2008 – after the inclusion of private healthcare providers into the public health insurance plan, but before the introduction of tight restrictions on the private healthcare delivery sector – the relationship between private healthcare provider organisations and the government were smooth. To exemplify, both private healthcare providers and the government referred to private hospitals as national resources, which were presented as no different from public hospitals. However, relations became tense after the government introduced new regulations that put an end to the uncontrolled growth of private healthcare provision and its ability to attract a significant share of specialist medical doctors.

The introduction of strict regulations on opportunities for capital accumulation in private healthcare delivery resulted in the consolidation of private sector interests and a more active role for private healthcare provider organisations to advocate for these interests behind closed doors. Since then, OHSAD has concentrated on three strategic areas to influence the reform: the pricing policy of the SGK, the level of the cap on additional payments and the number of specialist positions allotted to private hospitals. Given that public opinion is still in favour of public sector dominance in healthcare delivery, OHSAD was unable to reach out to the public to put pressure upon the government. Instead, OHSAD chose to express its demands to the healthcare bureaucracy and the representatives of the government, without using a confrontational discourse.

In fact, over the course of the reform, private healthcare provider organisations in general and OHSAD in particular can be considered partially successful in influencing the components of the reform that affected them the most. Throughout the implementation of the HTP, the level of the cap on additional payments and the number of available positions for specialist medical doctors in private hospitals increased.

Private healthcare provider organisations, however, failed to succeed in realising their demands when those demands were in direct conflict with government priorities. For instance, despite the insistence of private healthcare provider organisations on improving the pricing policy of the SGK, neither the pricing policy nor the level of prices changed substantially. This failure was mainly due to the fact that the realisation of this demand would have directly increased the financial burden on the public budget.

While the success of private healthcare provider organisations so far may seem incremental, they will have a critical impact on healthcare politics and policy change in the near future. As the Chilean example also shows (Ewig and Kay 2011), a strengthened private sector in healthcare may lead to 'lock-in effect' and create an obstacle to a revival of a public option in the future. In fact, their presence has already altered the trajectory of healthcare policy. Rather than pressuring private healthcare providers to work with SGK prices, the government chose to appease them by transferring to patients (those who were willing to use private hospitals with their public health insurance) the financial burden originating from private healthcare providers' demand for better revenues. In other words, the government prioritised meeting its public budget targets rather than keeping the level of out-of-pocket payments and the level of income-based inequalities in access to healthcare services low.

Given that the AK Party has transformed into a cartel party and that there are few political channels left which would allow for the representation of patients' interests in healthcare policy-making, I argue that patients' interests, which were previously partially represented by political parties in a competitive electoral atmosphere, are now increasingly becoming 'repressed structural interests'. The nascent healthcare politics scene is one where political actors with pro-public approaches to healthcare policy have been disempowered, while political actors with sectoral interests have been strengthened. This changing landscape of healthcare politics may work against the popular components of the HTP in the near future.

In conclusion, the HTP was a common product of the controlled populism and the pro-market healthcare reform approach. With the introduction of the HTP, the power distribution on which Turkey's healthcare system is based is changing. While governments were always the strongest party in healthcare politics prior to the reform, they still had to operate within a competitive electoral system with volatile electoral support and medical doctors and their organisation used to have significant leverage. However, after the reform, private healthcare provider organisations appeared as actors with considerable leverage and had an ability to effect changes in the reform. In contrast to the collaboration the government had with private healthcare provider organisations, it excluded the TTB from the reform process and characterised it as the culprit of all ills of the healthcare system before the HTP.

Private actors are not newcomers to the domain of healthcare. They have been major global actors in pharmaceuticals and health technology sectors. While private actors in healthcare delivery were not significant actors in most state and societal healthcare systems, including Turkey's, they were already strong in private healthcare systems such as the one in the United States. A recent trend that has manifested itself in the global wave of reforms leading to the privatisation in healthcare delivery strengthens private actors in healthcare market and politics. This trend, also visible in the case of Turkey, positions the politics of regulation as the main mode of healthcare politics in the near future. This idea is in line with Béland's belief that ideational analysis should explore the changing perspectives of policymakers on the proper public-private mix in healthcare (Béland 2010, p. 629).

The HTP led to a significant shift in the perception of a variety of actors and in the discourse on healthcare services, marking a new period of marketisation in the healthcare system of Turkey. One of the manifestations of this shift has been visible in the CHP-run Şişli municipality, a central district in Istanbul where the standard of living is high (Şeker 2015). Under the auspices of its social democratic mayor, the Şişli municipality introduced a Şişli health card to all residents of the district, which provides them a 'discount' of up to 50 per cent when they apply to 'sponsor' private hospitals (2016). The municipality presents this campaign as a 'revolution in the conduct of welfare municipality'. In fact, the Şişli health card is not breaking new ground, despite its claim to the contrary; it simply gives a new name to the incorporation of private hospitals into the public health insurance plan as a result of the HTP. Its novelty lies in the social democrat mayor's adoption of HTP discourse and his aggrandisement of it by relabelling individuals' legal entitlement as part of their public health insurance as a 'discount'. Rather than developing and mobilising a critique of the marketisation trend in healthcare, this example demonstrates how a social democrat mayor chose to use the popularity of the reform for his own political benefit and work within the new system.

Not all actors have come to terms with the marketisation dynamic that the HTP continues to create. The Pensioners Association of Turkey (*Türkiye Emekliler Derneği*), for example, brought an action against the drastic rise in 2013 in the cap on additional payments – from 90 per cent of the SGK prices to 200 per cent – that private hospitals were entitled to charge patients who were using public health insurance (TRTHaber 2013). The Council of State, however, ordered a peremptory nonsuit by a majority vote (Medimagazin 2015). Similar to criticism levelled by the Pensioners Association, the Patients' Rights Activists Association (*Hasta Hakları Aktivistleri Derneği*) declared that the drastic rise in 2013 in the level of the cap on additional payments, combined with user fees in public hospitals and additional payments for medications, undermined citizens' constitutional right to healthcare and that it is against patients' rights (2013).

Despite the above-mentioned critiques of the increasing marketisation that the reform has generated, increasing the role of personal income in access to healthcare has not met with strong popular resistance so far. This may be explained partly on the basis of a gradual adaptation to a marketised healthcare model, especially in the context of economic growth and increasing per capita income. 'Privatised Keynesianism', as Streeck suggests, enabled citizens to cover previously socialised risks by using generous consumer credit opportunities that were available to them (2014); this has long served to delay the emergence of conflicts over social policy issues. With per capita incomes and economic growth rate in Turkey starting to stagnate, more conflicts between patients and private hospitals on additional payments will surely emerge. Patient opposition may put pressure on the government to regulate private hospitals to the benefit of patients (e.g. a regulation that would increase the fine on private hospitals that overcharge patients or lead to stricter enforcement of fines) or, albeit less likely, it might strengthen political actors pushing for a public option. Low-income patients may continue to avoid user charges by applying for emergency services in cases where there is no real emergency – this tactic accounts for almost one-third of all outpatient visits to public hospitals (Medikal Akademi 2014).

Available theories on the politics of social policies and healthcare draw heavily on empirical studies of advanced capitalist countries, which reduce their ability to explain the politics of social policies and healthcare in emerging market economies (Walt et al. 2008, p. 309). The theorisation of the politics of social policies and healthcare in emerging market economies also remains in the contours of welfare regime typologies (e.g. Rudra 2007; Gough 2004). The limited number of empirical studies available on the issues under consideration contributes to the underdeveloped theorisation of welfare politics in emerging market economies. I believe this book contributes to the body of knowledge that will pave the way to theorisation attempts in the future.

References

Ağartan, T. I. (2012). Marketization and universalism: crafting the right balance in the Turkish healthcare system. *Current Sociology*, 60(4), 456–471.

Akdağ, E. (2012, May 28). SGK'lıya kaç, özel hastanelere tut! (Run public insuree, catch private hospitals!) *Aksiyon*.

Akıncı, F., Mollahaliloğlu, S., Gürsöz, H., and Öğücü, F. (2012). Assessment of the Turkish healthcare system reforms: a stakeholder analysis. *Health Policy*, 107(1), 21–30.

Akkoyunlu, K., and Öktem, K. (2016). Existential insecurity and the making of a weak authoritarian regime in Turkey. *Southeast European and Black Sea Studies*, 16(4), 505–527.

Alford, R. R. (1975). *Healthcare politics: ideological and interest group barriers to reform*. Chicago and London: The University of Chicago Press.

Béland, D. (2010). Policy change and healthcare research. *Journal of Health Politics, Policy and Law*, 35(4), 615–641.

Belediyesi, Şişli. (2016). *Şişli sağlık kart (Şişli health card)*. http://www.sislisaglikkart.com/Accessed 12 December 2016.

Buğra, A. (1997). *Devlet ve işadamları (State and businessmen)*. Istanbul: İletişim.

Buğra, A., Savaşkan, O. (2014). *New capitalism in Turkey: the relationship between politics, religion and business*. Cheltenham and Northampton: Edward Elgar.

Çarkoğlu, A. (2002). The rise of the new generation pro-Islamists in Turkey: the Justice and Development Party phenomenon in the November 2002 elections in Turkey. *South European Society and Politics*, 7(3), 123–156.

Ewig, C., and Kay, S. J. (2011). Postretrenchment politics: policy feedback in Chile's health and pension reforms. *Latin American Politics and Society*, 53(4), 67–99.

Gough, I. (2004). Social policy regimes in the developing world. In P. Kennett (ed..), *A Handbook of comparative social policy* (pp. 205–226). Cheltenham Northampton: Edward Elgar.

Hasta Hakları Aktivistleri Derneği (Patients Rights Activists Association). (2013, May 7). Fark ücretlerinin yüzde 200'e çıkarılması, anayasa ve hasta haklarına aykırıdır (Increasing additional payments to 200 per cent is against the constitution and patients rights). İstanbul: Hasta Hakları Aktivistleri Derneği.

Katz, R. S., and Mair, P. (1995). Changing models of party organization and party democracy: The emergence of cartel party. *Party Politics*, 1(1), 5–28.

Keyder, Ç. (2007b). *Türkiye'de devlet ve sınıflar (State and Class in Turkey)*. Istanbul: İletişim.

Medikal Akademi. (2014, April 8). Acil servislere başvuran hasta sayısı günlük 200 bini geçti, ancak yüzde 70'i acil değil (Number of patients applying to emergency services exceeded 200 thousand per day, yet 70 per cent of them lacks an emergency situation. Istanbul: Medikal Akademi.

Medimagazin. (2015, May 13). Danıştay: Özel hastaneler yüzde 200 fark almaya devam edecek (The Council of State: Private hospitals will continue to charge 200 per cent additionally). *Medimagazin*.

Öniş, Z. (2012). The triumph of conservative globalism: the political economy of the AKP Era. *Turkish Studies*, 13(2), 135–152.

Pierson, P. (1996). The new politics of the welfare state. *World Politics*, 48(2), 143–179.

Polanyi, K. (2001). *Great transformation: the political and economic origins of our time*. Boston: Beacon Press.

Rothman, D.J., Mcdonald, W.J., Berkowitz, C.D., Chimonas, S.C., Deangelis, C. D., Hale, R.W., Nissen, S.E., Osborn, J.E., Scully, Jr, J. D, Thomson, G.E, and Wofsy, D. (2009). Professional medical associations and their relationships with industry: a proposal for controlling conflict of interest. *JAMA*, 301(13), 1367–1372.

Rudra, N. (2007). Welfare states in developing countries: unique or universal?. *The Journal of Politics*, 69(2), 378–396.

Schmitter, P. (1974). Still the century of corporatism?. *The Review of Politics*, 36(1), 85–131.

Şeker, M. (2015). Quality of Life Index: A Case Study of Istanbul. *Ekonometri ve İstatistik e-Dergisi*, 23, 1–15.

Silva, P. (1991). Technocrats and Politics in Chile: from the Chicago Boys to the CIEPLAN Monks. *Journal of Latin American Studies, 23*(2), 385–410.

Somer, M. (2016). Understanding Turkey's democratic breakdown: old vs. new and indigenous vs. global authoritarianism. *Southeast European and Black Sea Studies*, 16(4), 1–23.

Sparkes, S. P., Bump, J. B., and Reich, M. R. (2015). Political strategies for health reform in Turkey: extending veto point theory. *Health Systems & Reform*, 1(4), 263–275.

Streeck, W. (2014). *Buying time: the delayed crisis of democratic capitalism.* London and New York: Verso.

TRTHaber. (2013, November 18). Özel hastanelerin fark ücreti Danıştay'a taşındı (Additional payments of private hospitals were brought to the Council of State). *TRTHaber.*

Walt, G., Shiffman, J., Schneider, H., Murray, S.F., and Brugha, R. (2008). 'Doing' health policy analysis: methodological and conceptual reflections and challenges. *Health Policy and Planning*, 23(5), 308–317.

Wendt, C., Frisina, L., and Rothgang, H. (2009). Healthcare system types: a conceptual framework for comparison. *Social Policy & Administration*, 43(1), 70–90.

Yılmaz, V. (2013). Changing origins of inequalities in access to healthcare in Turkey: from occupational status to income?. *New Perspectives on Turkey*, 48, 53–75.

List of Interviews

Interview no. 1 (2011). Recorded face-to-face in-depth interview. *Civil servant-Green Card Office (5 August 2011)*. Samsun.

Interview no. 2 (2011). Recorded focus group. *Pollsters worked for a nationwide survey on Green Card users (5 August 2011)*. Samsun.

Interview no. 3 (2011). Recorded face-to-face in-depth interview. *Hospital manager of one branch of a nationwide private hospital chain (5 August 2011)*. Samsun.

Interview no. 4 (2011). Recorded focus group. *Pollsters worked for a nationwide survey on Green Card users (9 August 2011)*. Adana.

Interview no. 5 (2011). Recorded face-to-face in-depth interview. *Citizen whose application to Green Card was denied (9 August 2011)*. Adana.

Interview no. 6 (2011). Recorded face-to-face in-depth interview. *Citizen whose application to Green Card was denied (9 August 2011)*. Adana.

Interview no. 7 (2011). Recorded face-to-face in-depth interview. *Civil servant in Green Card Office (9 August 2011)*. Adana.

Interview no. 8 (2011). Recorded face-to-face in-depth interview. *Hospital manager of one branch of a nationwide private hospital chain and a former member of healthcare reform team (9 August 2011)*. Adana.

Interview no. 9 (2011). Unrecorded face-to-face in-depth interview – personal interview notes available. *Specialist medical doctor and the head of Turkish Medical Association (13 August 2011)*. Ankara.

Interview no. 10 (2011). Recorded face-to-face in-depth interview. *Hospital owner and the head of health sector union in the Union of*

V. Yilmaz, *The Politics of Healthcare Reform in Turkey*,
DOI 10.1007/978-3-319-53667-5

Chamber and Commodity Exchanges in Turkey (13 August 2011). Ankara.

Interview no. 11 (2011). Unrecorded face-to-face in-depth interview – personal interview notes available. *Ph.D. candidate specialised in Turkey's health sector affiliated with a public university in Berlin (20 September 2011).* Istanbul.

Interview no. 12 (2011). Recorded face-to-face in-depth interview. *Specialist medical doctor, owner of a private clinic and the head of Association for Medical Doctors in the Private Sector (24 September 2011).* Istanbul.

Interview no. 13 (2011). Recorded face-to-face in-depth interview. *Professor of public health in a public university (1 October 2011).* Ankara.

Interview no. 14 (2011). Recorded face-to-face in-depth interview. *Specialist medical doctor and former head of Turkish Medical Association (5 October 2011).* Istanbul.

Interview no. 15 (2011). Recorded face-to-face in-depth interview. *Specialist medical doctor and the head of Right to Health Movement Association (5 October 2011).* Istanbul.

Interview no. 16 (2011). Recorded face-to-face in-depth interview. *Member of health staff in a public hospital and an active member of the Association for Human Health and Education (7 October 2011).* Istanbul.

Interview no. 17 (2011). Recorded face-to-face in-depth interview. *Assistant specialist medical doctor and an active member of the Association for Human Health and Education (7 October 2011).* Istanbul.

Interview no. 18 (2011). Recorded face-to-face in-depth interview. *Professor of public health in a public university and an active member of Izmir Medical Chamber (11 October 2011).* Izmir.

Interview no. 19 (2011). Unrecorded face-to-face in-depth interview – personal interview notes available. *Accountant in Turkey branch of an international private hospital chain (21 October 2011).* Istanbul.

Interview no. 20 (2011). Recorded face-to-face in-depth interview. *Professor of medicine, president of a private medical university, a specialist medical doctor and a former member of healthcare reform team (26 October 2011).* Istanbul.

Interview no. 21 (2011). Recorded face-to-face in-depth interview. *Senior economist in the World Bank and team leader in World Bank's health sector reform project in Turkey (1 November 2011).* Ankara.

Interview no. 22 (2011). Recorded face-to-face in-depth interview. *Senior economist in the World Bank and former team leader in World Bank's health sector reform project in Turkey (1 November 2011)*. Ankara.

Interview no. 23 (2011). Recorded face-to-face in-depth interview. *Family physician and secretary general of Istanbul Family Physicians Association (4 November 2011)*. Istanbul.

Interview no. 24 (2011). Recorded face-to-face in-depth interview. *Specialist medical doctor and head of Private Hospitals and Health Institutions Association (4 November 2011)*. Istanbul.

Interview no. 25 (2011). Unrecorded in-depth interview via teleconference – personal interview notes available. *Senior economist, head of health sector in the World Bank headquarters, former team leader in World Bank's health sector reform project in Turkey (10 November 2011)*. via teleconference.

Interview no. 26 (2011). Unrecorded face-to-face in-depth interview – personal interview notes available. *Professor of medicine in a public university and head of Human Health and Education Foundation (18 November 2011)*. Istanbul.

Interview no. 27 (2011). Recorded face-to-face in-depth interview. *Specialist medical doctor and owner of a private hospital (18 November 2011)*. Istanbul.

Interview no. 28 (2011). Unrecorded face-to-face in-depth interview – personal interview notes available. *Specialist medical doctor and a member of executive board in Turkish Medical Association (20 November 2011)*. Istanbul.

Interview no. 29 (2011). Recorded face-to-face in-depth interview. *Medical doctor and the president of Health and Social Services Labourers Union (21 November 2011)*. Ankara.

Interview no. 30 (2011). Unrecorded face-to-face in-depth interview – personal interview notes available. *Social security investigator and the head of Health Insurances Department at Social Security Institution (21 November 2011)*. Ankara.

Interview no. 31 (2011). Recorded face-to-face in-depth interview. *Specialist medical doctor and head of Revolutionary Health Workers Union (29 November 2011)*. Istanbul.

Interview no. 32 (2011). Recorded face-to-face in-depth interview. *General director of a public university hospital, former member of World Bank team in health sector reform project, former member of healthcare reform team (30 November 2011)*. Istanbul.

Interview no. 33 (2013). Unrecorded face-to-face in-depth interview – personal interview notes available. *High level state official working for the Ministry of Finance (4 January 2013)*. Ankara.

Public speech no. 1 (2011). Personal notes of the interviewee's public speech taken during the Supplementary Health Insurance Conference. *Turkey branch manager of an international private health insurance company (21 October 2011)*. Istanbul.

Public speech no. 2 (2011). Personal notes of the interviewee's public speech taken during the Supplementary Health Insurance Conference. *President of the Association of the Insurance and Reinsurance Companies in Turkey (21 October 2011)*. Istanbul.

Public speech no. 3 (2011). Recorded public speech in "Transformation of Turkey's Healthcare System" Workshop organised by the author at Bogazici University. *Professor of sociology in a public university and expert on healthcare policy in Turkey (25 November 2011)*. Istanbul.

Public speech no. 4 (2011). Recorded public speech in "Transformation of Turkey's Healthcare System" Workshop organised by the author at Bogazici University. *World Bank expert on healthcare reform in Turkey (25 November 2011)*. Istanbul.

Public speech no. 5 (2011). Recorded public speech in "Transformation of Turkey's Healthcare System" Workshop organised by the author at Bogazici University. *Specialist medical doctor in a private hospital, former head of curative healthcare services department at the Ministry of Health, former member of healthcare reform team (25 November 2011)*. Istanbul.

Index

V. Yilmaz, *The Politics of Healthcare Reform in Turkey*,
DOI 10.1007/978-3-319-53667-5

The manufacturer's authorised representative in the EU is Springer Nature Customer Service Centre GmbH, Europaplatz 3, 69115 Heidelberg, Germany. If you have any concerns regarding our products, please contact ProductSafety@springernature.com

Printed and bound by CPI Group (UK) Ltd, Croydon, CR0 4YY

30/09/2026

02225688-0003